THE RIGHT TO
DISSENT

Lawyers' Rights Watch Canada, 2017

Lawyers' Rights Watch Canada (LRWC) [2017]

ISBN: 978-0-9939149-0-4

Lawyers' Rights Watch Canada

Vancouver, B.C.

www.lrwc.org; lrwc@portal.ca

The Right to Dissent was researched and written by Lois Leslie BSocSc(Hons) LLB LLM, with editing assistance from Connor Bildfell BCom JD, and Gail Davidson LLB. Layout and design by Christopher Gully.

All photos are licensed under Creative Commons (CC BY 2.0), cropped from original. Credits to Flickr users by page number: Sally T. Buck (iv); earthjustice.org (9); Mohamed Azazy (14); Thomas Hawk (17, 27, 98, 152); Stever Rainwater (22); Sister Marches (24); Fibonacci Blue (33); earthjustice.org (101); S.L.M. (102).

TABLE OF CONTENTS

ACRONYMS & ABBREVIATIONS

ACHPR:	African Commission on Human and Peoples' Rights
ACHR:	American Convention on Human Rights
AU:	African Union
Banjul Charter:	African Charter on Human and Peoples' Rights
CAT:	Convention against Torture and Other Cruel, Inhuman or Degrading Treatment or Punishment
	UN Committee against Torture
CEDAW:	Convention on the Elimination of All Forms of Discrimination against Women
	UN Committee on the Elimination of All Forms of Discrimination against Women
CERD:	Committee on the Elimination of Racial Discrimination
CESCR:	Committee on Economic, Social and Cultural Rights
COE:	Council of Europe
CRC:	Convention on the Rights of the Child
	UN Committee on the Rights of the Child
CRPD:	Convention on the Rights of Persons with Disabilities
DDPA:	Durban Declaration and Programme of Action
ECHR:	European Convention on Human Rights
ECtHR:	European Court of Human Rights
HRC:	United Nations Human Rights Council
HR Committee:	Human Rights Committee
IACtHR:	Inter-American Court of Human Rights
IACHR:	Inter-American Commission on Human Rights
ICCPR:	International Covenant on Civil and Political Rights
ICERD:	International Convention on the Elimination of All Forms of Racial Discrimination
ICESCR:	International Covenant on Economic, Social and Cultural Rights
ICRMW:	International Convention on the Protection of the Rights of All Migrant Workers and Members of Their Families
OAS:	Organization of American States
SR:	Special Rapporteur
UDHR:	Universal Declaration of Human Rights
UN:	United Nations
WGAD:	UN Working Group on Arbitrary Detention

FOREWORD

Freedom of expression, freedom of association and the right to peaceful assembly are often compartmentalized and discussed individually, with little regard to their interdependence.

However, these fundamental human rights are bound together by their role in articulating, protecting, and promoting rights to participate in public affairs, to criticize, and to secure meaningful remedies for violations of those rights and of the rule of law.

This unifying theme of dissent distinguishes *The Right to Dissent* from other publications that address these themes. It is in the struggle to occupy public space, offer differing viewpoints, or take power where none was being ceded, that these rights take on their real meaning and significance.

Freedom of expression has been written about extensively, yet dissenting activities are often framed only in terms of free speech and the right to receive information without examining the connections to freedom of association. Even less on the right to peaceful assembly in the context of protest and dissent.

Indeed, the rights to freedom of association outside the context of labour rights and the right to peaceful assembly are among the most under-theorized areas of all rights and freedoms. In recent years, it has become disturbingly clear that the right to peaceful assembly is, in many respects, poorly understood – and certainly the most poorly protected.

From the raucous G20 summits and protests to the Occupy Movement, and from the Arab and Maple Spring to activists promoting democratic reform and protecting land and environmental rights, freedom of peaceful assembly has been heavily controlled by both state and non-state actors through prior restraints, ways and means restrictions, regulatory restrictions, criminal law powers and, in many cases, brute force.

The Right to Dissent emphasizes that all of these rights, even those that we most closely associate with civil and political rights, require the state not only to refrain from infringing rights but also to take positive steps to ensure that these rights are respected, protected and fulfilled.

In this respect, the crux of the Guide is located in the following passage:

The guarantee of the right to dissent and to participate in peaceful protest is not found in any single formulated right in international law, but rather is firmly anchored in a number of distinct but interconnected and mutually enforcing fundamental rights, which include the right to freedom of expression, the rights to freedom of association and peaceful assembly and the right to participate in public affairs. (Emphasis added).

In particular, the right to information is addressed as an intrinsic component of all of the fundamental freedoms that are discussed in the Guide, noting that positive duties fall on the state to ensure a legislative framework that guarantees a right to access, receive and share information.

Citizens must be able to make informed choices and understand the laws that are being enforced against them, as well as having the legal means to challenge those laws in appropriate circumstances.

In short, the state is responsible for fostering an enabling environment for the exercise of rights. The right to information, in turn, underpins the right to participation which forms the backbone of citizens' engagement and of democracy and its widest sense.

All of the rights and freedoms discussed in the Guide are woven together with equality rights and non-discrimination principles which emphasize the importance of protecting the rights of the most vulnerable and marginalized, including human rights defenders, LGBT people, minorities, indigenous peoples, people with disabilities and others whose voices are unfairly restricted or diminished or drowned out by more powerful perspectives.

One of these powerful perspectives is the pervasive and pernicious discourse surrounding "too many rights", too many remedies, and the perception that human rights advocacy and activism has gone too far.

In response, *The Right to Dissent* methodically and comprehensively demonstrates the need to consider emerging concepts that deal with new technologies and the realities that are faced by many of the most disenfranchised people around the world, as well as the civil society organizations and human rights defenders who work to protect them.

The Right to Dissent is an important addition to the literature on dissent, and on many of its most important constituent elements. By offering a thorough analysis of international human rights law, it will enable practitioners and citizens to claim their rights and participate more effectively in the project of democracy.

Pearl Eliadis, B.C.L., L.L.B., B.C.L. (Oxon)
Principal, Law Office of Pearl Eliadis (Montreal)

> " If freedom of expression is the grievance system of democracies, the right to protest and peaceful assembly is democracy's megaphone.
>
> It is the tool of the poor and the marginalized – those who do not have ready access to the levers of power and influence, those who need to take to the streets to make their voices heard.

International Network of Civil Liberties Organizations (INCLO), "Take Back the Streets": Repression and criminalization of protest around the world (October 2013)

INTRODUCTION

Throughout history, people have been engaging in public demonstrations and protests in order to effect change, often in the face of brutal resistance and suppression. The ability of individuals and groups to express dissent and to peacefully protest is, in fact, vital to a healthy, functioning human society. Tolerance of the right to be critical, to assemble freely to express grievances or aspirations and to mobilize for change contributes to a more secure society by allowing tensions to be defused in productive ways and enabling people to have a say in matters of public interest and to influence public policy and hold governments accountable.

In addition to fostering an engaged citizenry, peaceful protests play a critical role in protecting and promoting a broad range of human rights. As noted recently by SRs Maina Kiai and Christoph Heyns,

> [peaceful assemblies] can be instrumental in amplifying the voices of people who are marginalized or who present an alternative narrative to established political and economic interests. Assemblies present ways to engage not only with the State, but also with others who wield power in society, including corporations, religious, educational and cultural institutions, and with public opinion in general.[1]

The exercise of the rights to dissent and protest furthers the promotion and protection of other rights by generating visibility and momentum of issues and concerns; informing and changing public opinion; engaging the media in amplifying the voice of dissent; accelerating change and reform processes; and achieving social objectives in changing legislation, policies, decisions, actions and attitudes.[2]

International human rights law protects the right to dissent and protest through the guarantee of a set of universally-recognized rights, including rights to freedom of expression and opinion, association, peaceful assembly

---

1   UN, HRC, *Joint report of the Special Rapporteur on the rights to freedom of peaceful assembly and of association and the Special Rapporteur on extrajudicial, summary or arbitrary executions on the proper management of assemblies*, 4 February 2016, A/HRC/31/66, para. 6.

2   UN, General Assembly, *Report of the Special Representative of the Secretary-General on the situation of human rights defenders, Hina Jilani*, 13 August 2007, A/62/225, para. 7.

and the right to participate in public affairs. The OHCHR notes that these fundamental freedoms

> enable people to share ideas, form new ones, and join together with others to claim their rights. It is through the exercise of these public freedoms that we make informed decisions about our economic and social development. It is through these rights that we can take part in civic activity and build democratic societies. To restrict them undermines our collective progress.[3]

Despite these protections, the freedom to express opinions about issues of concern in a peaceful manner, including through public protests, "without fear of reprisals or of being intimidated, harassed, injured, sexually assaulted, beaten, arbitrarily arrested and detained, tortured, killed or subjected to enforced disappearance"[4] remains an illusory right for many across the globe. Peaceful protests are too often viewed as a threat, to be suppressed, rather than as a healthy and legitimate exercise of democratic rights, and, in many cases, advances in human rights protections are resisted or being rolled back.

A 2013 collaborative report by a group of ten domestic civil liberties and human rights organizations on how governments have responded to diverse kinds of protest and public assembly found "a very concerning pattern of government conduct: the tendency to transform individuals exercising a fundamental democratic right – the right to protest – into a perceived threat that requires a forceful government response".[5] The nine case studies from nine countries spread over four continents detailed in the report document instances of "unnecessary legal restrictions, discriminatory responses, criminalization of leaders, and unjustifiable – at times deadly – force".[6] Common themes that emerge from the case studies include excessive use of force, lethal deployment of "less-than-lethal" weapons, the criminalization of community leaders, and the use of anti-terror laws

---

3   UN OHCHR, *Civil Society Space and the United Nations Human Rights System: A Practical Guide for Civil Society,* 2014, p. 1.
4   UN, HRC resolution 22/10, *The promotion and protection of human rights in the context of peaceful protests,* 9 April 2013, A/HRC/22/10, Preamble.
5   International Network of Civil Liberties Organizations, *"Take back the streets": Repression and criminalization of protest around the world,* October 2013, p.1.
6   *Ibid.*

and regulatory frameworks to facilitate repression and discrimination and override internationally protected rights. The participants in the study reported that across the regions where their organizations operate,

> States are engaged in concerted efforts to roll back advances in the protection and promotion of human rights – and often, regressive measures impacting the right to protest follows in lockstep. And across the globe, social movements are pushing for change and resisting the advancement of authoritarian policies; dozens, hundreds, thousands or hundreds of thousands of individuals are marching in the roads and occupying the public space. In rural areas across the global south, there are a variety of demands, calling for access to land or resisting the exploitation of natural resources that threaten indigenous peoples' or peasants' territories. In urban settings, housing shortages or lack of basic services spark social protests and upheavals. Even in developed economies, there are disturbing tensions provoked by the contraction of the economy, globalization policies and the social and political exclusion of migrants. Students' movements all over the globe are demanding the right to education.[7]

In 2011, UN SR on extrajudicial, summary or arbitrary executions Christof Heyns reported that, based on a study of some 76 countries, many domestic legal systems do not adhere to international standards in respect of the use of force during demonstrations.[8]

A 2015 report, "State of democracy, human rights and the rule of law in Europe"[9] revealed, among other things, worsening conditions for free media and, in many places, deteriorating safety of journalists, with "disproportionate tactics employed to suppress dissent";[10] undue restriction on the freedom of assembly and the use of excessive force to disperse demonstrations and arrest demonstrators;[11] a perception among

---

7   *Ibid.*
8   UN, HRC, *Report of the Special Rapporteur on extrajudicial, summary or arbitrary executions, Christof Heyns,* 23 May 2011, A/HRC/ 17/28, summary.
9   COE, Secretary General of the Council of Europe, *State of democracy, human rights and the rule of law in Europe: A shared responsibility for democratic security in Europe,* 19 May 2015.
10   *Ibid,* para. 7.
11   *Ibid,* para. 11.

some member states that civil society organizations are a threat to state security;[12] a lack of mechanisms to enable meaningful public consultation and participation;[13] and, in the worst cases, "governments [that] are attempting – through legislation and various restrictive practices – to control citizen initiatives, including protests".[14]

National security considerations are often cited as a justification for the adoption of a state of emergency or other stricter rules to clamp down on or void the rights to peaceful protest.[15] Other obstacles to public and political participation exist in the form of direct and indirect discrimination and inequalities in access to the enjoyment of other human rights.[16] The OHCHR finds that discrimination, unequal treatment, harassment and restrictions of the rights to public and political participation are often directed against human rights defenders and civil society organizations advocating for the rights of marginalized groups.[17] According to the OHCHR, those most at risk of such treatment include

> people and organizations engaged in defending the rights of persons with disabilities, youth and children, women, lesbian, gay, bisexual, transgender and intersex people, members of minority groups, indigenous peoples, internally displaced persons, and non-nationals such as refugees, asylum seekers and migrant workers.[18]

While States have clear duties under international human rights law to respect, protect and fulfill the rights of individuals and groups to engage in dissent and peaceful protest, better compliance with international standards is required. In particular, there is a need to actively encourage and enable the right to demonstrate and peacefully protest and to prevent harm.

---

12   *Ibid,* para. 53.
13   *Ibid,* para. 53.
14   *Ibid,* para. 53.
15   UN, HRC, *Report of the Special Rapporteur on the rights to freedom of peaceful assembly and of association, Maina Kiai,* 21 May 2012, A/HRC/20/27, para. 21.
16   UN, HRC, *Report of the Office of the United Nations High Commissioner for Human Rights on factors that impede equal political participation and steps to overcome those challenges,* 30 June 2014, A/HRC/27/29, para. 3.
17   *Ibid,* para. 85.
18   *Ibid,* para. 85.

Growing international concern over the alarming prevalence of State repression of the right to peaceful protest and the use of force to disperse demonstrations has led to a number of developments at the international and regional levels. These developments are aimed at better promoting and protecting the right to dissent and protest, as well as strengthening the normative content of the right, including the rights to freedom of expression, freedom of assembly and of association and freedom to participate in the conduct of public affairs.[19]

SR on extrajudicial, summary or arbitrary executions Christof Heyns observed that the response to dissent and protest is not simply a matter of enforcing standards applicable to the use of force, but rather how to deal with dissent.[20] As Mr. Heyns notes, this "illusive problem has plagued humanity throughout history: how should those in power handle contestation?"[21] As the SR pointed out, the standards applicable to the use of force cannot be dealt with in isolation. An equally important question is how demonstrations and peaceful assemblies should be enabled and encouraged as a critical component of democracy.

A vitally important step in enabling peaceful protests and preventing harm is to ensure, at the State level, better understanding of, and compliance with, international standards protecting the right to peaceful protest. When the right to peaceful assembly is suppressed, there is a higher risk for demonstrations to escalate and turn violent.[22]

In a 2010 resolution, the HRC reaffirmed the importance of the rights to freedom of peaceful assembly and of association to "the full enjoyment of civil and political rights, and economic, social and cultural rights" and as "essential components of democracy".[23] The HRC recognized further

---

19   SRs on freedom of opinion and expression exist under each of the UN, OAS and AU human rights systems.
20   *Report of the Special Rapporteur on extrajudicial, summary or arbitrary executions (A/HRC/17/28)*, para. 12.
21   *Ibid.*
22   UN HRC, *Report of the United Nations High Commissioner for Human Rights on Effective measures and best practices to ensure the promotion and protection of human rights in the context of peaceful protests*, 21 January 2013, A/HRC/22/28, para. 21.
23   UN, HRC, *Resolution 15/21 on the rights to freedom of peaceful assembly and of association*, 6 October 2010, A/HRC/RES/15/21, preamble.

that the exercise of the rights to freedom of peaceful assembly and of association "free of restrictions, subject only to the limitations permitted by international law, in particular international human rights law, is indispensable to the full enjoyment of these rights, particularly where individuals may espouse minority or dissenting religious or political beliefs".[24]

In 2010, the HRC appointed an SR on the rights to freedom of peaceful assembly and of association, with the mandate to, inter alia, "make recommendations on ways and means to ensure the promotion and protection of the rights to freedom of peaceful assembly and of association in all their manifestations"; work with governments, NGOs, relevant stakeholders and others to promote and protect the rights to freedom of peaceful assembly and of association; and to report on violations of these rights, wherever they may occur, as well as on "discrimination, threats or use of violence, harassment, persecution, intimidation or reprisals directed at persons exercising these rights".[25] In 2008, the HRC extended the mandate on the situation of human rights defenders as an SR on the situation of human rights defenders.[26]

At the regional level, in 2004, the ACHPR appointed an SR on Freedom of Expression in Africa[27] and an SR on human rights defenders in Africa.[28] In 2011, the IACHR created an Office of the Rapporteur on the Situation of Human Rights Defenders.[29]

In 2013, the HRC adopted a resolution on "The promotion and protection of human rights in the context of peaceful protests", which urged States "to facilitate peaceful protests by providing protestors with access to

---

24   *Ibid.*

25   *Ibid*, para. 5.

26   UN, HRC, *Resolution 7/8 on the mandate of the Special Rapporteur on the situation of human rights defenders,* 27 March 2008, A/HRC/7/8.

27   ACHPR, Resolution 71: *Mandate and Appointment of a Special Rapporteur on Freedom of Expression in Africa,* 7 December 2004, online <http://www.achpr.org/sessions/36th/resolutions/71/>.

28   ACHPR, Resolution 69: *Protection of Human Rights Defenders in Africa,* 4th June 2004, online <http://www.achpr.org/sessions/35th/resolutions/69/>.

29   OAS, IACHR, Rapporteurship on Human Rights Defenders, online <http://www.oas.org/en/iachr/defenders/default.asp>.

public space and protecting them, where necessary, against any forms of threats"[30] and to "avoid using force during peaceful protests, and to ensure that, where force is absolutely necessary, no one is subject to excessive or indiscriminate use of force".[31]

In his first thematic report to the HRC, UN SR on the rights to freedom of peaceful assembly and of association Maina Kiai noted that the rights to freedom of peaceful assembly and of association are constitutionally guaranteed in most countries and that, in many States, specific domestic laws further govern the exercise of these rights. However, the SR found that, in many instances, domestic legislation listed grounds additional to those already prescribed by international human rights law or was ambiguous. The SR warned against arbitrary interpretations of such grounds for restriction. He further cautioned against an environment in which the enjoyment of rights to association and assembly are seriously impeded.[32]

Problems identified by the HR Committee on the implementation of the right to freedom of assembly include:

- bans on demonstrations;

- unjustified restrictions on demonstrations;

- unnecessary requirements to obtain authorizations that affect the enjoyment of freedom of assembly;

- lack of remedies to appeal decisions denying the authorization to hold demonstrations;

- arrest of protestors amounting to arbitrary detention;

- legislation contravening international human rights law by obstructing and punishing the exercise of freedom of assembly and the right to protest and establishing procedures that infringe on the actual ability to enjoy the right to peaceful assembly; and

- legislation on counter-terrorism with definitions of "terrorism" so

---

30   UN, HRC resolution 22/10, *The promotion and protection of human rights in the context of peaceful protests,* 9 April 2013, A/HRC/22/10, para. 4.

31   *Ibid,* para. 7.

32   UN, HRC, *Report of the Special Rapporteur on the rights to freedom of peaceful assembly and of association, Maina Kiai,* 21 May 2012, A/HRC/20/27, para. 20.

broad that they might jeopardize legitimate activities in a democratic society, in particular participation in public demonstrations.[33]

In addition, new technologies have changed the way in which people protest, challenging traditional notions about what constitutes a peaceful assembly and creating gaps in legal protections, including protection of rights to privacy and access to information. As the UN SRs stated in their joint report:

> The full and free exercise of the right to freedom of peaceful assembly is possible only where an enabling and safe environment for the general public, including for civil society and human rights defenders, exists and where access to spaces for public participation is not excessively or unreasonably restricted. Barriers to forming and operating associations, weak protection from reprisals for those exercising and defending human rights, excessive and disproportionate punishments for violations of the law, and unreasonable restrictions on the use of public spaces all negatively affect the right to freedom of peaceful assembly.[34]

The duty of States to respect, protect and fulfill international human rights

Under international law, States must respect and ensure the rights of all persons to participate in public affairs by engaging in the rights to dissent and protest. The obligation to respect means that States must refrain from restricting the exercise of the rights where such restriction is not expressly allowed under international law. The obligation to ensure is a positive duty that requires States to both fulfill and to protect rights.[35] The protection of rights requires that positive measures be taken to prevent actions by non-

---

33   UN General Assembly, *Report of the Special Representative of the Secretary-General on the situation of human rights defenders, Hina Jilani*, 13 August 2007, A/62/225, para. 20.
34   UN HRC, *Joint report of the Special Rapporteur on the rights to freedom of peaceful assembly and of association and the Special Rapporteur on extrajudicial, summary or arbitrary executions on the proper management of assemblies*, 4 February 2016, A/HRC/31/66, para. 7.
35   ECtHR, *Case of Plattform "Ärzte Für Das Leben" v. Austria*, App. no. 10126/82, Judgment of 21 June 1988.

" A free society is characterised by its willingness to tolerate dissent, as expressed also through protest action. As such, a free society may experience some discomfort with dissent.

This is a healthy attitude because dissenters in such a society would not have to resort to attacking the system as such. In a free society, the desire to engage in extreme measures largely disappears. Life would be more secure in such a society.

SR on extrajudicial, summary or arbitrary executions Christof Heyns, 23 May 2011 (A/HRC/17/28, para. 141)

State actors that could interfere with their exercise. In order to fulfill rights, States are obligated to create, facilitate or provide the necessary conditions for the enjoyment of the rights.[36]

States' duties to guarantee the exercise of these rights flow from obligations under domestic law and in international treaties to which they are parties. The *Vienna Convention on the Law of Treaties* specifies that States Parties are bound by their treaty obligations and all treaty obligations must be performed in good faith (*pacta sunt servanda*).[37] Article 27 of the *Vienna Convention* reads: "A party may not invoke the provisions of its internal law as justification for its failure to perform a treaty." Thus, under international human rights law, States not only have a negative obligation not to obstruct access to judicial and other remedies, but also have a positive duty to organize their domestic law to ensure that all persons can access those remedies.

To the extent that internationally protected human rights laws are considered to be peremptory norms of general international law (*jus cogens*), no derogation by States is permitted.[38]

International human rights treaties contain provisions requiring a State Party: to ensure to all individuals within its territories and subject to its jurisdiction the rights and freedoms set out in the treaty, without distinction of any kind; to take the necessary steps to give full effect to those rights and freedoms; and to ensure the enforcement of appropriate remedies in the event of a treaty violation.[39]

The IACtHR commented on this general obligation under *ACHR* Article 1(1)

---

36   UN, HRC, *Joint report of the Special Rapporteur on the rights to freedom of peaceful assembly and of association and the Special Rapporteur on extrajudicial, summary or arbitrary executions on the proper management of assemblies*, 4 February 2016, A/HRC/31/66, para. 14.

37   UN, *Vienna Convention on the Law of Treaties*, 23 May 1969, UN, Treaty Series, vol. 1155, p. 331 [*Vienna Convention*], Article 26.

38   Article 53 of the *Vienna Convention* defines a peremptory norm of international law as "a norm accepted and recognized by the international community of States as a whole as a norm from which no derogation is permitted and which can be modified only by a subsequent norm of general international law having the same character."

39   See, for example, *ICCPR* Article 2.

in *Velasquez Rodriguez Case*[40]:

The first obligation assumed by the States Parties under [ACHR] Article 1(1) is " 'to respect the rights and freedoms' recognized by the [ACHR]. The exercise of public authority has certain limits which derive from the fact that human rights are inherent attributes of human dignity and are, therefore, superior to the power of the State...

'The protection of human rights, particularly the civil and political rights set forth in the [ACHR], is in effect based on the affirmation of the existence of certain inviolable attributes of the individual that cannot be legitimately restricted through the exercise of governmental power. These are individual domains that are beyond the reach of the State or to which the State has but limited access. Thus, the protection of human rights must necessarily comprise the concept of the restriction of the exercise of state power...'

The second obligation of the States Parties is to "ensure" the free and full exercise of the rights recognized by the [ACHR] to every person subject to its jurisdiction. This obligation implies the duty of the States Parties to organize the governmental apparatus and, in general, all the structures through which public power is exercised, so that they are capable of juridically ensuring the free and full enjoyment of human rights. As a consequence of this obligation, the States must prevent, investigate and punish any violation of the rights recognized by the Convention and, moreover, if possible attempt to restore the right violated and provide compensation as warranted for damages resulting from the violation.

The obligation to ensure the free and full exercise of human rights is not fulfilled by the existence of a legal system designed to make it possible to comply with this obligation - it also requires the government to conduct itself so as to effectively ensure the free and full exercise of human rights.[41]

Where treaty bodies and human rights tribunals have examined alleged violations of specific treaty provisions, the jurisprudence of these bodies

---

40   IACtHR, *Velasquez Rodriguez Case,* Judgment of July 29, 1988, (Ser. C) No. 4 (1988).
41   *Ibid,* paras. 165-167.

provides a rich body of interpretive law and/or persuasive authority concerning States' obligations under international human rights law.[42]

As indicated by the HR Committee, States also have a legal interest in the performance by other States Parties of their obligations under human rights treaties, flowing from the fact that the "rules concerning the basic rights of the human person" are *erga omnes* (owed to all) obligations, and from States' obligation, under the *United Nations Charter*, to promote universal respect for, and observance of, human rights and fundamental freedoms for all persons, without distinction.[43]

Many human rights norms have acquired the force of customary international law. Such norms constitute further binding legal obligations on States.

Finally, there are numerous other UN and regional human rights instruments relevant to the right to dissent, including Declarations, Guidelines, Statements of Principle, Resolutions and Recommendations. While not binding *per se* on States, these secondary instruments provide important sources for interpreting and understanding States' international legal obligations arising from treaty obligations as well as normative guidance for States in developing domestic public policy that complies with generally accepted international human rights standards and principles.

---

42   In considering the impact of the findings of UN Treaty Bodies, the International Law Association concluded "treaty body output has become a relevant interpretive source for many national courts in the interpretation of constitutional and statutory guarantees of human rights, as well as in interpreting provisions which form part of domestic law, as well as for international tribunals. While national courts have generally not been prepared to accept that they are formally bound by committee interpretations of treaty provisions, most courts have recognised that, as expert bodies entrusted by the States parties with functions under the treaties, the treaty bodies' interpretations deserve to be given considerable weight in determining the meaning of a relevant right and the existence of a violation": International Law Association, Berlin Conference (2004), *Final Report on the Impact of Findings of the United Nations Human Rights Treaty Bodies*, para. 175 [footnotes omitted].
43   UN, HR Committee, *CCPR General Comment No. 31, Article 2 (The Nature of the General Legal Obligation Imposed on States Parties to the Covenant)*, 29 March 2004, CCPR/C/21/Rev.1/Add.13, para. 2.

The purpose of this Guide

This Guide to the Right to Dissent has been developed for the purpose of promoting the rule of law through enhancing knowledge and awareness of international human rights law concerning the rights to participate in public affairs by engaging in public debate, criticism, opposition and dissent. It is anticipated that access to this knowledge by a broad range of users—including lawyers, activists, human rights workers, police, judges, government officials and interested members of the public—will enable and promote better compliance with international standards.

This Guide explains the international legal standards and underlying principles and interpretations of the standards that comprise the international legal framework for the right to dissent and protest. It includes observations, jurisprudence, comments and recommendations from UN treaty bodies; opinions and recommendations of Special Procedures of the HRC; and jurisprudence from regional courts and bodies, including the ECtHR, the IACtHR, the IACHR and the ACHPR.

The following section of the Guide sets out the legal standards which make up the right to dissent and protest at international law including: freedom of opinion and expression; freedom of peaceful assembly and association; the right to take part in the conduct of public affairs; the right to promote and protect human rights and fundamental freedoms; and the right to a remedy. Also considered are rights to equality and non-discrimination, rights to privacy, and rights to life, liberty and security of the person as well as the specific rights of children and vulnerable persons as these rights are engaged in the exercise of the right to dissent and protest. This is followed by a discussion of the general approach by the treaty bodies and regional human rights courts in interpreting the scope of these specific rights.

The final section of this guide reviews the scope and interpretation of the right to dissent and protest, as a right in itself. Readers are reminded to read this section together with the scope of the individual rights which make up the right to dissent and protest.

All of the international standards referred to in the Guide are set out in Appendix A.

" Peaceful protests are a fundamental aspect of a vibrant democracy. States should recognize the positive role of peaceful protests as a means to strengthen human rights and democracy.

They should guarantee the rights to freedom of peaceful assembly, freedom of association and freedom of opinion and expression, which are essential components of democracy and indispensable to the full enjoyment of all human rights.

Report of the United Nations High Commissioner for Human Rights to the Human Rights Council, 21 January 2013 (A/HRC/22/28, para. 77)

FOUNDATION OF THE RIGHT TO DISSENT IN INTERNATIONAL LAW

The international human right of individuals and groups to peacefully protest and express their dissent, individually and collectively, involves a number of internationally-protected rights, including rights to freedom of expression, opinion and belief; freedom of association and peaceful assembly; the right to participate in public affairs; bodily integrity, which includes the right to security, the right to be free from cruel, inhuman or degrading treatment or punishment, and the right to life; dignity; privacy; and an effective remedy for all human rights violations. States have an obligation to ensure all persons enjoy these fundamental rights equally and without discrimination of any kind.

States have the primary responsibility to respect, protect and fulfill the rights to dissent and protest, including protecting persons against the interference of their rights by others. *ICCPR* Article 2(1) reads as follows:

> 2. (1) Each State Party to the present Covenant undertakes to respect and to ensure to all individuals within its territory and subject to its jurisdiction the rights recognized in the present Covenant, without distinction of any kind...

Definition of "protest"

The term "protest" is not defined in international law. For the purpose of this Guide, we have adopted the definition proposed by the charitable organization ARTICLE 19 in its 2015 Policy Brief, *The Right to Protest: Principles on protection of human rights in protests*[44]:

> A protest is the individual or collective expression of oppositional, dissenting, reactive or responsive views, values or interests. As such, a protest may encompass, *inter alia*:
>
> > i Individual or collective actions, as well as spontaneous or simultaneous protests in the manner, form and for the

---

44   ARTICLE 19, *The Right to Protest: Principles on protection of human rights in protests* (Policy Brief, 2015).

duration of one's choosing, including through the use of digital technologies;

ii An individual or collective expression relating to any cause or issue;

iii Actions targeting any audience, including public authorities, private entities or individuals or the general public;

iv Actions in any location, including public or privately owned places, as well as online;

v Actions involving various degrees and methods of organisation, including where there is no clear organisational structure, hierarchy or pre-determined form or duration;[45]

Right to freedom of opinion and expression

An essential aspect of the right to dissent is the right to freely hold and express a dissenting opinion or belief without fear of reprisal by the State, subject only to specific limitations as are provided by law and are necessary to protect the rights or reputations of others, or to protect national security, public order, public health or morals.

The HR Committee has stated that

the freedoms of information and expression are cornerstones in any free and democratic society. It is the essence of such societies that citizens must be allowed to inform themselves about alternatives to the political system/parties in power, and that they may criticize or openly and publicly evaluate their Governments without fear of interference or punishment by the Government, subject to certain restrictions set out in article 19, paragraph 3, of the [*ICCPR*].[46]

Inter-American case law has explained that the inter-American legal

---

45   *Ibid*, p. 11.

46   HR Committee, Communication No. 1173/2003, *Benhadj v. Algeria,* Views adopted on 20 July 2007, para. 8.10.

> **Freedom of information is a fundamental human right and is the touchstone of all the freedoms to which the United Nations is consecrated.**
>
> *UN General Assembly Resolution 59(1)*

framework places a high value on freedom of expression because

> it is based on a broad concept of the autonomy and dignity of the individual, and because it takes into account the instrumental value of freedom of expression for the exercise of all other fundamental rights, as well as its essential role within democratic systems...[47]

As the IACHR has observed,

> It is evident that the right to freedom of expression and thought guaranteed in the [ACHR] is inextricably connected to the very existence of a democratic society. ... [f]ull and free discussion keep a society from becoming stagnant and unprepared for the stresses and strains that work to tear all civilizations apart.[48]

In the view of UN SR on the promotion and protection of the right to freedom of opinion and expression, Mr. Abid Hussain,

> the right to seek, receive and impart information is not merely a corollary of freedom of opinion and expression; it is a right in and of itself. As such, it is one of the rights upon which free and democratic societies depend. It is also a right that gives meaning to the right to participate...[49]

Freedom of opinion and expression is guaranteed in the *UDHR*, in the *ICCPR*, in regional human rights treaties as well as in a number of other instruments.

Article 19 of the *UDHR* provides that:

> 19. Everyone has the right to freedom of opinion and expression; this

---

47   Office of the SR for Freedom of Expression of the IACHR, "The Inter-American Legal Framework regarding the Right to Freedom of Expression", OEA Ser.L/V/II, December 30, 2009, para. 5.

48   IACHR, Annual Report 1994. OEA/Ser.L/V.88. Doc. 9 rev. 1. 17 February 1995. Chapter V, citing Dennis v. U.S., 341 U.S. 494, 584 (1951) (Douglas, J., dissenting).

49   UN, Economic and Social Council, Commission on Human Rights, *Civil And Political Rights including the question of: Freedom of Expression, Report of the Special Rapporteur on the promotion and protection of the right to freedom of opinion and expression, Mr. Abid Hussain, submitted in accordance with Commission resolution 1999/36*, E/CN.4/2000/63 18 January 2000, para. 42.

right includes freedom to hold opinions without interference and to seek, receive and impart information and ideas through any media and regardless of frontiers.

Under the *ICCPR*,

19. (1) Everyone shall have the right to hold opinions without interference.

(2) Everyone shall have the right to freedom of expression; this right shall include freedom to seek, receive and impart information and ideas of all kinds, regardless of frontiers, either orally, in writing or in print, in the form of art, or through any other media of his choice.

(3) The exercise of the rights provided for in paragraph 2 of this article carries with it special duties and responsibilities. It may therefore be subject to certain restrictions, but these shall only be such as are provided by law and are necessary:

(a) For respect of the rights or reputations of others;

(b) For the protection of national security or of public order (ordre public), or of public health or morals.

20. (1) Any propaganda for war shall be prohibited by law.

(2) Any advocacy of national, racial or religious hatred that constitutes incitement to discrimination, hostility or violence shall be prohibited by law.

The legal framework for protection of the right to freedom of expression under the inter-American human rights system[50] is thought to provide the greatest scope and the broadest guarantees to the right to freedom of thought and expression, with more limited restrictions to the free circulation of information, opinions and ideas to those found in comparable provisions the UN and European human rights systems.[51] The right to freedom of thought and expression under the *ACHR*, which shall not be subject to prior

---

50   This includes Article 13 of the ACHR, Article IV of the *American Declaration of the Rights and Duties of Man* and Article 4 of the *Inter-American Democratic Charter.*

51   Office of the SR for Freedom of Expression of the IACHR, "The Inter-American Legal Framework regarding the Right to Freedom of Expression", OEA Ser.L/V/II, December 30, 2009, paras. 3-5.

censorship, includes the right to "seek information".

Article 13 of the *ACHR* provides that:

13. (1) Everyone has the right to freedom of thought and expression. This right includes freedom to seek, receive, and impart information and ideas of all kinds, regardless of frontiers, either orally, in writing, in print, in the form of art, or through any other medium of one's choice.

(2) The exercise of the right provided for in the foregoing paragraph shall not be subject to prior censorship but shall be subject to subsequent imposition of liability, which shall be expressly established by law to the extent necessary to ensure:

(a) respect for the rights or reputations of others; or

(b) the protection of national security, public order, or public health or morals.

(3) The right of expression may not be restricted by indirect methods or means, such as the abuse of government or private controls over newsprint, radio broadcasting frequencies, or equipment used in the dissemination of information, or by any other means tending to impede the communication and circulation of ideas and opinions.

(4) Notwithstanding the provisions of paragraph 2 above, public entertainments may be subject by law to prior censorship for the sole purpose of regulating access to them for the moral protection of childhood and adolescence.

(5) Any propaganda for war and any advocacy of national, racial, or religious hatred that constitute incitements to lawless violence or to any other similar action against any person or group of persons on any grounds including those of race, color, religion, language, or national origin shall be considered as offenses punishable by law.

Article 32 of the *Arab Charter of Human Rights* states:

32. (1) The present Charter guarantees the right to information and to freedom of opinion and expression, as well as the right to seek, receive and impart information and ideas through any medium, regardless of geographical boundaries.

(2) Such rights and freedoms shall be exercised in conformity with the fundamental values of society and shall be subject only to such limitations as are required to ensure respect for the rights or reputation of others or the protection of national security, public order and public health or morals.

Right to freedom of peaceful assembly and association

The rights to freedom of expression and to participate in public affairs are further protected and served by international law guarantees of the rights to peaceful assembly and to freedom of association.

As with the right to freedom of expression, the rights to peaceful assembly and to freedom of association under the *ICCPR* may be restricted only for the purpose of protecting national security, public safety, public order, public health or morals or the rights and freedoms of others. Any restrictions imposed must be prescribed by law and be "necessary in a democratic society".

Under *UDHR* Article 20 (1),

20. (1) Everyone has the right to freedom of peaceful assembly and association.

ICCPR Articles 21 and 22 state:

21. The right of peaceful assembly shall be recognized. No restrictions may be placed on the exercise of this right other than those imposed in conformity with the law and which are necessary in a democratic society in the interests of national security or public safety, public order (ordre public), the protection of public health or morals or the protection of the rights and freedoms of others.

22. (1) Everyone shall have the right to freedom of association with others, including the right to form and join trade unions for the protection of his interests.

(2) No restrictions may be placed on the exercise of this right other than those which are prescribed by law and which are necessary in a democratic society in the interests of national security or public safety,

" The rights to freedom of peaceful assembly and of association are not always the most popular of rights for people who are not actually exercising them. But there is a reason that the international community has collectively enshrined them as fundamental rights.

They are among the best tools to address social conflict. They allow underrepresented groups to amplify their voices; they give dispossessed people a channel for engagement and a stake in society; and above all they allow us to thrash out our disagreements in a peaceful—even if messy—manner.

United Nations, Statement by the UN Special Rapporteur on the rights to freedom of peaceful assembly and of association at the conclusion of his visit to the Republic of Korea (Seoul, 29 January 2016)

public order (ordre public), the protection of public health or morals or the protection of the rights and freedoms of others. This article shall not prevent the imposition of lawful restrictions on members of the armed forces and of the police in their exercise of this right.

Article 11 of the *ECHR* provides:

11. (1) Everyone has the right to freedom of peaceful assembly and to freedom of association with others, including the right to form and to join trade unions for the protection of his interests.

(2) No restrictions shall be placed on the exercise of these rights other than such as are prescribed by law and are necessary in a democratic society in the interests of national security or public safety, for the prevention of disorder or crime, for the protection of health or morals or for the protection of the rights and freedoms of others. This Article shall not prevent the imposition of lawful restrictions on the exercise of these rights by members of the armed forces, of the police or of the administration of the State.

The word "peaceful" is absent from Article 11 of the *African Charter on Human and Peoples' Rights*:

11. Every individual shall have the right to assemble freely with others. The exercise of this right shall be subject only to necessary restrictions provided for by law in particular those enacted in the interest of national security, the safety, health, ethics and rights and freedoms of others.

Right to take part in the conduct of public affairs

The equal right to participate directly or indirectly in political and public affairs is intimately connected to rights to peaceful assembly and association, freedom of expression and opinion and the rights to education and to information.[52]

The OHCHR has observed that

---

52   HR Committee, *CCPR General Comment No. 25 Article 25 (Participation in Public Affairs and the Right to Vote)*, 12 July 1996, CCPR/C/21/Rev.1/Add.7, para. 26.

"Political and public participation rights play a crucial role in the promotion of democratic governance, the rule of law, social inclusion and economic development, as well as in the advancement of all human rights.

The right to directly and indirectly participate in political and public life is important in empowering individuals and groups, and is one of the core elements of human rights-based approaches aimed at eliminating marginalization and discrimination.

Report of the Office of the UN High Commissioner for Human Rights to HRC, 30 June 2014 (A/HRC/27/29, para. 2)

[i]ncreasingly, international human rights mechanisms are acknowledging the rights of all people to be fully involved in and to effectively influence public decision-making processes that affect them. These public participation rights encompass the rights to be consulted at each phase of legislative drafting and policymaking, to voice criticism and to submit proposals aimed at improving the functioning and inclusivity of all governmental bodies engaged in the conduct of public affairs. This wider interpretation of the right to political and public participation is particularly apparent in relation to the rights of persons with disabilities and in connection with indigenous peoples, minorities and the role of civil society organizations.[53]

Article 21(1) of the *UDHR* provides that

21. (1) Everyone has the right to take part in the government of his country, directly or through freely chosen representatives.

Article 25 of the *ICCPR* recognizes and protects the right of every citizen to take part in the conduct of public affairs, the right to vote and to be elected and the right to have access to public service. In contrast with other rights and freedoms recognized by the *ICCPR* (which are ensured to all individuals within the territory and subject to the jurisdiction of the State), *ICCPR* Article 25 applies only to citizens. In addition to ensuring that the conditions for obtaining citizenship are not directly or indirectly discriminatory, States must also take measures to guarantee that non-citizens, including migrants (regardless of their migration status), non-permanent residents, refugees, stateless persons and asylum seekers enjoy other participation rights such as the freedom of association and peaceful assembly, expression and opinion, and the rights to information and education.[54]

Article 25 of the *ICCPR* states:

25. Every citizen shall have the right and the opportunity, without any of the distinctions mentioned in article 2 and without unreasonable restrictions:

---

53   UN, HRC, *Report of the United Nations High Commissioner for Human Rights on factors that impede equal political participation and steps to overcome those challenges*, A/HRC/27/29 (30 June 2014), para. 21.
54   *Ibid*, para. 37.

(a) To take part in the conduct of public affairs, directly or through freely chosen representatives;

(b) To vote and to be elected at genuine periodic elections which shall be by universal and equal suffrage and shall be held by secret ballot, guaranteeing the free expression of the will of the electors;

(c) To have access, on general terms of equality, to public service in his country.

Article 8 of the *UN Declaration on the Right and Responsibility of Individuals, Groups and Organs of Society to Promote and Protect Universally Recognized Human Rights and Fundamental Freedoms* provides:

8. (1) Everyone has the right, individually and in association with others, to have effective access, on a non-discriminatory basis, to participation in the government of his or her country and in the conduct of public affairs.

(2) This includes, inter alia, the right, individually and in association with others, to submit to governmental bodies and agencies and organizations concerned with public affairs criticism and proposals for improving their functioning and to draw attention to any aspect of their work that may hinder or impede the promotion, protection and realization of human rights and fundamental freedoms.

Right to promote and protect human rights and fundamental freedoms

Under the *UN Declaration on the Right and Responsibility of Individuals, Groups and Organs of Society to Promote and Protect Universally Recognized Human Rights and Fundamental Freedoms*, Article 1,

1. Everyone has the right, individually and in association with others, to promote and to strive for the protection and realization of human rights and fundamental freedoms at the national and international levels.

The right of individuals to be free from reprisal as a consequence of communications or cooperation with UN treaty bodies is protected under

" Exclusion, marginalization and discrimination cannot be effectively addressed unless all people are provided with meaningful opportunities to exercise their rights to participate in political and public life and other related rights.

Report of the Office of the UN High Commissioner for Human Rights to the HRC, 30 June 2014 (A/HRC/27/29, para. 41)

Optional Protocols to *ICESCR, CRC* and *CEDAW*.[55]

Right to equality and non-discrimination

Under international human rights law, States must ensure that the rights and fundamental freedoms guaranteed by all persons within their territories and subject to their jurisdiction are enjoyed equally and without distinction of any kind.

Each of the core international human rights treaties explicitly prohibits both formal (*de jure*) and substantive (*de facto*) discrimination.

Articles 2 and 7 of the *UDHR* state:

> 2. Everyone is entitled to all the rights and freedoms set forth in this Declaration, without distinction of any kind, such as race, colour, sex, language, religion, political or other opinion, national or social origin, property, birth or other status. Furthermore, no distinction shall be made on the basis of the political, jurisdictional or international status of the country or territory to which a person belongs, whether it be independent, trust, non-self-governing or under any other limitation of sovereignty.

> 7. All are equal before the law and are entitled without any discrimination to equal protection of the law. All are entitled to equal protection against any discrimination in violation of this Declaration and against any incitement to such discrimination.

Under the *ICCPR*,

> 2. (1) Each State Party to the present Covenant undertakes to respect and to ensure to all individuals within its territory and subject to its jurisdiction the rights recognized in the present Covenant, without distinction of any kind, such as race, colour, sex, language, religion, political or other opinion, national or social origin, property, birth or

---

55 *Optional Protocol to the International Covenant on Economic, Social and Cultural Rights,* Article 13; *Optional Protocol to the Convention on the Rights of the Child on a communications procedure,* Article 4; *Optional Protocol to the Convention on the Elimination of All Forms of Discrimination against Women,* Article 11.

other status.

3. The States Parties to the present Covenant undertake to ensure the equal right of men and women to the enjoyment of all civil and political rights set forth in the present Covenant.

26. All persons are equal before the law and are entitled without any discrimination to the equal protection of the law. In this respect, the law shall prohibit any discrimination and guarantee to all persons equal and effective protection against discrimination on any ground such as race, colour, sex, language, religion, political or other opinion, national or social origin, property, birth or other status.

Article 7 of *CEDAW* provides:

7. States Parties shall take all appropriate measures to eliminate discrimination against women in the political and public life of the country and, in particular, shall ensure to women, on equal terms with men, the right:...

(b) To participate in the formulation of government policy and the implementation thereof and to hold public office and perform all public functions at all levels of government;

(c) To participate in non-governmental organizations and associations concerned with the public and political life of the country.

The *Durban Declaration and Programme of Action*[56] urges States to

promote, as appropriate, effective and equal access of all members of the community, especially those who are victims of racism, racial discrimination, xenophobia and related intolerance, to the decision-making process in society at all levels and in particular at the local level, and also urges States and encourages the private sector to facilitate their effective participation in economic life;[57]

---

56   UN, *Durban Declaration and Programme of Action, Adopted at the World Conference Against Racism, Racial Discrimination, Xenophobia and Related Violence,* 8 September 2001, online <http://www.un.org/WCAR/durban.pdf>.
57   *Ibid,* para. 113.

Rights of children and vulnerable groups

Special measures may be required to ensure the protection and fulfillment of the rights of children and other vulnerable groups in the effective exercise of their rights to dissent.

ICCPR Article 24 provides:

24. (1) Every child shall have, without any discrimination as to race, colour, sex, language, religion, national or social origin, property or birth, the right to such measures of protection as are required by his status as a minor, on the part of his family, society and the State.

Under *CRC* Article 2,

2. (1) States Parties shall respect and ensure the rights set forth in the present Convention to each child within their jurisdiction without discrimination of any kind, irrespective of the child's or his or her parent's or legal guardian's race, colour, sex, language, religion, political or other opinion, national, ethnic or social origin, property, disability, birth or other status.

(2) States Parties shall take all appropriate measures to ensure that the child is protected against all forms of discrimination or punishment on the basis of the status, activities, expressed opinions, or beliefs of the child's parents, legal guardians, or family members.

CRPD Article 29 states:

29. States Parties shall guarantee to persons with disabilities political rights and the opportunity to enjoy them on an equal basis with others, and shall undertake to:

(a) Ensure that persons with disabilities can effectively and fully participate in political and public life on an equal basis with others, directly or through freely chosen representatives...

Right to privacy

Persons exercising their right to dissent are entitled to the full protection of their rights to privacy under international law.

UDHR Article 12 provides:

12. No one shall be subjected to arbitrary interference with his privacy, family, home or correspondence, nor to attacks upon his honour and reputation. Everyone has the right to the protection of the law against such interference or attacks.

ICCPR Article 17 states:

17. (1) No one shall be subjected to arbitrary or unlawful interference with his privacy, family, home or correspondence, nor to unlawful attacks on his honour and reputation.

(2) Everyone has the right to the protection of the law against such interference or attacks.

Right to life, liberty and security of the person

The right to express dissent and to participate in public affairs through peaceful protest may engage individual rights to life, liberty and security of the person (as well as due process rights) when authorities respond with the use of force or powers of arrest or fail to protect protesters from harm by others.

UDHR Article 3 states:

3. Everyone has the right to life, liberty and security of person.

ICCPR Article 9 (1) provides:

9. (1) Everyone has the right to liberty and security of person. No one shall be subjected to arbitrary arrest or detention. No one shall be deprived of his liberty except on such grounds and in accordance with such procedure as are established by law.

Right to a remedy

International human rights law provides the right to an effective remedy to all persons whose rights and freedoms have been violated.

UDHR Article 8 provides:

8. Everyone has the right to an effective remedy by the competent

national tribunals for acts violating the fundamental rights granted him by the constitution or by law.

The *ICCPR* states:

2. (3) Each State Party to the present Covenant undertakes:

(a) To ensure that any person whose rights or freedoms as herein recognized are violated shall have an effective remedy, notwithstanding that the violation has been committed by persons acting in an official capacity;

(b) To ensure that any person claiming such a remedy shall have his right thereto determined by competent judicial, administrative or legislative authorities, or by any other competent authority provided for by the legal system of the State, and to develop the possibilities of judicial remedy;

(c) To ensure that the competent authorities shall enforce such remedies when granted.

Interpretation

Freedom of opinion and expression

The right to freedom of opinion and expression includes the freedom to hold an opinion without interference and the freedom to seek, receive and impart information and ideas of all kinds, regardless of frontiers. Freedom of expression includes the negative freedom not to speak.[58]

The right to freedom of expression does not exist in isolation. All rights are interrelated, interdependent and indivisible. Freedom of expression is linked with the right to peaceful assembly and association and freedom of thought, conscience, and religion, in particular.

Commenting on the interpretation of *ICCPR* Article 19, in *CCPR General Comment No. 34*, the HR Committee observes that

[f]reedom of opinion and freedom of expression are indispensable

---

58   Eur. Comm. HR, *Case of K. v. Austria*, App. no. 16002/90, Judgment of 13 October 1992.

" Freedom of expression constitutes the primary and basic element of the public order of a democratic society, which is not conceivable without free debate and the possibility that dissenting voices be fully heard.

ACtHR, Compulsory Membership in an Association Prescribed by Law for the Practice of Journalism (Arts. 13 and 29 of the American Convention on Human Rights) (Advisory Opinion OC-5/85 of November 13, 1985, para. 69)

conditions for the full development of the person. They are essential for any society. They constitute the foundation stone for every free and democratic society. The two freedoms are closely related, with freedom of expression providing the vehicle for the exchange and development of opinions.[59]

As affirmed by the ECtHR in *Case of Perna v. Italy*,[60] and repeated by the IACtHR,[61]

Freedom of expression constitutes one of the essential foundations of a democratic society and one of the basic conditions for its progress and for each individual's self-fulfillment. Subject to paragraph 2 of Article 10 [of the *ECHR*], it is applicable not only to "information" or "ideas" that are favourably received or regarded as inoffensive or as a matter of indifference, but also to those that offend, shock or disturb. Such are the demands of that pluralism, tolerance and broadmindedness without which there is no "democratic society". As set forth in [*ECHR*] Article 10, this freedom is subject to exceptions, which must, however, be construed strictly, and the need for any restrictions must be established convincingly...[62]

Dual dimension

Freedom of expression has both an individual dimension and a collective or social dimension. There is an individual right to freedom of expression comprising the right of each person to hold opinions; to share thoughts, ideas and information; and to seek out and receive information. The collective right is the right of society to obtain and receive any information; to know the thoughts, ideas and information communicated by others that is of public interest; and to be well-informed.[63] A specific act of expression

---

59   HR Committee, *CCPR General Comment No. 34, Article 19: Freedoms of opinion and expression*, 12 September 2011, CCPR/C/GC/34, para. 2, [footnotes omitted].
60   ECtHR, *Case of Perna v. Italy*, App. no. 48898/99, Judgment of 6 May 2003.
61   See, for example, IACtHR, *Case of Herrera-Ulloa v. Costa Rica, Preliminary Objections, Merits, Reparations and Costs*, Judgment of July 2, 2004, para. 113.
62   ECtHR, *Case of Perna v. Italy*, App. no. 48898/99, Judgment of 6 May 2003, para. 39.
63   Office of the SR for Freedom of Expression of the IACHR, "The Inter-American Legal Framework regarding the Right to Freedom of Expression", OEA Ser.L/V/II, December 30,

involves both dimensions simultaneously; they are interdependent and of equal importance and must be guaranteed simultaneously, in full.[64]

The ACtHR explained the two dimensions of the right to freedom of expression in *Compulsory Membership in an Association Prescribed by Law for the Practice of Journalism*[65]:

> In its individual dimension, freedom of expression goes further than the theoretical recognition of the right to speak or to write. It also includes and cannot be separated from the right to use whatever medium is deemed appropriate to impart ideas and to have them reach as wide an audience as possible. When the [ACHR] proclaims that freedom of thought and expression includes the right to impart information and ideas through "any... medium," it emphasizes the fact that the expression and dissemination of ideas and information are indivisible concepts...
>
> In its social dimension, freedom of expression is a means for the interchange of ideas and information among human beings and for mass communication. It includes the right of each person to seek to communicate his own views to others, as well as the right to receive opinions and news from others...[66]

The ECtHR has confirmed the essential role of the press in a democratic society. In the *Case of Gawęda v. Poland*,[67] the ECtHR stated that

> [a]lthough [the press] must not overstep certain bounds, in particular in respect of the reputation and rights of others, its duty is nevertheless to impart – in a manner consistent with its obligations and responsibilities – information and ideas on all matters of public interest... Not only does it have the task of imparting such information and ideas: the public also has a right to receive them. Were it otherwise, the press would be

---

2009, para. 13.

64   *Ibid,* para. 16.

65   ACtHR, *Compulsory Membership in an Association Prescribed by Law for the Practice of Journalism* (Arts. 13 and 29 of the American Convention on Human Rights), Advisory Opinion OC-5/85, November 13, 1985.

66   *Ibid,* paras. 31-32.

67   ECtHR, *Case of Gawęda v. Poland,* App. no. 26229/95, Judgment of 14 March 2002.

unable to play its vital role of "public watchdog"... [68]

The right to hold an opinion without interference

Under *ICCPR* Article 19(1), all forms of opinion are protected, including opinions of a political, scientific, historic, moral or religious nature.[69] The right to hold an opinion permits no exceptions or restrictions and includes the right to change one's opinion. No person may be subject to the impairment of their rights under the *ICCPR* on the basis of his or her actual, perceived or supposed opinions. Any form of effort to coerce the holding or not holding of any opinion is prohibited.[70] Freedom to express an opinion includes the freedom not to express one's opinion.[71]

The right to seek and receive information and ideas

The right to seek and receive is part of the public's right of access to information. It includes access to communications of every form that are capable of transmission to others, subject to the provisions in *ICCPR* Article 19(3) and Article 20, which prohibits propaganda for war and the advocacy of national, racial or religious hatred that constitutes incitement to discrimination, hostility or violence.

While access to the internet is not specifically protected as a human right, access to the internet is essential to enjoy the right to freedom of expression, as well as other rights, such as the right to education; the right to freedom of association and assembly; the right to full participation in social, cultural and political life; and the right to social and economic development. States therefore have a positive obligation to promote or to facilitate the enjoyment of the right to freedom of expression and the means necessary to exercise this right, which includes the internet.[72]

---

68   *Ibid*, para. 34.
69   HR Committee, *CCPR General Comment No. 34, Article 19: Freedoms of opinion and expression*, 12 September 2011, CCPR/C/GC/34, para. 9.
70   HR Committee, Communication No. 878/1999, *Yong-Joo Kang v. Republic of Korea*, Views adopted on 15 July 2003, para. 7.2.
71   HR Committee, *CCPR General Comment No. 34, Article 19: Freedoms of opinion and expression*, 12 September 2011, CCPR/C/GC/34, para. 10.
72   UN General Assembly, *Report of the Special Rapporteur on the promotion and protection of the right to freedom of opinion and expression, Frank La Rue*, A/66/290 (10

The right to impart information and ideas of all kinds through any media and regardless of frontiers

Presumption of protection of all forms of expression

As a matter of principle, the protection given by international law to the right to freedom of expression embraces all forms of expression, notwithstanding their content, disseminated by any individual, group or type of media.

In *CCPR General Comment No. 34*, the HR Committee states that *ICCPR* Article 19(2) protects

> all forms of expression and the means of their dissemination. Such forms include spoken, written and sign language and such non-verbal expression as images and objects of art. Means of expression include books, newspapers, pamphlets, posters, banners, dress and legal submissions. They include all forms of audio-visual as well as electronic and internet-based modes of expression [footnotes omitted].[73]

"Expression" under *ECHR* Article 10 is not limited to words, written or spoken, but extends to pictures,[74] images[75] and actions intended to express an idea or to present information. In some circumstances, dress may also fall under *ECHR* Article 10.[76]

Under the inter-American human rights system, the forms of expression protected include:

- the right to speak and to express one's thoughts, ideas, information or opinions orally, in the language of one's choice;

- the right to express oneself in written or printed form, in the language of one's choice;

August 2011), para. 61.

73   HR Committee, *CCPR General Comment No. 34, Article 19: Freedoms of opinion and expression*, 12 September 2011, CCPR/C/GC/34, para. 12.

74   ECtHR, *Müller and Others v. Switzerland*, App. no. 10737/84, Judgment of 24 May 1988, para. 27.

75   ECtHR, *Chorherr v. Austria*, App. no. 13308/87, Judgment of 25 August 1993, para. 23.

76   Eur. Comm. HR, *Stevens v. the United Kingdom*, App. No. 11674/85, Judgment of 3 March 1986.

- the right to disseminate spoken or written expressions or thoughts, information, ideas or opinions, through the appropriate means of one's choosing, in order to reach as many people as possible;

- the right to artistic and symbolic expression, to the dissemination of artistic expression and to access to art, in all its forms;

- the right to seek, receive and have access to expressions, ideas, opinions and information of all kinds;

- the right of access to information about oneself contained in public or private databases or registries, with the corresponding right to update, correct or amend it; and

- the right to possess information, whether written or in any other medium, to transport such information, and to distribute it.[77]

Presumption of protection of all types of expression

In principle, all types of expression are protected, independent of their content.

The right to freedom of expression under *ICCPR* Article 19(2) includes the expression and receipt of communications of every form of idea and opinion capable of transmission to others, subject to the restrictions set out in the *ICCPR*. The HR Committee has determined that Article 19(2) embraces, *inter alia*, political discourse, commentary on one's own and on public affairs, canvassing, discussion of human rights, journalism, cultural and artistic expression, teaching, and religious discourse, and may also include commercial advertising.[78] The scope of *ICCPR* Article 19(2) includes expression that may be regarded as deeply offensive.[79]

The general presumption of coverage of all expressive speech is explained, in the context of the inter-American human rights system, by the State's

---

77   Office of the SR for Freedom of Expression of the IACHR, "The Inter-American Legal Framework regarding the Right to Freedom of Expression", OEA Ser.L/V/II, December 30, 2009, paras 22-29.

78   HR Committee, *CCPR General Comment No. 34, Article 19: Freedoms of opinion and expression,* 12 September 2011, CCPR/C/GC/34, para. 11.

79   See HR Committee, Communication No. 736/1997, *Malcolm Ross v. Canada,* Views adopted on 18 October 2000.

"primary duty of content-neutrality", which requires States "to guarantee that, in principle, there are no persons, groups, ideas or means of expression excluded *a priori* from public debate".[80] The rule that freedom of expression guaranteed under the *ACHR* embraces speech that is "offensive, shocking, unsettling, unpleasant or disturbing to the State or to any segment of the population...is required by the pluralism, tolerance and spirit of openness without which a democratic society cannot exist".[81]

Under the *ECHR*, the only content restriction applied by the European Commission on Human Rights (later merged with ECtHR), dealt with the dissemination of ideas promoting racism and Nazi ideology, and inciting to hatred and racial discrimination.[82] The European Commission relied on *ECHR* Article 17 (prohibition of abuse of rights) and held that freedom of expression may not be used in order to lead to the destruction of the rights and freedoms granted by the *ECHR*, in this case "the basic order of freedom and democracy".[83]

Specifically protected speech

While all forms of expression are protected in principle, certain types of speech receive special protection because of their importance to the exercise of other rights or to the proper functioning and preservation of democracy. Cases under the inter-American system have identified the following types of expression warranting special protection:

- political speech and speech involving matters of public interest;

- speech regarding public officials in the exercise of their duties and candidates for public office; and

- speech that is an element of the identity or personal dignity of the person expressing himself or herself.[84]

---

80   Office of the SR for Freedom of Expression of the IACHR, "The Inter-American Legal Framework regarding the Right to Freedom of Expression", OEA Ser.L/V/II, December 30, 2009, para. 30.
81   *Ibid*, para. 31.
82   Eur. Comm. HR, *Kühnen v. the Federal Republic of Germany*, Application No. 12194/86, Judgment (admissibility) of 12 May 1988.
83   *Ibid*, para. 1.
84   Office of the SR for Freedom of Expression of the IACHR, "The Inter-American Legal

The importance of monitoring the conduct of public affairs in a democratic society means there is a "narrower margin for any restriction of political debate or discourse on matters of public interest".[85] In *Tristán Donoso v. Panama*, the IACtHR reiterated that

> [i]n its constant case law, [the IACtHR] has repeatedly upheld the protection of freedom of expression regarding opinions and statements on matters of which society has a legitimate interest to be informed, in order to be aware of anything that bears on the performance of the State or impacts on general interests or rights, or of anything having significant consequences...[86]

When speech that is critical of or offensive to public officials or individuals involved in shaping public policy results in unjustified attacks on an official's honour, the official is entitled to judicial protection; however, such protection must be "in accordance with the principles of democratic pluralism"[87] and must be afforded through mechanisms that do not stifle criticism or result in self-censorship, in turn obstructing public debate on issues of interest to society.[88]

Under the *ICCPR*, "free communication of information and ideas about public and political issues between citizens, candidates and elected representatives is essential".[89]

The ECtHR has observed that "freedom of political debate is at the very core of the concept of a democratic society which prevails throughout the [*ECHR*]" and it is incumbent on the press, therefore, to impart information

---

Framework regarding the Right to Freedom of Expression", OEA Ser.L/V/II, December 30, 2009, para. 32.

85   *Ibid*, para. 35. See also ECtHR, *Case of Stankov and the United Macedonian Organisation Ilinden v. Bulgaria*, App. nos. 29221/95 and 29225/95, Judgment of 2 January 2002 (Final), para. 88.

86   IACtHR, *Case of Tristán Donoso v. Panamá, Preliminary Objection, Merits, Reparations, and Costs*, Judgment of 27 January 2009, para. 121.

87   IACtHR, *Case of Herrera-Ulloa v. Costa Rica, Preliminary Objections, Merits, Reparations and Costs*, Judgment of July 2, 2004, para. 128.

88   *Ibid*, para. 133.

89   HR Committee, *CCPR General Comment No. 34, Article 19: Freedoms of opinion and expression*, 12 September 2011, CCPR/C/GC/34, para. 20.

and ideas on political issues as well as other areas of public interest.[90] "Not only does the press have the task of imparting such information and ideas: the public also has a right to receive them".[91]

Rulings of the ECtHR indicate that, in matters of public controversy or public interest, or where criticism is aimed at government, strong words and harsh criticism will be tolerated to a greater degree by the court.[92] In the *Case of Arslan v. Turkey*,[93] the ECtHR recalled that

> there is little scope under [Article 10(2) of the *ECHR*] for restrictions on political speech or on debate on questions of public interest... Furthermore, the limits of permissible criticism are wider with regard to the government than in relation to a private citizen or even a politician. In a democratic system the actions or omissions of the government must be subject to the close scrutiny not only of the legislative and judicial authorities but also of public opinion.[94]

The case law of the inter-American system has held that freedom of expression includes the right to denounce human rights violations committed by public officials. In a case involving allegations of victimization for revealing the existence of a "death squad", the IACHR found that

> [t]he right of free expression also includes the right to analyze critically and to oppose. This protection is broader, however, when the statements made by a person deal with alleged violations of human rights. In such a case, not only is a person's individual right to transmit or disseminate information being violated, the right of the entire community to receive information is also being undermined.[95]

---

90   ECtHR, *Case of Lingens v. Austria,* App. no. 9815/82, Judgment of 8 July 1986, para. 42.
91   *Ibid,* para. 41.
92   See, for example, ECtHR, *Case of Thorgeir Thorgeirson v. Iceland, App. no.* 13778/88, Judgment of 25 June 1992; ECtHR, *Case of Jersild v. Denmark,* App. no. 15890/89, Judgment of 23 September 1994.
93   ECtHR, *Case of Arslan v. Turkey, App. no. 23462/94, Judgment of 8 July 1999.*
94   *Ibid,* para. 46.
95   IACHR, *Report No. 20/99. Case 11.317. Merits. Rodolfo Robles Espinoza and Sons.* Peru. February 23, 1999, para. 148.

Freedom of expression includes right to information

Implicit in the right to freedom of expression is the public's right to open access to information held by public bodies. Such information includes records held by a public body, regardless of the form in which the information is stored, its source and the date of production, as well as records held by any other entity so long as they are carrying out a public function.[96]

The right of access to information includes the right of the media to access information on public affairs and the right of the general public to receive media output.[97]

Individuals also have the right to know, in an intelligible form, whether (and if so, what) personal data is stored in automatic data files and for what purposes, and the right to have records rectified where they contain incorrect personal data or data collected or processed contrary to the law.[98]

The HR Committee also suggests that States should proactively put in the public domain government information of public interest and make every effort to ensure easy, prompt, effective and practical access to that information. Fees for requests for information should not be such as to constitute an unreasonable impediment to access to information.[99]

The right to access information, according to the IACHR, is

> a fundamental requirement for guaranteeing transparency and good public administration of the government and other State authorities... It fosters the rendition of accounts and transparency in State administration and prevents corruption and authoritarianism. In addition, free access to information is a measure that allows citizens to adequately exercise their political rights in a representative and participatory democracy.[100]

---

96   HR Committee, *CCPR General Comment No. 34, Article 19: Freedoms of opinion and expression,* 12 September 2011, CCPR/C/GC/34, para. 18.

97   *Ibid,* para. 18. See also ECtHR, *Case of the Sunday Times v. the United Kingdom,* App. no. 6538/74, Judgment of 26 April 1979, para. 65.

98   *Ibid, CCPR General Comment No. 34,* para. 18.

99   *Ibid,* para. 19.

100   IACHR, *Annual Report of the Office of the Special Rapporteur for Freedom of*

In the *Case of Claude-Reyes et al. v. Chile*,[101] the ACtHR held the right to seek and receive information in *ACHR* Article 13 "protects the right of all individuals to request access to State-held information, with the exceptions permitted by the restrictions established in the [ACHR]".[102] The information should be provided without the need to prove direct interest or personal involvement in order to obtain it, except in cases in which a legitimate restriction is applied.

Right to truth

The "right to truth", distinct from the right to access information and from the right to freedom of expression, has emerged in response to the need to access information concerning serious human rights violations. The "right to truth" has been acknowledged in HRC Resolutions[103] and in UN General Assembly Resolution 68/165.[104]

In the case of *Lucio Parada Cea, et al v. El Salvador*,[105] the IACHR found that

> the "right to the truth" arises as a basic and indispensable consequence for all States Parties, given that not knowing the facts related to human rights violations means that, in practice, there is no system of protection capable of guaranteeing the identification and possible punishment of those responsible... The "right to the truth" is a collective right which allows a society to gain access to information essential to the development of democratic systems, and also an individual right for the relatives of the victims, allowing for a form of reparation, especially in cases where the Amnesty Law is enforced. The [ACHR] protects the right to gain access to and obtain information, especially in cases of the disappeared, in regard to which the Court and the Commission

---

Expression, OEA/Ser.L/V/II. Doc. 149, 31 December 2013, Chapter V, pp. 533-534.

101   IACtHR, *Case of Claude-Reyes et al. v. Chile, Merits, Reparations and Costs*, Judgment of September 19, 2006.

102   *Ibid*, para. 77.

103   See UN, HRC resolution 21/7, *Right to the truth*, A/HRC/RES/21/7 (10 October 2012); UN, HRC resolution 12/12, A/HRC/RES/12/12 (12 October 2009).

104   UN General Assembly resolution 68/165. *Right to the truth*, A/RES/68/165 (21 January 2014).

105   IACHR, *Report No. 1/99, Case 10.480, Lucio Parada Cea, et al, v. El Salvador*, 27 January 1999.

have established that the State is obligated to determine the person's whereabouts.[106]

Relationship between right to freedom of expression and other fundamental rights

The rights to freedom of opinion and expression form a basis for the full enjoyment of a wide range of other human rights, including the right to freedom of assembly and association.[107] In its *General Comment No. 25*[108] on *ICCPR* Article 25 (the right to take part in the conduct of public affairs), para. 25, the HR Committee states:

> In order to ensure the full enjoyment of rights protected by [*ICCPR*] article 25, the free communication of information and ideas about public and political issues between citizens, candidates and elected representatives is essential. This implies a free press and other media able to comment on public issues without censorship or restraint and to inform public opinion. It requires the full enjoyment and respect for the rights guaranteed in articles 19, 21 and 22 of the [*ICCPR*], including freedom to engage in political activity individually or through political parties and other organizations, freedom to debate public affairs, to hold peaceful demonstrations and meetings, to criticize and oppose, to publish political material, to campaign for election and to advertise political ideas.

In commenting on the relationship between *ICCPR* Articles 19 and 20 (propaganda for war and advocacy of national, racial or religious hatred), the HR Committee explains that the two provisions are compatible with and complement each other. The expression described in *ICCPR* Article 20 is subject to restriction pursuant to *ICCPR* Article 19. What distinguishes the acts addressed in Article 20 is that they must be prohibited by law.[109]

---

106   *Ibid*, paras. 150-151.
107   HR Committee, *CCPR General Comment No. 34, Article 19: Freedoms of opinion and expression*, 12 September 2011, CCPR/C/GC/34, para. 4.
108   HR Committee, *CCPR General Comment No. 25, Article 25: The Right to Participate in Public Affairs, Voting Rights and the Right of Equal Access to Public Service*, 12 July 1996, CCPR/C/21/Rev.1/Add.7, para. 25.
109   HR Committee, *CCPR General Comment No. 34, Article 19: Freedoms of opinion and expression*, 12 September 2011, CCPR/C/GC/34, paras. 50-51.

According to the OAS SR for Freedom of Expression Catalina Botero Merino, similar provisions contained in *ACHR* Article 13(5) relating to propaganda for war and advocacy of national, racial or religious hatred are not protected expression under the *ACHR*.[110] Also excluded from protection under ACHR Article 13 are incitements to genocide[111] and child pornography.[112]

States have positive and negative duties

States have an obligation both to promote, by creating a legal and social environment in which the exercise of the right to freedom of expression is possible, and to protect the right, by preventing the interference with the exercise of freedom of expression and access to information.

In *Ozgur Gundem v. Turkey*,[113] the ECtHR noted that the effective exercise of the right to freedom of expression may entail positive as well as negative duties on the part of the State:

The Court recalls the key importance of freedom of expression as one of the preconditions for a functioning democracy. Genuine, effective exercise of this freedom does not depend merely on the State's duty not to interfere, but may require positive measures of protection, even in the sphere of relations between individuals...In determining whether or not a positive obligation exists, regard must be had to the fair balance that has to be struck between the general interest of the community and the interests of the individual, the search for which is called for throughout the [*ECHR*]. The scope of this obligation will inevitably vary, having regard to the diversity of situations obtaining in Contracting States, the difficulties involved in policing modern societies and the choices which must be made in terms of priorities and resources. Nor must such an obligation be interpreted in such a way as to impose an impossible or disproportionate burden on the authorities.[114]

---

110   Office of the SR for Freedom of Expression of the IACHR, "The Inter-American Legal Framework regarding the Right to Freedom of Expression", OEA Ser.L/V/II, December 30, 2009, paras. 57-58.
111   *Ibid,* para. 59.
112   *Ibid,* para. 60.
113   ECtHR, *Ozgur Gundem v. Turkey,* App. no. 23144/93, Judgment of 16 March 2000.
114   *Ibid,* paras. 42-43.

State duty to protect against impairment of rights and freedoms by private persons or entities

States have an obligation to ensure that persons are protected from any acts by private persons or entities that would impair the enjoyment of the freedoms of opinion and expression to the extent that these rights are amenable to application between private persons or entities.[115] In *Gauthier v. Canada*, the HR Committee held that the State party had allowed a private organization to control access to the Parliamentary press facilities, without intervention, resulting in a violation of Mr. Gauthier's rights to freedom of expression under *ICCPR* Article 19.[116]

Restrictions on the right to express an opinion, idea or information strictly limited

International law outlines a cumulative three-part test that must be met for the legitimate and legal restriction of the right to the freedom of expression. Any restriction must:

- be provided by law, which is clear and accessible to everyone;

- be proven as necessary and legitimate to protect one or more of the grounds for restriction explicitly and exhaustively set out in the respective treaty; and

- be proven to be a proportionate measure and the least restrictive means to achieve the purported aim.

Restriction must be provided by law

Any restriction imposed on the exercise of the right to freedom of expression must, first of all, be provided for by pre-existing law. The law must meet certain requirements of precision and clarity, so that individuals can foresee the consequences of their actions, and must be applied in an objective, non-discriminatory manner.

---

115   HR Committee, *CCPR General Comment No. 34, Article 19: Freedoms of opinion and expression,* 12 September 2011, CCPR/C/GC/34, para. 7.
116   HR Committee, Communication No. 633/1995, *Robert W. Gauthier v. Canada,* Views adopted on 5 May 1999, para. 13.6.

For the purposes of *ICCPR* Article 19(3), a norm, to be characterized as a "law", must be formulated with sufficient precision to enable an individual to regulate his or her conduct accordingly.[117] Laws imposing restrictions or limitations must be accessible, concrete, clear and unambiguous, such that they can be understood by everyone and applied to everyone.[118] Laws imposing restrictions or limitations must not be arbitrary or unreasonable and must not be used as a means of political censorship or of silencing criticism of public officials or public policies.[119]

A law may not confer unfettered discretion on those charged with its execution and must provide sufficient guidance to those charged with their execution to enable them to ascertain what sorts of expression are properly restricted.[120] Laws restricting the right to freedom of expression must be compatible with the provisions, aims and objectives of the *ICCPR*.[121] It is for the State party to demonstrate the legal basis for any restrictions imposed on freedom of expression.[122] Finally, the law must clearly "set out the remedy against or mechanisms for challenging the illegal or abusive application of that limitation or restriction," including judicial review by an independent court or tribunal.[123]

The types of information or expression that may be restricted under international human rights law in relation to offline content also apply to online content. Similarly, any restriction applied to the right to freedom of expression exercised through the internet must also comply with human rights law.[124]

---

117 HR Committee, Communication No. 578/1994, *Leonardus Johannes Maria de Groot v. The Netherlands*, 14 July 1995, para. 4.3.

118 UN, General Assembly, *Report of the Special Rapporteur on the promotion and protection of the right to freedom of opinion and expression, Frank La Rue*, A/HRC/ (14/23), 20 April 2010, para. 79(d).

119 *Ibid*, para. 79(f).

120 HR Committee, *CCPR General Comment No. 34, Article 19: Freedoms of opinion and expression*, 12 September 2011, CCPR/C/GC/34, para. 25.

121 *Ibid*, para. 26. See HR Committee, Communication No. 488/1992, *Toonen v. Australia*, Views adopted on 31 March 1994, para. 8.2.

122 *Ibid, CCPR General Comment No. 34*, para. 27.

123 UN General Assembly, *Report of the Special Rapporteur on the promotion and protection of the right to freedom of opinion and expression, Frank La Rue*, A/HRC/ (14/23), 20 April 2010, para. 79(e).

124 UN General Assembly, *Report of the Special Rapporteur on the promotion and*

Any legislation restricting the right to freedom of expression must be applied by a body that is independent of any political, commercial or other unwarranted influences in a manner that is neither arbitrary nor discriminatory, and with adequate safeguards against abuse, including the possibility of challenge and remedy against abuse in the legislation's application.[125]

Under *ECHR* Article 10(2), the "prescribed by law" requirement demands that the law be adequately accessible and that it be formulated with sufficient precision to enable the citizen to regulate his or her conduct. For example, in *Altuğ Taner Akçam v Turkey*,[126] the ECtHR found that there was a violation of *ECHR* Article 10 because the domestic legislation prohibiting expression, Article 301 of the Turkish Criminal Code, was too broad and vague, meaning an individual could not foresee what the consequences of an action might entail. The ECtHR has accepted that common-law rules[127] or principles of international law[128] constitute a legal basis for the interference with the right to freedom of expression.

Under the *ACHR*, a restriction must be established, in advance, by an express and precise definition in a law.[129] The restriction imposed must serve compelling objectives authorized by the ACHR and be necessary to achieve those objectives.

In the *Case of Usón Ramírez v. Venezuela*,[130] the IACtHR found that ambiguity in the criminal law used to convict a retired military officer of slander "raises doubts and opens possibilities for the abuse of discretion

---

protection of the right to freedom of opinion and expression, Frank La Rue, A/66/290 (10 August 2011), para. 15.

125 *Ibid*, para. 17.

126 ECtHR, *Case of Altuğ Taner Akçam v Turkey,* App. no. 27520/07, Judgment of 25 January 2012 (Final), para. 95.

127 ECtHR, *Case of the Sunday Times v. the United Kingdom,* App. no. 6538/74, Judgment of 26 April 1979, para. 47.

128 ECtHR, *Case of Groppera Radio Ag and Others v. Switzerland,* App. no. 10890/84, Judgment of 28 March 1990, para. 68.

129 ACtHR, *Compulsory Membership in an Association Prescribed by Law for the Practice of Journalism* (Arts. 13 and 29 of the American Convention on Human Rights), Advisory Opinion OC-5/85, November 13, 1985, paras. 39-40.

130 IACtHR, *Case of Francisco Usón Ramírez v. Venezuela, Preliminary Objections, Merits, Reparations, and Costs,* Judgment of November 20, 2009.

by the authority, particularly undesirable when the criminal liabilities of individuals shall be established and it is penalized in a manner that seriously affects fundamental goods such as freedom".[131]

A law restricting freedom of expression must be of general application. The ACHPR has ruled that laws made to apply specifically to one individual or legal personality raise the serious danger of discrimination and lack of equal treatment before the law guaranteed by Article 3 of the *Banjul Charter*.[132] Overly broad limitations are also illegitimate.[133]

Restriction must be necessary to protect the legitimate ground

"exhaustive list"

The only grounds for restricting the exercise of the right to freedom of expression are those set out in the international and regional human rights instruments. States may not create additional grounds in domestic legislation.

The *ECHR* again narrows the definition of a limitation, requiring the three-part test to apply to any "formalities, conditions, restrictions or penalties" under *ECHR* Article 10(2).

Under *ICCPR* Article 19(3), restrictions on the right to freedom of expression must be provided by law and necessary for "respect of the rights and reputations of others" or for "the protection of national security or of public order (ordre public), or of public health or morals". No exception or restriction to the right to hold opinions is permitted under the *ICCPR*. Restrictions are not allowed on grounds not specified in *ICCPR* Article 19(3), even if such grounds would justify restrictions to other rights protected in the *ICCPR*. Restrictions must be applied only for those purposes for which they were prescribed and must be directly related to the specific need on which they are predicated.[134]

---

131   *Ibid*, para. 56.
132   ACHPR, *Media Rights Agenda, Constitutional Rights Project, Media Rights Agenda and Constitutional Rights Project v. Nigeria, Communication* Nos. 105/93, 128/94, 130/94 and 152/96 (1998), para. 71.
133   ACHR, *Constitutional Rights Project and Others v. Nigeria*, Communication Nos. 140/94, 141/94 and 145/95 (2000), para. 40.
134   HR Committee, *CCPR General Comment No. 34, Article 19: Freedoms of opinion and*

ICCPR grounds for restriction

"respect of the rights and reputations of others"

Under *ICCPR* Article 19(3)(a), the term "rights" includes human rights as recognized in the *ICCPR* and more generally in international human rights law.[135] The term "others" relates to other persons individually or as members of a community.[136] This ground includes types of expression that States are bound under *ICCPR* Article 20 to prohibit by law[137] as well as expression that is not punishable criminally, but may justify restriction through civil suit, such as defamation.[138]

Frank La Rue, the UN SR on the promotion and protection of the right to freedom of opinion and expression, believes that it is important to make a clear distinction between three types of expression:

(a) expression that constitutes an offence under international law and can be prosecuted criminally; (b) expression that is not criminally punishable but may justify a restriction and a civil suit; and (c) expression that does not give rise to criminal or civil sanctions, but still raises concerns in terms of tolerance, civility and respect for others. These different categories of content pose different issues of principle and call for different legal and technological responses.[139]

The SR cautioned, however, against criminalizing laws, such as defamation laws, aimed at protecting the reputation of individuals, "as criminalization can be counter-effective and the threat of harsh sanctions exert a significant chilling effect on the right to freedom of expression".[140]

Laws that prohibit incitement to national, racial or religious hatred must

---

expression, 12 September 2011, CCPR/C/GC/34, para. 22.

135   *Ibid,* para. 28.

136   See HR Committee, Communication No. 736/1997, *Malcolm Ross v. Canada,* Views adopted on 18 October 2000, para. 11.5.

137   HR Committee, *CCPR General Comment No. 34, Article 19: Freedoms of opinion and expression,* 12 September 2011, CCPR/C/GC/34, paras. 50-51.

138   UN General Assembly, *Report of the Special Rapporteur on the promotion and protection of the right to freedom of opinion and expression, Frank La Rue,* A/66/290 (10 August 2011), para. 18.

139   *Ibid.*

140   *Ibid,* para. 40.

be formulated in a way that makes clear that the law's sole purpose is to protect individuals from hostility, discrimination or violence, rather than to protect belief systems, religions or institutions as such from criticism.[141] SR Frank La Rue observes that

[t]he right to freedom of expression implies that it should be possible to scrutinize, openly debate and criticize, even harshly and unreasonably, ideas, opinions, belief systems and institutions, including religious ones, as long as this does not advocate hatred that incites hostility, discrimination or violence against an individual or a group of individuals.[142]

"protection of national security or of public order (ordre public), or of public health or morals"

It is not compatible with *ICCPR* Article 19(3) to invoke provisions relating to national security to suppress, or withhold from the public, information of legitimate public interest that does not harm national security, or to prosecute journalists, researchers, environmental activists, human rights defenders, or others, for having disseminated such information.[143]

Principle 3 of the *Global Principles on National Security and the Right to Information (Tshwane Principles)*[144] states that

[n]o restriction on the right to information on national security grounds may be imposed unless the government can demonstrate that: (1) the restriction (a) is prescribed by law and (b) is necessary in a democratic society (c) to protect a legitimate national security interest; and (2) the law provides for adequate safeguards against abuse, including prompt, full, accessible, and effective scrutiny of the validity of the restriction

---

141   *Ibid,* para. 30.
142   *Ibid.*
143   HR Committee, *CCPR General Comment No. 34, Article 19: Freedoms of opinion and expression,* 12 September 2011, CCPR/C/GC/34, para. 30. *HR Committee, Concluding Observations on the Russian Federation,* 1 December 2003, CCPR/CO/79/RUS, para. 21.
144   Open Society Justice Initiative, *The Global Principles on National Security and the Right to Information (The Tshwane Principles),* 12 June 2013 (New York: Open Society Foundations, 2013).

by an independent oversight authority and full review by the courts.[145]

Even if a State Party may introduce a permit system intended to strike a balance between an individual's freedom of speech and the general interest in maintaining public order in a certain area, such a system must not operate in a way that is incompatible with Article 19 of the *ICCPR*.[146]

Domestic criminal laws that prohibit incitement to terrorism must meet the three-part test of restrictions to the right of freedom of expression, that is, the laws

(a) must be limited to the incitement of conduct that is truly terrorist in nature, as properly defined; [footnote omitted] (b) must restrict the right to freedom of expression no more than is necessary for the protection of national security, public order and safety or public health or morals; (c) must be prescribed in law in precise language, including by avoiding reference to vague terms such as "glorifying" or "promoting" terrorism; (d) must include an actual (objective) risk that the act incited will be committed; (e) should expressly refer to two elements of intent, namely intent to communicate a message and intent that this message incite the commission of a terrorist act; and (f) should preserve the application of legal defences or principles leading to the exclusion of criminal liability by referring to "unlawful" incitement to terrorism.[147]

In the view of the HR Committee, offences such as "encouragement of terrorism"[148] and "extremist activity"[149] risk unnecessary and disproportionate interferences with freedom of expression. States should ensure that powers to protect information genuinely related to matters of

---

145   *Ibid*, Principle 3.
146   HR Committee, Communication No. 1157/2003, *Patrick Coleman v. Australia*, Views adopted on 17 July 2006, para. 7.3.
147   UN General Assembly, *Report of the Special Rapporteur on the promotion and protection of the right to freedom of opinion and expression, Frank La Rue*, A/66/290 (10 August 2011), para. 34.
148   HR Committee, *Concluding observations on the United Kingdom of Great Britain and Northern Ireland*, 30 July 2008, CCPR/C/GBR/CO/6, para. 26.
149   HR Committee, *Concluding observations on Russia*, 24 November 2009, CCPR/C/RUS/CO/6, para. 24.

national security are narrowly utilized and limited to instances where the release of such information would be harmful to national security.[150]

With respect to protection of morals, the concept of morals "derives from many social, philosophical and religious traditions; consequently, limitations... for the purpose of protecting morals must be based on principles not deriving exclusively from a single tradition".[151] Any such limitations must be understood in the light of universality of human rights and the principle of non-discrimination.

Grounds for restriction under regional instruments

Article 10(2) of the *ECHR* contains a greater number of legitimate aims which may limit the exercise of the right to freedom of expression when "prescribed by law" and "necessary in a democratic society", namely, "national security, territorial integrity or public safety", "the prevention of disorder or crime", "the protection of health or morals", "the protection of the reputation or rights of others", "preventing the disclosure of information received in confidence", or "maintaining the authority and impartiality of the judiciary".

Under *ACHR* Article 13(2), the exercise of the right to freedom of thought and expression "shall not be subject to prior censorship but shall be subject to subsequent imposition of liability, which shall be expressly established by law to the extent necessary to ensure: a. respect for the right or reputations of others; or b. the protection of national security, public order, or public health or morals".

In *Case of Ivcher-Bronstein v. Peru*, the IACtHR held that "[w]hen evaluating an alleged restriction or limitation to freedom of expression, the Court should not restrict itself to examining the act in question, but should also examine this act in the light of the facts of the case as a whole, including the circumstances and context in which they occurred".[152]

---

150   HR Committee, *Concluding observations on the United Kingdom of Great Britain and Northern Ireland,* 30 July 2008, CCPR/C/GBR/CO/6, para. 24.

151   HR Committee, *CCPR General Comment No. 34, Article 19: Freedoms of opinion and expression,* 12 September 2011, CCPR/C/GC/34, para. 32.

152   IACtHR, *Case of Ivcher-Bronstein v. Peru,* Judgment of February 6, 2001 (Merits,

In *Tristán Donoso*, the IACtHR held that, in considering the legitimacy of limitations on freedom of expression under the *ACHR*, "the Judiciary must take into account the context in which the statements involving matters of public interest are made; the judge shall 'assess the respect of the rights and reputations of others in relation to the value in a democratic society of open debate regarding matters of public interest or concern.'"[153]

An interference with freedom of expression can take many different forms, but censorship prior to publication, expressly prohibited only under the *ACHR*, is seen by the courts and treaty bodies as the most dangerous threat to the exercise of the right, and as such requires the most careful scrutiny.[154] Criminal penalties, even those consisting of relatively small fines, could constitute an implicit censorship.

Courts at the regional level have also confirmed the supervisory role of the courts in determining in each case whether an expression posed a real and serious danger to national security. Under the *ECHR*, where an expression has been limited for being an "incitement to violence", the court must look at the interference in light of the case as a whole, including the content of the impugned statements and the context in which they were made.

In the *Case of Sürek v. Turkey (No. 3)*,[155] the ECtHR found that while references to "Kurdistan" and to the existence of a national liberation struggle could not, on their own, justify an interference with the applicant's rights, descriptions of the struggle as a "war directed against the forces of the Republic of Turkey", and assertions that "[w]e want to wage a total liberation struggle", made in the context of a security situation in southeast Turkey, "must be seen as capable of inciting to further violence in the region" and were therefore lawfully restricted.[156]

By contrast, in the *Case of Sürek v. Turkey (No. 4)*,[157] where the impugned articles described Turkey as "the real terrorist" and as "the enemy" the

---

Reparations and Costs), para. 154.

153   IACtHR, *Case of Tristán Donoso v. Panamá, Preliminary Objection, Merits, Reparations, and Costs,* Judgment of 27 January 2009, para. 123.

154   ECtHR, *Gaweda v. Poland,* App. no. 26229/95, Judgment of 14 March 2002, para. 35.

155   ECtHR, *Case of Sürek v. Turkey (No. 3),* App. No. 24735/94, Judgment of 8 July 1999.

156   *Ibid,* paras. 38-43.

157   ECtHR, *Case of Sürek v. Turkey (No. 4),* App. No. 24762/94), Judgment of 8 July 1999.

ECtHR found this language "more a reflection of the hardened attitude of one side to the conflict, rather than a call to violence", and the statement that "it is time to settle accounts" must be seen "in the context of the overall literary and metaphorical tone of the article".[158] The ECtHR also found that "the domestic authorities failed to have sufficient regard to the public's right to be informed of a different perspective on the situation in Southeastern Turkey, irrespective of how unpalatable that perspective may be for them".[159]

Decisions of the ECtHR indicate that once in the public arena, information on national security may not be prohibited, withdrawn or the authors of dissemination punished.[160]

In *Kühnen v. Federal Republic of Germany*, criminal proceedings taken in response to a publication advocating national socialism were found not to violate *ECHR* Article 10, as the impugned publication aimed at impairing the basic order of freedom and democracy and therefore was contrary to the basic values underlying the *ECHR*.[161]

The ECtHR has found that, although the margin of appreciation of states is wider with respect to "morals", it is not unlimited: the national authorities do not have an unfettered and an unreviewable discretion.[162]

With respect to "hate speech", the ECtHR has stressed that

the "duties and responsibilities" which accompany the exercise of the right to freedom of expression by media professionals assume special significance in situations of conflict and tension. Particular caution is called for when consideration is being given to the publication of views of representatives of organisations which resort to violence against the State lest the media become a vehicle for the dissemination of hate

---

158   *Ibid,* para. 58.
159   *Ibid.*
160   See ECtHR, *Case of Observer and Guardian v. the United Kingdom,* App. no. 13585/88, Judgment of 26 November 1991; ECtHR, *Case of Vereniging Weekblad Bluf! v. the Netherlands,* App. no. 16616/90, Judgment of 9 February 1995.
161   Eur. Comm. HR, *Kühnen v. the Federal Republic of Germany,* Application No. 12194/86, Judgment (admissibility) of 12 May 1988.
162   ECtHR, *Open Door and Dublin Well Woman v. Ireland,* App. no. 64/1991/316/387-388, Judgment of 23 September 1992, para. 68.

speech and the promotion of violence. At the same time, where such views cannot be categorised as such, Contracting States cannot with reference to the protection of territorial integrity or national security or the prevention of crime or disorder restrict the right of the public to be informed of them by bringing the weight of the criminal law to bear on the media.[163]

The ACHPR has confirmed that the *Banjul Charter* does not contain a derogation clause and, therefore, limitations on the rights and freedoms enshrined in the *Banjul Charter* cannot be justified by emergencies or special circumstances.[164] The only legitimate reasons for limitations of the rights and freedoms of the *Banjul Charter* are those found in Article 27(2), that is, that the rights of the Charter "shall be exercised with due regard to the rights of others, collective security, morality and common interest".[165]

Under the *ACHR*, where limitations to freedom of expression are imposed for the protection of the rights of others, it is necessary for those rights to be clearly harmed or threatened.[166] In any case where there is an actual abuse of freedom of expression that causes harm to the rights of others, the means least restrictive to freedom of expression must be used to repair that harm.[167]

For purposes of limitations to freedom of expression under the ACHR, the ACtHR defines "public order" as "the conditions that assure the normal and harmonious functioning of institutions based on a coherent system of values and principles".[168] According to the ACtHR,

that same concept of public order in a democratic society requires the

---

163   ECtHR, *Case Of Erdoğdu and İnce v. Turkey*, App. nos. *25067/94 and 25068/94*, Judgment of 8 July 1999, para. 54.

164   ACHR, *Constitutional Rights Project and Others v. Nigeria*, Communication Nos. 140/94, 141/94 and 145/95 (2000), para. 41.

165   *Ibid.*

166   Office of the SR for Freedom of Expression of the IACHR, *"The Inter-American Legal Framework regarding the Right to Freedom of Expression"*, OEA Ser.L/V/II, December 30, 2009, para. 77.

167   *Ibid,* para 79.

168   ACtHR, *Compulsory Membership in an Association Prescribed by Law for the Practice of Journalism* (Arts. 13 and 29 of the American Convention on Human Rights), Advisory Opinion OC-5/85, November 13, 1985, para. 64.

guarantee of the widest possible circulation of news, ideas and opinions as well as the widest access to information by society as a whole. Freedom of expression constitutes the primary and basic element of the public order of a democratic society, which is not conceivable without free debate and the possibility that dissenting voices be fully heard. In this sense, the Court adheres to the ideas expressed by the European Commission of Human Rights when, basing itself on the Preamble of the European Convention, it stated

> "that the purpose of the High Contracting Parties in concluding the Convention was not to concede to each other reciprocal rights and obligations in pursuance of their individual national interests but... to establish a common public order of the free democracies of Europe with the object of safeguarding their common heritage of political traditions, ideals, freedom and the rule of law..."

It is also in the interest of the democratic public order inherent in the [ACHR] that the right of each individual to express himself freely and that of society as a whole to receive information be scrupulously respected. [169]

In the case of violations of human rights or humanitarian law, the IACtHR has stated that States cannot use the protection of national security or public order as grounds to refuse providing judicial or other authorities information required as part of an ongoing investigation or proceeding.[170]

A limitation under the *ACHR* may not constitute direct or indirect mechanisms of prior censorship.[171]

"necessary"

A limitation that is in accordance with a clear law serving a legitimate aim will not pass the test unless it can be convincingly established that it is truly necessary to achieve that aim. The necessity for any limitation

---

169   *Ibid*, para. 69.
170   IACtHR, *Myrna Mack Chang v Guatemala. Merits, Reparations and Costs.* Judgment of 25 November 2003, Series C, No. 101, I/A Court HR, para. 180.
171   IACtHR, *Case of Kimel v. Argentina, Merits, Reparations and Costs,* Judgment of 2 May 2008, para. 54.

is judged within the context of the needs of a democratic society and its institutions. A limitation must be directly related to the specific need on which it is predicated and must be proportionate to that need and applied in an objective and non-discriminatory manner. In exercising its supervisory jurisdiction, the court must look at the interference in the light of the case as a whole, including the content of the impugned statements and the context in which they were made.

Both the *ICCPR* and *ECHR* preface the limitation provision with the statement that the exercise of the right to freedom of expression carries with it "duties and responsibilities". In *Maximilian Rommelfanger v. the Federal Republic of Germany*,[172] the European Commission of Human Rights found that even where an individual assumes special duties and responsibilities of loyalty through a valid contract of employment, domestic law must take account of the necessity to secure the employee's freedom of expression against unreasonable demands of his employer.[173] In *Case of Wille v. Liechtenstein*,[174] the applicant, a high-ranking judge, complained that, on account of the views expressed by him in the course of a public lecture on constitutional law, the Prince of Liechtenstein announced his intention not to re-appoint the applicant to a public office. In finding a violation of the right to freedom of expression under *ECHR* Article 10(2), the ECtHR ruled that

> the Court must bear in mind that, whenever the right of freedom of expression of persons in such a position is at issue, the "duties and responsibilities" referred to in [*ECHR* Article 10(2)] assume a special significance since it can be expected of public officials serving in the judiciary that they should show restraint in exercising their freedom of expression in all cases where the authority and impartiality of judiciary are likely to be called in question. Nevertheless the Court finds that an interference with the freedom of expression of a judge in a position such as the applicant's calls for close scrutiny on the part of the Court.[175]

---

172   Eur. Comm. HR, *Maximilian Rommelfanger v. the Federal Republic of Germany*, App. No. 12242/86, 6 September 1989.
173   *Ibid.*
174   ECtHR, *Case of Wille v. Liechtenstein*, App. no. 28396/95, Judgment of 28 October 1999.
175   *Ibid*, para. 64.

"in a democratic society"

The courts and treaty bodies have determined that the necessity for any limitation must be judged in terms of the legitimate needs of democratic societies and institutions.

Under Article 32 of the *Arab Charter of Human Rights*, the right to information and to freedom of opinion and expression shall be exercised "in conformity with the fundamental values of society" and subject to only those restrictions "required" (to ensure respect for the rights or reputation of others or the protection of national security, public order, public health or morals.)

The requirement that the necessity for any limitation on the right to freedom of expression must be determined within the context of a democratic society is explicitly provided for in *ECHR* Article 10(2). In the *Case of Handyside v. the United Kingdom*,[176] the ECtHR found that it was impossible to find in the domestic law of the various Contracting States a uniform European conception of morals. Therefore, States should be left a margin of appreciation in interpreting whether a particular measure is "necessary". At the same time, the ECtHR stressed that the test of "necessity" is a strict one:

> [W]hilst the adjective "necessary", within the meaning of [*ECHR*] Article 10 para. 2 ...is not synonymous with "indispensable"... the words "absolutely necessary" and "strictly necessary"..., neither has it the flexibility of such expressions as "admissible", "ordinary"... "useful"... "reasonable"... or "desirable".[177]

The ECtHR further stated that the court's supervisory functions oblige it to pay the utmost attention to the principles characterizing a "democratic society". In particular, it held that:

> Freedom of expression constitutes one of the essential foundations of such a society, one of the basic conditions for its progress and for the development of every man. Subject to [*ECHR*] paragraph [10]2...,

---

176   ECtHR, *Case of Handyside v. the United Kingdom,* App. no. 5493/72, Judgment of 7 December 1976.
177   *Ibid,* para. 48.

it is applicable not only to "information" or "ideas" that are favourably received or regarded as inoffensive or as a matter of indifference, but also to those that offend, shock or disturb the State or any sector of the population. Such are the demands of that pluralism, tolerance and broadmindedness without which there is no "democratic society". This means, amongst other things, that every "formality", "condition", "restriction" or "penalty" imposed in this sphere must be proportionate to the legitimate aim pursued.[178]

In the *Case of Sergey Kuznetsov v. Russia*,[179] the ECtHR ruled, in relation to the right to peaceful assembly under *ECHR* Article 11, "the only necessity capable of justifying an interference with the rights enshrined in [*ECHR* Article 11] is one that may claim to spring "from democratic society" and that "[a]ccordingly, States must not only safeguard the right to assemble peacefully but also refrain from applying unreasonable indirect restrictions upon that right. In view of the essential nature of freedom of assembly and its close relationship with democracy there must be convincing and compelling reasons to justify an interference with this right".[180]

In *Compulsory Membership in an Association Prescribed by Law for the Practice of Journalism*, the ACtHR commented on the absence of the phrase "in a democratic society" in ACHR Article 13:

It is true that the [*ECHR*] uses the expression "necessary in a democratic society," while Article 13 of the [ACHR] omits that phrase. This difference in wording loses its significance, however, once it is recognized that the [*ECHR*] contains no clause comparable to Article 29 of the [ACHR], which lays down guidelines for the interpretation of the [ACHR] and prohibits the interpretation of any provision of the treaty "precluding other rights and guarantees... derived from representative democracy as a form of government."[181]

---

178   *Ibid*, para. 49.
179   ECtHR, *Case of Sergey Kuznetsov v. Russia*, App. no. 10877/04, Judgment of 23 January 2009 (Final).
180   *Ibid*, para. 39.
181   ACtHR, *Compulsory Membership in an Association Prescribed by Law for the Practice of Journalism* (Arts. 13 and 29 of the American Convention on Human Rights), Advisory Opinion OC-5/85, November 13, 1985, para. 44.

Referring also to Article XXVIII of the *American Declaration of the Rights and Duties of Man*, which provides that "[t]he rights of man are limited by the rights of others, by the security of all, and by the just demands of the general welfare and the advancement of democracy", the ACtHR concluded:

> The just demands of democracy must consequently guide the interpretation of the [ACHR] and, in particular, the interpretation of those provisions that bear a critical relationship to the preservation and functioning of democratic institutions.[182]

"pressing social need"

The word "necessary" in *ICCPR* Article 19(3) means that the limitation or restriction must address a "pressing pubic or social need which must be met in order to prevent the violation of a legal right that is protected to an even greater extent".[183] In *Ross v. Canada*, the HR Committee determined that the removal of the author from a teaching position could be considered a restriction necessary to protect the right and freedom of Jewish children to have a school system free from bias, prejudice and intolerance.[184]

In *Sunday Times v. the United Kingdom*, interfering with the publication of an article about the distillers of thalidomide while legal actions against the distillers were on-going did not correspond to a sufficiently pressing social need that outweighed the public interest in freedom of expression within the meaning of the *ECHR*.[185]

In order to prove that an interference was necessary in a democratic society, the domestic courts as well as the ECtHR must be satisfied that a "pressing social need" requiring that particular limitation on the exercise of the right to freedom of expression existed.[186] Any restriction under *ECHR* Article 10

---

182   *Ibid.*
183   UN General Assembly, *Report of the Special Rapporteur on the promotion and protection of the right to freedom of opinion and expression, Frank La Rue*, A/HRC/ (14/23), 20 April 2010, para. 79(g)(ii).
184   HR Committee, Communication No. 736/1997, *Malcolm Ross v. Canada*, Views adopted on 18 October 2000, para. 11.6.
185   ECtHR, *Case of the Sunday Times v. the United Kingdom*, App. no. 6538/74, Judgment of 26 April 1979, para. 67.
186   ECtHR, *Case of Observer and Guardian v. the United Kingdom*, App. no. 13585/88, Judgment of 26 November 1991, para. 59.

"must be narrowly interpreted and the necessity for any restrictions must be convincingly established."[187]

The term "necessary" under *ACHR* Article 13(2) has been interpreted to mean that there is a clear and compelling need for its imposition and that it cannot reasonably be accomplished by any other means less restrictive to human rights. In *Compulsory Membership in an Association Prescribed by Law for the Practice of Journalism*, the ACtHR found that

> [t]he "necessity" and, hence, the legality of restrictions imposed under [ACHR] Article 13(2) on freedom of expression, depend upon a showing that the restrictions are required by a compelling governmental interest. Hence if there are various options to achieve this objective, that which least restricts the right protected must be selected. Given this standard, it is not enough to demonstrate, for example, that a law performs a useful or desirable purpose; to be compatible with the Convention, the restrictions must be justified by reference to governmental objectives which, because of their importance, clearly outweigh the social need for the full enjoyment of the right Article 13 guarantees.[188]

The restriction must be proportionate to the value to be protected

Restrictions must not be overbroad. Restrictive measures must conform to the principle of proportionality – they must be appropriate to achieve their protective function, be the least intrusive measure among those which might achieve the protective function, and be proportionate to the value to be protected.[189] The principle of proportionality applies to both the law and its application. In *Rafael Marques de Morais v. Angola*,[190] the HR Committee found that the arrest, 40-day detention and conviction of a journalist for writing articles critical of the president, even if it had a basis in Angolan law

---

187   ECtHR, *Case of Thorgeir Thorgeirson v. Iceland*, App. no. 13778/88, Judgment of 25 June 1992, para. 63.

188   ACtHR, *Compulsory Membership in an Association Prescribed by Law for the Practice of Journalism* (Arts. 13 and 29 of the American Convention on Human Rights), Advisory Opinion OC-5/85, November 13, 1985, para. 46.

189   HR Committee, *CCPR General Comment No. 34, Article 19: Freedoms of opinion and expression*, 12 September 2011, CCPR/C/GC/34, para. 34.

190   HR Committee, Communication No. 1128/2002, *Rafael Marques de Morais v. Angola*, Views adopted on 29 March 2005.

and was in pursuit of a legitimate aim, such as protecting the president's rights and reputation or public order, was not proportionate to that aim. The HR Committee observed that,

> Given the paramount importance, in a democratic society, of the right to freedom of expression and of a free and uncensored press or other media, [footnote omitted] the severity of the sanctions imposed on the author cannot be considered as a proportionate measure to protect public order or the honour and the reputation of the President, a public figure who, as such, is subject to criticism and opposition. [191]

The principle of proportionality must also take account of the form of expression at issue as well as the means of its dissemination. For instance, the value placed by the *ICCPR* on uninhibited expression is particularly high in circumstances of public debate in a democratic society concerning figures in the political domain.[192]

In *Gauthier v Canada*, the HR Committee found that failing to issue Mr. Gauthier a full membership to the Parliamentary Press Gallery was neither necessary nor proportionate to the alleged goal of maintaining the effective operation of Parliament and public order.[193]

Any restrictions on the operation of websites, blogs or any other internet-based, electronic or other such information dissemination system, including systems to support such communication, such as internet service providers or search engines, are only permissible to the extent that they are compatible with *ICCPR* Article 19(3).[194] Permissible restrictions generally should be content-specific; generic bans on the operation of certain sites and systems are not compatible with the *ICCPR*. It is a violation of *ICCPR* Article 19 to prohibit a site or an information dissemination system from publishing material solely on the basis that it may be critical of the

---

191 *Ibid,* para. 6.8. See also HR Committee, Communication No. 1157/2003, *Patrick Coleman v. Australia,* Views adopted on 17 July 2006, para. 7.3.

192 HR Committee, Communication No. 1180/2003, *Mr. Zeljko Bodrožić v. Serbia and Montenegro,* Views adopted on 31 October 2005, para. 7.2.

193 HR Committee, Communication No. 633/1995, *Robert W. Gauthier v. Canada,* Views adopted on 5 May 1999, para. 13.6.

194 HR Committee, *CCPR General Comment No. 34, Article 19: Freedoms of opinion and expression,* 12 September 2011, CCPR/C/GC/34, para. 43.

government or the political or social system espoused by the government.[195]

Where States restrict prohibited expression on the internet through blocking of content, they should "provide full details regarding the necessity and justification for blocking a particular website" and "determination of what content should be blocked should be undertaken by a competent judicial authority or a body which is independent of any political, commercial, or other unwarranted influences to ensure that blocking is not used as a means of censorship".[196]

In *Constitutional Rights Project and Others v. Nigeria*, the ACHPR ruled that the "justification of limitations must be strictly proportionate with and absolutely necessary for the advantages which follow. Most important, a limitation may not erode a right such that the right itself becomes illusory".[197]

Under the *ACHR*, a restriction of the right to freedom of expression "must be proportionate and closely tailored to the accomplishment of the legitimate governmental objective necessitating it".[198]

The onus is on the State to justify restriction

The burden is on the State to prove that a limitation is justified.[199] When a State invokes a legitimate ground for restriction of the right to freedom of expression, it must demonstrate in specific and individualized fashion the precise nature of the threat, the necessity and proportionality of the specific action taken, in particular by establishing a direct and immediate

---

195   HR Committee, *Concluding observations on the Syrian Arab Republic,* 9 August 2005, CCPR/CO/84/SYR, para. 13.

196   UN General Assembly, *Report of the Special Rapporteur on the promotion and protection of the right to freedom of opinion and expression, Frank La Rue,* A/66/290 (10 August 2011), para. 38.

197   ACHR, *Constitutional Rights Project and Others v. Nigeria,* Communication Nos. 140/94, 141/94 and 145/95 (2000), para. 42.

198   ACtHR, *Compulsory Membership in an Association Prescribed by Law for the Practice of Journalism* (Arts. 13 and 29 of the American Convention on Human Rights), Advisory Opinion OC-5/85, November 13, 1985 para. 46.

199   See, for example, ACHPR, *Media Rights Agenda, Constitutional Rights Project, Media Rights Agenda and Constitutional Rights Project v. Nigeria,* Communication Nos. 105/93, 128/94, 130/94 and 152/96 (1998), para. 71.

connection between the expression and the threat.[200]

Derogation in time of public emergency

Under the *ICCPR*, States may temporarily suspend certain rights, including the right to freedom of expression, where a state of emergency threatens the life of the nation. *ICCPR* Article 4(1) provides:

> 4. (1) In times of public emergency which threatens the life of the nation and the existence of which is officially proclaimed, the States Parties to the present Covenant may take measures derogating from their obligations under the present Covenant to the extent strictly required by the exigencies of the situation, provided that such measures are not inconsistent with their other obligations under international law and do not involve discrimination solely on the ground of race, colour, sex, language, religion or social origin.

Any derogation of rights must be in accordance with *ICCPR* Article 4. In *CCPR General Comment No. 29*,[201] the HR Committee notes, on the interpretation of Article 4, that "[m]easures derogating from the provisions of the [*ICCPR*] must be of an exceptional and temporary nature"[202], are allowed "only if and to the extent that the situation constitutes a threat to the life of the nation"[203] and must be a proportionate response to the threat.[204] A state of emergency is invalid under *ICCPR* Article 4 if it is declared for the sole aim of restricting freedom of expression and preventing criticism of those who hold power.[205]

---

200   HR Committee, *CCPR General Comment No. 34, Article 19: Freedoms of opinion and expression,* 12 September 2011, CCPR/C/GC/34, para. 36 [footnotes omitted]; UN General Assembly, *Report of the Special Rapporteur on the promotion and protection of the right to freedom of opinion and expression, Frank La Rue,* A/66/290 (10 August 2011), para. 16.
201   HR Committee, *CCPR General Comment No. 29, Article 4: States of Emergency,* U.N. Doc. CCPR/C/21/Rev.1/Add.11 (2001).
202   *Ibid,* para. 2.
203   *Ibid,* para. 3.
204   *Ibid,* para. 4.
205   UN General Assembly, *Report of the Special Rapporteur on the promotion and protection of the right to freedom of opinion and expression, Frank La Rue,* A/HRC/ (14/23), 20 April 2010, para. 79(j).

Restriction must not impair the right itself

In *General Comment No. 34*, the HR Committee noted that *ICCPR* Article 19(3) expressly provides that the exercise of the right to freedom of expression carries with it special duties and responsibilities, and for this reason

> two limitative areas of restrictions on the right are permitted, which may relate either to respect of the rights or reputations of others or to the protection of national security or of public order (ordre public) or of public health or morals. However, when a State party imposes restrictions on the exercise of freedom of expression, these may not put in jeopardy the right itself. The Committee recalls that the relation between right and restriction and between norm and exception must not be reversed. [footnote omitted] The Committee also recalls the provisions of article 5, paragraph 1, of the [*ICCPR*] according to which "nothing in the present [*ICCPR*] may be interpreted as implying for any State, group or person any right to engage in any activity or perform any act aimed at the destruction of any of the rights and freedoms recognized herein or at their limitation to a greater extent than is provided for in the present [*ICCPR*]".[206]

Types of expression that should not be restricted

As stipulated in HRC resolution 12/16 (para. 5 (p) (i)), the following types of expression should never be subject to restrictions:

- discussion of government policies and political debate;
- reporting on human rights, government activities and corruption in government;
- engaging in election campaigns, peaceful demonstrations or political activities, including for peace or democracy; and
- expression of opinion and dissent, religion or belief, including by persons belonging to minorities or vulnerable groups.

In their *Joint Declaration on Universality and the Right to Freedom of*

---

206   HR Committee, *CCPR General Comment No. 34, Article 19: Freedoms of opinion and expression*, 12 September 2011, CCPR/C/GC/34, para. 21.

Expression,[207] the SRs on Freedom of Expression of the UN, OAS, ACHPR, and the Organization for the Security and Cooperation of Europe's Representative on the Freedom of the Media (OSCE RFM) stated that certain types of legal restrictions on freedom of expression can never be justified by reference to local traditions, culture and values, but rather constitute human rights violations:

i. Laws which protect religions against criticism or prohibit the expression of dissenting religious beliefs.

ii. Laws which prohibit debate about issues of concern or interest to minorities and other groups which have suffered from historical discrimination or prohibit speech which is an element of the identity or personal dignity of these individuals and/or groups.

iii. Laws which provide for special protection against criticism for officials, institutions, historical figures, or national or religious symbols.[208]

Exceptional types of expression that States are required to prohibit

International law prohibits five categories of expression: child pornography;[209] direct and public incitement to commit genocide;[210] advocacy of national, racial or religious hatred that constitutes incitement to discrimination, hostility or violence;[211] dissemination of ideas based on racial superiority or hatred and incitement to racial discrimination;[212] and

---

207   UN, OAS, OSCE, ACHPR, *Joint Declaration on Universality and the Right to Freedom of Expression,* 6 May 2014.

208   *Ibid,* para (1)(f).

209   The dissemination of child pornography is explicitly prohibited under the *Optional Protocol to the Convention on the Rights of the Child on the sale of children, child prostitution and child pornography,* Article 3.

210   Direct and public incitement to commit genocide is prohibited under the *Convention on the Prevention and Punishment of the Crime of Genocide,* Article 3; *Rome Statute of the International Criminal Court,* Article 25(3)(e); *Statue of the International Criminal Tribunal for the Former Yugoslavia,* Article 4(3)(c); *Statute of the International Criminal Tribunal for Rwanda,* Article 2(3)(c).

211   Under *ICCPR,* Article 20, States must prohibit by law "any propaganda for war" and "any advocacy of national, racial or religious hatred that constitutes incitement to discrimination, hostility or violence".

212   *ICERD,* Article 4.

incitement to terrorism.[213]

Domestic laws prohibiting these categories of expression must still meet the test described above for limiting the right to freedom of expression.

Freedom of peaceful assembly and association

The HR Committee has not developed general comments on *ICCPR* Article 21 (freedom of assembly) or *ICCPR* Article 22 (freedom of association) and has relatively little jurisprudence on either right. In 2010, the HRC appointed a SR on the rights to freedom of peaceful assembly and of association. In his first thematic report, SR Maina Kiai stated that

> [t]he rights to freedom of peaceful assembly and of association serve as a vehicle for the exercise of many other civil, cultural, economic, political and social rights. The rights are essential components of democracy as they empower men and women to "express their political opinions, engage in literary and artistic pursuits and other cultural, economic and social activities, engage in religious observances or other beliefs, form and join trade unions and cooperatives, and elect leaders to represent their interests and hold them accountable"... Such interdependence and interrelatedness with other rights make them a valuable indicator of a State's respect for the enjoyment of many other human rights.[214]

UN SRs report that, alongside elections, assemblies can play a fundamental role in public participation, "holding governments accountable and expressing the will of the people as part of the democratic processes".[215]

The right to freedom of assembly has been described by the ECtHR as a

> fundamental right in a democratic society and, like the right to freedom of expression, is one of the foundations of such a society. Thus, it

---

213   *See* UN Security Council resolution 1624 (2005).
214   UN HRC, *Report of the Special Rapporteur on the rights to freedom of peaceful assembly and of association, Maina Kiai*, 21 May 2012, A/HRC/20/27, para. 12.
215   UN HRC, *Joint report of the Special Rapporteur on the rights to freedom of peaceful assembly and of association and the Special Rapporteur on extrajudicial, summary or arbitrary executions on the proper management of assemblies, 4 February 2016*, A/HRC/31/66, para. 5.

should not be interpreted restrictively...As such this right covers both private meetings and meetings in public thoroughfares as well as static meetings and public processions; in addition, it can be exercised by individuals and those organising the assembly... States must not only safeguard the right to assemble peacefully but also refrain from applying unreasonable indirect restrictions upon that...Lastly, the Court considers that, although the essential object of [ECHR] Article 11 is to protect the individual against arbitrary interference by public authorities with the exercise of the rights protected, there may in addition be positive obligations to secure the effective enjoyment of these rights.[216]

While rights to freedom of peaceful assembly and of association are clearly interrelated, interdependent and mutually reinforcing, they are also two separate rights and should be treated separately.[217]

Definition of "assembly"

For the purposes of *ICCPR* Article 21, an "assembly" is generally understood as meaning

an intentional and temporary gathering in a private or public space for a specific purpose, and can take the form of demonstrations, meetings, strikes, processions, rallies or sit-ins with the purpose of voicing grievances and aspirations or facilitating celebrations ... Even sporting events, music concerts and other such gatherings can potentially be included. While an assembly is defined as a temporary gathering, this may include long-term demonstrations, including extended sit-ins and "occupy"-style manifestations. Although an assembly has generally been understood as a physical gathering of people, it has been recognized that human rights protections, including for freedom of assembly, may apply to analogous interactions taking place online.[218]

---

216   ECtHR, *Djavit An v. Turkey,* App. No. 20652/92, Judgment of 9 July 2003 (Final), paras. 56-57.
217   UN HRC, *Report of the Special Rapporteur on the rights to freedom of peaceful assembly and of association, Maina Kiai,* 21 May 2012, A/HRC/20/27, para. 4.
218   UN HRC, *Joint report of the Special Rapporteur on the rights to freedom of peaceful assembly and of association and the Special Rapporteur on extrajudicial, summary or*

The right to freedom of peaceful assembly is held by each individual participating in an assembly and includes the right to plan, organize, promote and advertise an assembly in any lawful manner.[219]

The OSCE *Guidelines on Freedom of Peaceful Assembly*[220] define "assembly" to mean "the intentional and temporary presence of a number of individuals in a public place for a common expressive purpose".[221]

Definition of "association"

An "association" includes any groups of individuals or any legal entities brought together in order to collectively act, express, promote, pursue or defend a field of common interests.[222] The word "association" refers, *inter alia*, to civil society organizations, clubs, cooperatives, NGOs, religious associations, political parties, trade unions, foundations or even online associations.[223]

In *Sidiropoulos and Others v. Greece*, the ECtHR ruled "that citizens should be able to form a legal entity in order to act collectively in a field of mutual interest is one of the most important aspects of the right to freedom of association, without which that right would be deprived of any meaning".[224]

The right to form and join an association is an inherent part of the right to freedom of association.[225] No one can be compelled to belong to an association; associations should be free to choose their members and

---

arbitrary executions on the proper management of assemblies, 4 February 2016, A/ HRC/31/66, para. 10.

219   *Ibid, paras. 19-20.*

220   OSCE Office of Democratic Institutions and Human Rights (2010), *Guidelines on Freedom of Peaceful Assembly*, 2nd Edition (Warsaw: Organization for Security and Cooperation in Europe) ["OSCE Guidelines"]

221   *OSCE Guidelines, para. 1.2.*

222   UN General Assembly, *Report of the Special Representative of the Secretary-General on human rights defenders, Hina Jilani*, 1 October 2004, A/59/401, para. 46, online <http:// www.un.org/ga/59/documentation/list4.html>.

223   UN General Assembly, *Report of the Special Rapporteur on the rights to freedom of peaceful assembly and of association, Maina Kiai*, 21 May 2012, A/HRC/20/27, para. 52.

224   ECtHR, *Sidiropoulos and Others v. Greece*, App. no. 57/1997/841/1047, Judgment of 10 July 1998, para. 40.

225   UN HRC, *Report of the Special Rapporteur on the rights to freedom of peaceful assembly and of association, Maina Kiai*, 21 May 2012, A/HRC/20/27, para. 53.

whether to open to any membership.[226] Necessarily included in the right of association is the freedom not to associate with others. In no cases should membership in an association alone be taken as grounds for criminal charges.[227]

The right to freedom of association applies for the entire life of the association[228] and equally protects associations that are not registered.[229]

The HR Committee has observed that "the right to freedom of association relates not only to the right to form an association, but also guarantees the right of such an association freely to carry out its statutory activities. The protection afforded by [*ICCPR*] article 22 extends to all activities of an association".[230]

Relationship with right to freedom of expression

In *Stankov v. Bulgaria*, the ECtHR commented on the important interplay between the rights to freedom of assembly and association and the right to freedom of expression:

> The Court reiterates that notwithstanding its autonomous role and particular sphere of application, Article 11 of [*ECHR*] must also be considered in the light of Article 10. The protection of opinions and the freedom to express them is one of the objectives of the freedoms of assembly and association as enshrined in [*ECHR*] Article 11.[231]

---

226   OSCE/ODIHR, *Key Guiding Principles of Freedom of Association with an Emphasis on Non-Governmental Organizations*, para. 28.

227   See, for example, ACHPR, *International Pen and Others v. Nigeria*, Communication Nos. 137/94, 139/94, 154/96 and 161/97 (1998), paras. 107-110; ACHPR, *Malawi African Association and others v. Mauritania*, Communication Nos. 54/91, 61/91, 98/93, 164/97, 196/97 and 210/98 (2000), paras. 106-107.

228   ECtHR, *United Communist Party of Turkey and Others v. Turkey*, App. no. 133/1996/752/951, Judgment of 30 January 1998, para. 33.

229   UN HRC, *Report of the Special Rapporteur on the rights to freedom of peaceful assembly and of association, Maina Kiai*, 21 May 2012, A/HRC/20/27, para. 56.

230   HR Committee, Communication No. 1274/2004, *Korneenko et al. v. Belarus*, Views adopted on 31 October 2006, para. 7.2.

231   ECtHR, *Case of Stankov and the United Macedonian Organisation Ilinden v. Bulgaria*, App. nos. 29221/95 and 29225/95, Judgment of 2 January 2002 (Final), para. 85.

In the *Case of Schwabe and M.G. v. Germany*,[232] the ECtHR stated that it takes several elements into account in determining the relationship between the right to freedom of expression and the right to freedom of assembly to determine whether the main focus of a case should be on the right to freedom of assembly or the right to freedom of expression on its own.[233] Depending on the circumstances of the case, *ECHR* Article 11 has often been regarded by the ECtHR as the *lex specialis*, taking precedence for assemblies over *ECHR* Article 10.[234] In *Schwabe*, the ECtHR noted that, owing to their detention throughout the duration of the G8 summit, the applicants were unable to express their views together with the other demonstrators present to protest against the summit. They were also protesting against the prohibition on expressing their views concerning the detention of demonstrators as expressed on the banners. The ECtHR found, though, that the main focus of the complaints lay in their right to freedom of assembly as they were prevented from taking part in the demonstrations and expressing their views and therefore examined that part of the application under *ECHR* Article 11 alone. The ECtHR went on to hold, however, that "the issue of freedom of expression cannot in the present case be entirely separated from that of freedom of assembly. Notwithstanding its autonomous role and particular sphere of application, [*ECHR*] Article 11 must therefore also be considered in the light of [*ECHR*] Article 10".[235]

The ACHPR described the relationship between the rights to freedom of expression, freedom of assembly and of association under the *Banjul Charter* in *International Pen and Others v. Nigeria*:

There is a close relationship between the rights expressed in the Articles 9.2, 10.1 and 11. Communication 154 alleges that the actual reason for the trial and the ultimate death sentences was the peaceful expression of views by the accused persons. The victims were disseminating information and opinions on the rights of the people who live in the oil producing area of Ogoniland, through MOSOP and specifically a rally. These allegations have not been contradicted by the government,

---

232   See ECtHR, *Case of Schwabe and M.G. v. Germany,* App. nos. 8080/08 and 8577/08, Judgment of 01 March 2012 (Final).

233   *Ibid,* paras. 99-100.

234   *Ibid.*

235   *Ibid,* para. 101.

which has already been shown to be highly prejudiced against MOSOP, without giving concrete justifications. MOSOP was founded specifically for the expression of views of the people who live in the oil producing areas, and the rally was organised with this in view. The Government's actions is [sic] inconsistent with Article 9.2 implicit when it violated Articles 10.1 and 11.[236]

In *Mecheslav Gryb v. Belarus*,[237] an outspoken critic of the government was fined after participating in a peaceful rally and his lawyer's licence was not renewed. Noting the intimate connection between the acts protected by Articles 19 and 21 of the *ICCPR*, the HR Committee found that the government's actions had resulted in a violation of both articles.[238]

In the *Case of Sergey Kuznetsov v. Russia*, the ECtHR observed that "the protection of personal opinions, secured by [*ECHR*] Article 10, is one of the objectives of freedom of peaceful assembly as enshrined in [*ECHR*] Article 11. Accordingly, the issue of freedom of expression cannot be separated from that of freedom of assembly".[239]

Presumption in favour of holding assemblies

Because international law recognizes an inalienable right to take part in peaceful assemblies, it follows that there is a presumption in favour of holding peaceful assemblies.[240] Assemblies should be presumed lawful, subject to the permissible limitations set out in international human rights instruments.

The OSCE Guidelines provide that "[a]s a fundamental right, freedom of assembly should be enjoyed insofar as possible without regulation.

---

236   ACHPR, *International Pen and Others v. Nigeria,* Communication Nos. 137/94, 139/94, 154/96 and 161/97 (1998), para. 110.

237   HR Committee, Communication No. 1316/2004, *Mecheslav Gryb v. Belarus,* Views adopted on 26 October 2011.

238   *Ibid,* paras. 9.5 and 14.

239   ECtHR, *Case of Sergey Kuznetsov v. Russia,* App. no. 10877/04, Judgment of 23 January 2009 (Final), para. 23.

240   UN HRC, *Joint report of the Special Rapporteur on the rights to freedom of peaceful assembly and of association and the Special Rapporteur on extrajudicial, summary or arbitrary executions on the proper management of assemblies, 4 February 2016,* A/HRC/31/66, para. 18.

Anything not expressly forbidden by law should be presumed to be permissible".[241] The OSCE recommends that the presumption in favour of holding assemblies should be "clearly and explicitly established in law".[242]

Public protest, and freedom of assembly in general, should be regarded as equally legitimate uses of public space as the more routine purposes for which public space is used (such as commercial activity or for pedestrian and vehicular traffic).[243]

Presumption of "peacefulness"

In determining whether an assembly is protected under *ICCPR* Article 21, the peacefulness of an assembly should be presumed, and a broad interpretation of the term "peaceful" should be afforded.[244] Regard must be given to the manner in which the assembly is held and to the intentions of the participants.[245]

According to the UN High Commissioner for Human Rights, an assembly should be deemed peaceful "if its organizers and participants have peaceful intentions and do not use, advocate or incite violence".[246] The term "peaceful" should be interpreted to include conduct that may annoy or give offence to persons opposed to the ideas or claims that it is seeking to promote[247] and even include conduct that temporarily hinders, impedes or

---

241   *OSCE Guidelines,* para. 2.1.

242   *OSCE Guidelines,* para. 2.1.

243   *OSCE Guidelines,* para. 20. See also UN HRC, *Report of the Special Rapporteur on the rights to freedom of peaceful assembly and of association, Maina Kiai,* 21 May 2012, A/HRC/20/27, para. 41.

244   UN HRC, *Joint report of the Special Rapporteur on the rights to freedom of peaceful assembly and of association and the Special Rapporteur on extrajudicial, summary or arbitrary executions on the proper management of assemblies, 4 February 2016,* A/HRC/31/66, para. 18.

245   *Ibid,* para. 18.

246   UN HRC, *Report of the United Nations High Commissioner for Human Rights on Effective measures and best practices to ensure the promotion and protection of human rights in the context of peaceful protests,* 21 January 2013, A/HRC/22/28, para. 10. See also *OSCE Guidelines,* para. 1.2.

247   ECtHR, *Case of Plattform "Ärzte Für Das Leben" v. Austria,* App. no. 10126/82, Judgment of 21 June 1988, para. 32.

obstructs the activities of third parties.[248]

The notion of "peaceful assembly" does not cover a demonstration where the organizers and participants have violent intentions that result in public disorder.[249] The ECtHR has ruled that an assembly will be deemed peaceful as long as the participants remain peaceful, even if the organizers have not complied with all legal requirements prior to the assembly.[250] The Commission considers that the right to freedom of peaceful assembly is secured to everyone who organizes or participates in a peaceful demonstration.

Police have the duty to remove violent individuals in order to allow protesters to exercise their right to assemble and express themselves peacefully.[251]

The presumption in favour of holding peaceful assemblies should be clearly and explicitly established in the law.[252]

Right to access information

The ability to access information is essential to the effective exercise of the right to freedom of assembly and to ensure accountability. Information includes records held by a public body at any level or by private bodies performing public functions.[253] The public should have "easy, prompt, effective and practical access to such information, through proactive disclosure and the enactment of legislation to facilitate public access to

---

248   *OSCE Guidelines*, para. 1.3.

249   ECHR, *Case of M.C. v. the Federal Republic of Germany*, App. no. 13079/87, 6 March 1989 (Admissibility decision).

250   ECtHR, *Case of Oya Ataman v. Turkey*, App. no. 74552/01, Judgment of 5 December 2006, para. 39; ECtHR, *Case of Cisse v. France*, App. no. 51346/99, Judgment of 09/07/2002 (Final), para. 37.

251   *Report of the United Nations High Commissioner for Human Rights on Effective measures and best practices to ensure the promotion and protection of human rights in the context of peaceful protests*, 21 January 2013, A/HRC/22/28, para. 10.

252   *OSCE Guidelines*, para. 30.

253   UN HRC, *Joint report of the Special Rapporteur on the rights to freedom of peaceful assembly and of association and the Special Rapporteur on extrajudicial, summary or arbitrary executions on the proper management of assemblies, 4 February 2016, A/HRC/31/66*, para. 79.

information".[254]

State duty to facilitate the exercise of rights to freedom of assembly and association

The State duty to fulfill the rights to freedom of association and assembly require positive measures to facilitate the exercise of these rights, including establishing and maintaining an environment in which individuals exercising these rights may operate freely without undue bureaucratic regulation or fear that they may be subject to threats, acts of intimidation or violence.[255]

The OSCE Guidelines provide that the State should facilitate and protect assemblies "at the organizers' preferred location" and should ensure that organizers are not impeded in efforts to publicize assemblies.[256]

Under the *ACHR*, the competent institutions of the State have a duty to design operating plans and procedures that will facilitate the exercise of the right of assembly.[257] According to the IACHR, "[t]his involves everything from rerouting pedestrian and vehicular traffic in a certain area, to escorting those who are participating in the mass gathering or demonstration in order to guarantee their safety and make it possible for the activities involved to take place".[258]

Protection from interference by others

The State has a positive duty to take reasonable and appropriate measures to enable peaceful assemblies to take place without participants fearing physical violence.[259] The State's obligation to protect the exercise of peaceful assemblies includes the protection of participants from individuals or groups who aim at disrupting or dispersing such assemblies.[260] The obligation to

---

254   *Ibid*, para. 80.

255   UN HRC, *Report of the Special Rapporteur on the rights to freedom of peaceful assembly and of association, Maina Kiai*, 21 May 2012, A/HRC/20/27, para. 63.

256   *OSCE Guidelines*, para. 2.2.

257   OAS, IACHR, *Report on Citizen Security and Human Rights* (2009), OEA/Ser.L/V/II. Doc. 57, para. 193.

258   *Ibid*.

259   *OSCE Guidelines*, para. 5.3.

260   UN HRC, *Report of the Special Rapporteur on the rights to freedom of peaceful assembly and of association, Maina Kiai*, 21 May 2012, A/HRC/20/27, para. 33.

protect assemblies from disruption by others is the responsibility of the State and not of assembly organizers and should be explicitly stated in legislation.[261]

Assembly organizers and participants should not be considered or held liable for the unlawful conduct of others and should not be made responsible for the maintenance of public order.[262]

Policing of assemblies must be guided by human rights principles[263]

The OSCE Guidelines provide that policing of assemblies "must be guided by the human rights principles of legality, necessity, proportionality and non-discrimination and must adhere to applicable human rights standards".[264] The use of force must be regulated by domestic law, which should set out the circumstances under which its use is justified, including the need to provide adequate prior warnings.[265] Law enforcement personnel should face civil and/or criminal liability where the use of force was not authorized by law, or more force was used than was necessary in the circumstances, or when authorities failed to intervene when such intervention might have prevented other officers from using excessive force.[266]

Freedom from State interference

In addition to positive obligations to create the conditions in which individuals may exercise their rights to peacefully assemble and to associate, States also have negative obligations not to unduly obstruct the exercise of these rights.

Associations

Members should be free to determine their statutes, structure and activities and make decisions without State interference.[267] Associations should enjoy,

---

261   *Ibid.*
262   *Ibid,* para. 31; *OSCE Guidelines,* para. 5.7.
263   See the following section, under "Interpretation", for a more detailed discussion on policing peaceful protests.
264   *OSCE Guidelines,* para. 5.3.
265   *OSCE Guidelines,* para. 5.5.
266   *OSCE Guidelines,* para. 5.6.
267   UN HRC, *Report of the Special Rapporteur on the rights to freedom of peaceful assembly and of association, Maina Kiai,* 21 May 2012, A/HRC/20/27, para. 64.

inter alia, the rights to express opinion, disseminate information, engage with the public and advocate before governments and international bodies for human rights, for the preservation and development of a minority's culture[268] or for changes in law, including changes in the Constitution.[269]

In establishing procedures to create an association as a legal entity, governments must act in good faith and in a timely and non-selective manner. Procedures should be simple, non-onerous or even free of charge and expeditious.[270] Under the *ICCPR*, failure by a registration body to provide a response to a submission or application within a clear and short time limit should result in a presumption that associations are operating legally.[271] The ECtHR found that "significant delays in the registration procedure, if attributable to the Ministry of Justice, amounts to an interference with the exercise of the right of the association's founders to freedom of association".[272]

Any decision rejecting the submission or application must be clearly motivated and duly communicated in writing to the applicant.[273] Associations whose submissions or applications have been rejected should have the opportunity to challenge the decision before an independent and impartial court.[274]

Newly adopted laws should not request all previously registered associations to re-register.[275]

Assemblies and associations should not be subject to prior authorization

The exercise of fundamental freedoms should not be subject to previous

---

268   ECtHR, *Ouranio Toxo and Others v. Greece*, App. no. 74989/01, Judgment of 20 October 2005, para. 40.

269   ECtHR, *Zhechev v. Bulgaria*, App. no. 57045/00, Judgment of 21 June 2007.

270   UN HRC, *Report of the Special Rapporteur on the rights to freedom of peaceful assembly and of association, Maina Kiai*, 21 May 2012, A/HRC/20/27, para. 57.

271   *Ibid*, para. 60.

272   ECtHR, *Ismayilov v. Azerbaijan*, App. No. 4439/04, Judgment of 17 April 2008 (Final), para. 48.

273   UN HRC, *Report of the Special Rapporteur on the rights to freedom of peaceful assembly and of association, Maina Kiai*, 21 May 2012, A/HRC/20/27, para. 61.

274   *Ibid*.

275   CRC, *Concluding observations on Nepal*, CRC/C/15/Add.261, 21 September 2005, paras. 33 and 34.

authorizations by the authorities.[276] With respect to the establishment of an association, a "notification procedure", rather than a "prior authorization procedure", complies better with international human rights law (associations are automatically granted legal personality as soon as the authorities are notified by the founders that an organization was created).[277]

Any notification procedure imposed on the holding of an assembly must be for the purpose of facilitating the exercise of the right to freedom of assembly and to take measures to protect public safety and order and the rights and freedoms of others.[278]

Prior notification procedures in relation to the holding of an assembly should be subject to a "proportionality assessment, not unduly bureaucratic" and "be required a maximum of, for example, 48 hours prior to the day the assembly is planned to take place".[279] Prior notification should ideally be required only for large meetings or meetings that may disrupt road traffic.[280] Where the organizers fail to notify the authorities, the assembly should not be dispersed automatically and criminal sanctions should not be applied automatically.[281] Spontaneous assemblies should be exempted from prior notification.[282] Where notification is provided for two or more unrelated assemblies at the same time and place, each should be facilitated as best as

---

276   UN HRC, *Report of the Special Rapporteur on the rights to freedom of peaceful assembly and of association, Maina Kiai,* 21 May 2012, A/HRC/20/27, para. 28; UN HRC, *Joint report of the Special Rapporteur on the rights to freedom of peaceful assembly and of association and the Special Rapporteur on extrajudicial, summary or arbitrary executions on the proper management of assemblies,* 4 February 2016, A/HRC/31/66, para. 21.

277   UN HRC, *Report of the Special Rapporteur on the rights to freedom of peaceful assembly and of association, Maina Kiai,* 21 May 2012, A/HRC/20/27, para. 58.

278   *OSCE Guidelines,* para. 4.1; IACHR, *Report on the Situation of Human Rights Defenders in the Americas,* OEA/Ser.L/V.II.124, Doc. 5 rev. 1, 7 March 2006, para. 58.

279   UN HRC, *Report of the Special Rapporteur on the rights to freedom of peaceful assembly and of association, Maina Kiai,* 21 May 2012, A/HRC/20/27, para. 28.

280   *Ibid.* See *OSCE Guidelines,* para. 163.

281   UN HRC, *Report of the Special Rapporteur on the rights to freedom of peaceful assembly and of association, Maina Kiai,* 21 May 2012, A/HRC/20/27, para. 29.

282   *Ibid.* See also UN HRC, *Joint report of the Special Rapporteur on the rights to freedom of peaceful assembly and of association and the Special Rapporteur on extrajudicial, summary or arbitrary executions on the proper management of assemblies,* 4 February 2016, A/HRC/31/66, para. 23.

possible, ensuring no differential levels of restriction.[283]

A notification procedure should not function as a de facto request for authorization or as a basis for content-based regulation. Notification should not be expected for assemblies that do not require prior preparation by State authorities, such as those where only a small number of participants is expected, or where the impact on the public is expected to be minimal.[284]

The notification procedure(s) should be free of charge and widely accessible.[285]

Right to access funding and resources

Associations, both registered and unregistered, should be able to access funding freely, including the right to seek, secure and use funding and resources – human, material and financial - from domestic, foreign, and international entities, including individuals, civil society organizations, governments and international organizations.[286]

According to SR Maina Kiai, the term "resources" encompasses

> a broad concept that includes financial transfers (e.g., donations, grants, contracts, sponsorships, social investments, etc.); loan guarantees and other forms of financial assistance from natural and legal persons; in-kind donations (e.g., contributions of goods, services, software and other forms of intellectual property, real property, etc.); material resources (e.g. office supplies, IT equipment, etc.); human resources (e.g. paid staff, volunteers, etc.); access to international assistance, solidarity; ability to travel and communicate without undue interference and the right to benefit from the protection of the State.[287]

---

283   See *OSCE Guidelines*, para. 4.3.
284   UN HRC, *Joint report of the Special Rapporteur on the rights to freedom of peaceful assembly and of association and the Special Rapporteur on extrajudicial, summary or arbitrary executions on the proper management of assemblies*, 4 February 2016, A/HRC/31/66, para. 21
285   *Ibid*, para. 22.
286   UN HRC, *Report of the Special Rapporteur on the rights to freedom of peaceful assembly and of association, Maina Kiai*, 21 May 2012, A/HRC/20/27, para. 68.
287   UN HRC, *Report of the Special Rapporteur on the rights to freedom of peaceful assembly and of association, Maina Kiai*, 24 April 2013, A/HRC/23/39, para. 10.

Organizers of assemblies should not incur any financial charges for the provision of policing, medical, safety measures and other public services during an assembly.[288]

Right to monitor assemblies

The right to observe public assemblies is part of the more general right to receive information.[289] Freedom to monitor public assemblies should be guaranteed not only to all media professionals, but also to others, such as human rights activists, whose aim is to contribute to informed public debate. In *Steel and Morris v. United Kingdom*,[290] the ECtHR rejected the notion that the applicants should be afforded any less protection under *ECHR* Article 10 than a journalist:

> The Court considers, however, that in a democratic society even small and informal campaign groups, such as London Greenpeace, must be able to carry on their activities effectively and that there exists a strong public interest in enabling such groups and individuals outside the mainstream to contribute to the public debate by disseminating information and ideas on matters of general public interest such as health and the environment.[291]

Restrictions on exercise of rights to freedom of assembly and association strictly limited

The rights to peaceful assembly and freedom of association are fundamental rights that should be enjoyed without restriction to the greatest extent possible. Freedom is to be considered the rule and its restriction the exception. Any restriction must not impair the essence of the right.[292] The

---

288 UN HRC, *Report of the Special Rapporteur on the rights to freedom of peaceful assembly and of association, Maina Kiai*, 21 May 2012, A/HRC/20/27, para. 31; *OSCE Guidelines*, para. 5.2.
289 See, *inter alia*, ECtHR, *Case of Castells v. Spain*, App. no. 11798/85, Judgment of 23 April 1992, para. 43; ECtHR, *Case of Thorgeir Thorgeirson v. Iceland*, App. no. 13778/88, Judgment of 25 June 1992, para. 63.
290 ECtHR, *Case of Steel and Morris v. United Kingdom*, App. no. 68416/01, Judgment of 15 May 2005 (final).
291 *Ibid*, para. 89.
292 UN HRC, *Joint report of the Special Rapporteur on the rights to freedom of peaceful assembly and of association and the Special Rapporteur on extrajudicial, summary or*

only legitimate grounds for restricting the rights to freedom of assembly and association are those prescribed in international and regional human rights instruments.

As with the right to freedom of expression, the rights to freedom of assembly and association may only be restricted under *ICCPR* Articles 21 and 22 for the purpose of protecting national security, public safety, public order, the protection of public health or morals or the protection of the rights and freedoms of others. Any restrictions imposed must be prescribed by law and be "necessary in a democratic society".

In its *General Comment No. 34*, the HR Committee explains that any restrictions on the exercise of freedom of opinion and expression "must conform to the strict tests of necessity and proportionality" and "be applied only for those purposes for which they were prescribed and must be directly related to the specific need on which they are predicated".[293] In the context of an individual communication, the Committee pointed out that although *General Comment No. 34* refers to *ICCPR* Article 19, it also provides guidance with regard to elements of *ICCPR* Article 21.[294]

The ECtHR has ruled that the term "restrictions" in *ECHR* Article 11(2) "must be interpreted as including both measures taken before or during the public assembly, and those, such as punitive measures, taken after the meeting".[295]

The IACHR has underscored the fact that the rights to freedom of assembly and peaceful demonstration are protected under the *ACHR*:

> Hence, any measure that a State adopts to restrict the exercise of those rights must be established by law beforehand, and must also be only what is strictly necessary when circumstances warrant it. Any such

---

arbitrary executions on the proper management of assemblies, 4 February 2016, A/ HRC/31/66, para. 29. See also UN HRC, *CCPR General Comment No. 27 (1999): Article 12, Freedom of movement,* para. 13; UN, HR Committee, *CCPR General Comment No. 31, Article 2 (The Nature of the General Legal Obligation Imposed on States Parties to the Covenant),* 29 March 2004, CCPR/C/21/Rev.1/Add.13, para. 6.

293   See HR Committee, *CCPR General Comment No. 34, Article 19: Freedoms of opinion and expression,* 12 September 2011, CCPR/C/GC/34, para. 22.

294   HR Committee, Communication No. 1790/2008, *Govsha, Syritsa and Mezyak v. Belarus,* Views adopted on 27 July 2012, para. 9.4.

295   ECtHR, *Case of Sergey Kuznetsov v. Russia,* App. no. 10877/04, Judgment of 23 January 2009 (Final), para. 35.

measure must always be a proportional response to the end being sought.[296]

According to the IACHR, the interpretation of these limitations on the rights to freedom of assembly must be an objective one that establishes a "correlation between personal liberty and equality, solidarity and the general welfare...Such limitations cannot stray beyond the boundaries of reason, i.e., they cannot disregard, destroy or alter the right being limited."[297]

Lawfulness

To satisfy the requirement of lawfulness, any restrictions imposed on the rights to freedom of peaceful assembly and association must have a "legitimate and formal basis in law (the legality principle)".[298] This requirement applies also to the mandate and powers of the restricting authority.[299] The law itself must be sufficiently precise to enable an individual to assess whether or not his or her conduct would be in breach of the law, and also foresee the likely consequences of any such breach.[300] The law must be in conformity with international human rights standards.[301]

Necessary and proportionate

It is not sufficient that the laws serve the permissible purposes; they must also be necessary to protect them. Any restriction must conform to the principle of proportionality – it must be appropriate to achieve its protective function, it must be the least intrusive instrument among those

---

296   IACHR, *Annual Report 2007,* Chapter IV, Report on Venezuela, para. 268.

297   OAS, IACHR, *Report on Citizen Security and Human Rights* (2009), OEA/Ser.L/V/II. Doc. 57, para. 195.

298   UN HRC, *Joint report of the Special Rapporteur on the rights to freedom of peaceful assembly and of association and the Special Rapporteur on extrajudicial, summary or arbitrary executions on the proper management of assemblies, 4 February 2016,* A/HRC/31/66, para. 30.

299   See *OSCE Guidelines,* para. 35. See also ECtHR, *Hyde Park and others v. Moldova,* App. no. 33482/06, Judgment of 30 June 2009 (Final), paras. 25 and 30-31.

300   See ECtHR, *Hashman and Harrup v. the United Kingdom,* App. no. 25594/94, Judgment of 25 November 1999, para. 31; ECtHR, *Gillan and Quinton v. the United Kingdom,* App. no. 4158/05, Judgment of 12 January 2010, para. 76. See also *OSCE Guidelines,* para. 2.3.

301   *OSCE Guidelines,* para. 2.3.

which might achieve the desired result, and it must be proportionate to the interest involved.[302] This requires that the law be narrowly tailored to the specific aims and concerns of the authorities, and that it take into account an analysis of the full range of rights involved in the proposed assembly.[303]

The OSCE Guidelines indicate that

> "The principle of proportionality is a vehicle for conducting a balancing exercise. It does not directly balance the right against the reason for interfering with it. Instead, it balances the nature and extent of the interference against the reason for interfering." The extent of the interference should cover only the purpose that justifies it. Moreover, given that a wide range of interventions might be suitable, the least intrusive means of achieving the legitimate purpose should always be given preference.[304]

In determining the least intrusive instrument to achieve the desired result, authorities should consider a range of measures, with prohibition being a last resort. To this end, the SRs conclude that

> blanket bans, including bans on the exercise of the right entirely or on any exercise of the right in specific places or at particular times, are intrinsically disproportionate, because they preclude consideration of the specific circumstances of each proposed assembly.[305]

Under the *ECHR*, Contracting States have a certain margin of appreciation in assessing whether an interference is "necessary in a democratic society", "but it goes hand in hand with European supervision, embracing both

---

302   UN HRC Committee, *CCPR General Comment No. 27 (1999): Article 12, Freedom of movement*, para. 14; *OSCE Guidelines*, para. 2.4.

303   UN HRC, *Joint report of the Special Rapporteur on the rights to freedom of peaceful assembly and of association and the Special Rapporteur on extrajudicial, summary or arbitrary executions on the proper management of assemblies*, 4 February 2016, A/HRC/31/66, para. 30.

304   *OSCE Guidelines*, para. 39 [footnotes omitted].

305   UN HRC, *Joint report of the Special Rapporteur on the rights to freedom of peaceful assembly and of association and the Special Rapporteur on extrajudicial, summary or arbitrary executions on the proper management of assemblies*, 4 February 2016, A/HRC/31/66, para. 30. See also UN HRC, *Report of the Special Rapporteur on the rights to freedom of peaceful assembly and of association, Maina Kiai*, 24 April 2013, A/HRC/23/39, para. 63; *OSCE Guidelines*, para. 2.4.

the legislation and the decisions applying it".[306] The ECtHR has ruled that "[t]here is little scope under [*ECHR*] Article 10 – in the light of which *ECHR* Article 11 has to be construed...for restrictions on political speech or on debate on questions of public interest".[307] However, where there has been incitement to violence against an individual or a sector of the population, State authorities enjoy a wider margin of appreciation when examining the need for an interference with freedom of expression.[308]

The suspension and the involuntarily dissolution of an association should only be possible "when there is a clear and imminent danger resulting in a flagrant violation of national law, in compliance with international human rights law".[309] It should be strictly proportional to the legitimate aim pursued and used only when softer measures would be insufficient.

Similarly, the authorities may prohibit a peaceful assembly only when a less restrictive response would not achieve the legitimate aim(s) pursued by the authorities.[310] Under the OSCE Guidelines, when considering the necessity of any restrictions it must be acknowledged that assemblies are "as legitimate uses of public space as commercial activity or the movement of vehicular and pedestrian traffic".[311]

"Time, place and manner" restrictions regarding when, where and how an assembly may be conducted should never be used to undermine the message or expressive value of an assembly or to dissuade the exercise of the right to freedom of assembly.[312]

Organizers of peaceful assemblies should not be coerced to follow the authorities' suggestions if these would undermine the essence of their right

---

306   ECtHR, *Case of Schwabe and M.G. v. Germany,* App. nos. 8080/08 and 8577/08, Judgment of 1 March 2012 (Final), para. 113.
307   *Ibid.*
308   *Ibid.*
309   UN HRC, *Report of the Special Rapporteur on the rights to freedom of peaceful assembly and of association, Maina Kiai,* 21 May 2012, A/HRC/20/27, para. 75.
310   *Ibid,* para. 39.
311   *OSCE Guidelines,* para. 3.2.
312   UN HRC, *Joint report of the Special Rapporteur on the rights to freedom of peaceful assembly and of association and the Special Rapporteur on extrajudicial, summary or arbitrary executions on the proper management of assemblies,* 4 February 2016, A/ HRC/31/66, para. 34; *OSCE Guidelines,* para. 3.4.

to freedom of peaceful assembly.[313]

The ECtHR has held that the reasons adduced by national authorities to support any claim of proportionality must be "relevant and sufficient",[314] "convincing and compelling"[315] and based on "an acceptable assessment of the relevant facts".[316]

"rights and freedoms of others"

Case law of the ECtHR indicates that a high threshold will need to be overcome before it can be established that a public assembly will unreasonably infringe upon the rights and freedoms of others.[317]

"public order"

Neither a hypothetical risk of public disorder nor the presence of a hostile audience are legitimate grounds for prohibiting a peaceful assembly under the *ECHR*.[318]

Right to hold assembly within sight and sound of target audience

Where authorities propose reasonable alternatives to assembly organizers in compliance with international law, such alternatives "fundamentally should always be facilitated within 'sight and sound' of the target audience so that the message they (organizers and participants) want to convey reaches this target audience".[319] Counter-demonstrations should be facilitated, to the

---

313   UN HRC, *Report of the Special Rapporteur on the rights to freedom of peaceful assembly and of association, Maina Kiai*, 21 May 2012, A/HRC/20/27, para. 40.

314   See, for example, *Case of Makhmudov v. Russia*, App. no. 35082/04, Judgment of 26 October 2007 (Final), para. 65.

315   *Ibid*, para. 64.

316   ECtHR, *Case of Stankov and the United Macedonian Organisation Ilinden v. Bulgaria*, App. nos. 29221/95 and 29225/95, Judgment of 2 January 2002 (Final), para. 87.

317   See, for example, ECtHR, *Ashughyan v. Armenia*, App. no. 33268/03, Judgment of 1 December 2008 (Final), para. 90. Similarly, see ECtHR, *Balçık and Others v. Turkey*, App. no. 25/02, Judgment of 29 November 2007 (Final), para. 49; ECtHR, *Case of Oya Ataman v. Turkey*, App. no. 74552/01, Judgment of 5 December 2006, para. 38; ECtHR, *Nurettin Aldemir and others v. Turkey*, App. nos. 32124/02, 32126/02, 32129/02, 32132/02, 32133/02, 32137/02 and 32138/02, Judgment of 2 June 2008 (Final), para. 43.

318   *Case of Makhmudov v. Russia*, App. no. 35082/04, Judgment of 26 October 2007 (Final).

319   UN HRC, *Report of the Special Rapporteur on the rights to freedom of peaceful assembly and of association, Maina Kiai*, 24 April 2013, A/HRC/23/39, para. 60; OSCE

extent possible, within "sight and sound" of one another.[320]

Content-based restrictions face a high threshold

The OSCE Guidelines provide that assemblies "are held for a common expressive purpose and, thus, aim to convey a message. Restrictions on the visual or audible content of any message should face a high threshold and should only be imposed if there is an imminent threat of violence".[321]

Right to timely and fulsome reasons for any restriction

Whenever authorities decide to restrict an assembly, they should provide assembly organizers, in writing, with "timely and fulsome reasons" which should satisfy the strict test of necessity and proportionality of the restriction(s) imposed on the assembly pursuant to legitimate aims[322] and the possibility of an expedited appeal procedure.[323]

Right to appeal restriction

Organizers of an assembly should be able to appeal the imposition of restrictions before an independent and impartial court, which should make a decision promptly.[324]

The onus of justifying a limitation rests with the authority

When a State invokes national security or protection of public order to restrict an assembly, it must prove the precise nature of the threat and the specific risks posed.[325] It is not sufficient for the State to refer generally to the security situation. National, political or government interest is not synonymous with national security or public order.[326]

Guidelines, para. 3.5.
320   OSCE Guidelines, para. 4.4.
321   Ibid, para. 3.3.
322   UN HRC, Report of the Special Rapporteur on the rights to freedom of peaceful assembly and of association, Maina Kiai, 24 April 2013, A/HRC/23/39, para. 48.
323   Ibid, para. 64. UN HRC, Report of the Special Rapporteur on the rights to freedom of peaceful assembly and of association, Maina Kiai, 21 May 2012, A/HRC/20/27, para. 42.
324   UN HRC, Report of the Special Rapporteur on the rights to freedom of peaceful assembly and of association, Maina Kiai, 21 May 2012, A/HRC/20/27, para. 42.
325   HR Committee, Communication No. 1119/2002, Lee v. the Republic of Korea, Views adopted on 20 July 2005, para. 7.3.
326   UN HRC, Joint report of the Special Rapporteur on the rights to freedom of peaceful

Right to participate in public affairs

A recent report by the Office of the UN High Commissioner for Human Rights highlights the relationship between the right to participate in public affairs and other fundamental freedoms:

> Participation in political and public affairs underpins the realization of all human rights and is inextricably linked to them. It cannot be considered in a vacuum without taking into consideration structural issues such as poverty or literacy levels...the respect and full exercise of the rights to freedoms of opinion and expression, association and peaceful assembly, and the rights to information, education and access to justice, are prerequisites to an enabling environment for participation in the conduct of political and public affairs.[327]

In order to ensure the full, effective and equal enjoyment of participatory rights, States are required to adopt positive measures, "including through inclusive, meaningful and non-discriminatory processes and mechanisms".[328] Participatory mechanisms should conform to certain principles – they should be established by law; provide stakeholders with easy, prompt, effective and practical access to information in a timely and transparent manner; be sufficiently resourced, non-discriminatory, inclusive and designed so that even the most marginalized have the opportunity to voice their opinions.[329]

Public participation rights "encompass the right to be consulted at each

---

assembly and of association and the Special Rapporteur on extrajudicial, summary or arbitrary executions on the proper management of assemblies, 4 February 2016, A/ HRC/31/66, para. 31.

327   UN HRC, *Report of the Office of the United Nations High Commissioner for Human Rights on promotion, protection and implementation of the right to participate in public affairs in the context of the existing human rights law: best practices, experiences, challenges and ways to overcome them,* 23 July 2015, A/HRC/30/26, para. 13. See also UN, HRC, *Report of the United Nations High Commissioner for Human Rights on factors that impede equal political participation and steps to overcome those challenges,* A/HRC/27/29 (30 June 2014), paras. 22-30.

328   *Report of the Office of the United Nations High Commissioner for Human Rights on promotion, protection and implementation of the right to participate in public affairs (A/ HRC/30/26),* para. 5.

329   *Ibid,* para. 9.

phase of legislative drafting and policymaking; to voice opinions and criticism; and to submit proposals aimed at improving the functioning and inclusivity of all State bodies".[330]

The right of indigenous peoples to participate in public affairs has an additional collective aspect in international law, implying a right of the group as a people to exercise decision-making authority. The Expert Mechanism on Indigenous Peoples explains:

> With regard to participatory rights, international human rights law refers to the right to participate in public affairs in both general and specific forms, including as set out in various human rights treaties, such as in article 25 of the International Covenant on Civil and Political Rights and in the Indigenous and Tribal Peoples Convention, 1989 (No. 169) of the International Labour Organization (ILO). Participation in public affairs in its general form includes involvement in the conduct of public affairs. Electoral participation is only one specific expression of the right to participation. Moreover, the right to take part in public affairs is not limited to participation in formal political institutions, as it also includes participation in civil, cultural and social activities of a public nature. The right to participate in public affairs has conventionally been understood as a civil and political right of the individual. In the context of indigenous peoples, however, the right also takes on a collective aspect, implying a right of the group as a people to exercise decision-making authority.[331]

Scope of "the conduct of public affairs"

In *General Comment No. 25*, the HR Committee commented on the broad scope of "the conduct of public affairs" in *ICCPR* Article 25(a):

---

330   *Ibid*, para. 10. See *Convention on the Rights of Persons with Disabilities; Declaration on the Right and Responsibility of Individuals, Groups and Organs of Society to Promote and Protect Universally Recognized Human Rights and Fundamental Freedoms*, Art. 8. See also UN HRC, *Report of the independent expert on minority issues, Gay McDougall*, 7 January 2010, A/HRC/13/23, paras. 31-33 and 52.
331   UN HRC, Expert Mechanism on the Rights of Indigenous Peoples, *Expert Mechanism Advice No. 2 (2011): Indigenous peoples and the right to participate in decision-making*, A/HRC/18/42, para. 5.

The conduct of public affairs, referred to in [*ICCPR* Article 25] paragraph (a), is a broad concept which relates to the exercise of political power, in particular the exercise of legislative, executive and administrative powers. It covers all aspects of public administration, and the formulation and implementation of policy at international, national, regional and local levels. The allocation of powers and the means by which individual citizens exercise the right to participate in the conduct of public affairs protected by [*ICCPR*] article 25 should be established by the constitution and other laws.[332]

The CEDAW Committee, in its *General Recommendation No. 23* on *CEDAW*, states:

[*CEDAW*] Article 7 obliges States parties to take all appropriate measures to eliminate discrimination against women in political and public life and to ensure that they enjoy equality with men in political and public life. The obligation specified in article 7 extends to all areas of public and political life and is not limited to those areas specified in subparagraphs (a), (b) and (c). The political and public life of a country is a broad concept. It refers to the exercise of political power, in particular the exercise of legislative, judicial, executive and administrative powers. The term covers all aspects of public administration and the formulation and implementation of policy at the international, national, regional and local levels. The concept also includes many aspects of civil society, including public boards and local councils and the activities of organizations such as political parties, trade unions, professional or industry associations, women's organizations, community-based organizations and other organizations concerned with public and political life.[333]

The CEDAW Committee notes that *CEDAW* Article 7(b) requires parties to ensure that women have the right to participate fully in and be represented in public policy formulation in all sectors and at all levels. In the opinion of the CEDAW Committee, "this would facilitate the mainstreaming of gender

---

332   HR Committee, *CCPR General Comment No. 25 Article 25 (Participation in Public Affairs and the Right to Vote)*, 12 July 1996, CCPR/C/21/Rev.1/Add.7, para. 5.
333   CEDAW, *CEDAW General Recommendation No. 23: Political and Public Life*, 1997, A/52/38, para. 5.

issues and contribute a gender perspective to public policy-making".[334]

Relationship with other rights

When citizens take part in the conduct of public affairs, for example, "by exerting influence through public debate and dialogue with their representatives or through their capacity to organize themselves", they rely on the full enjoyment of other rights, such as the rights to freedom of expression and the free flow of information, and the rights to freely assemble and to associate with others.[335] The presence of a free press is vital to the exercise of the rights to participate in public affairs. The HR Committee states:

> In order to ensure the full enjoyment of rights protected by article 25, the free communication of information and ideas about public and political issues between citizens, candidates and elected representatives is essential. This implies a free press and other media able to comment on public issues without censorship or restraint and to inform public opinion. It requires the full enjoyment and respect for the rights guaranteed in articles 19, 21 and 22 of the Covenant, including freedom to engage in political activity individually or through political parties and other organizations, freedom to debate public affairs, to hold peaceful demonstrations and meetings, to criticize and oppose, to publish political material, to campaign for election and to advertise political ideas.[336]

Restrictions must be based on objective and reasonable criteria

Restrictions to the right to vote and to stand for elections must be objective, reasonable, non-discriminatory and provided for by law.[337] With regard to other political rights, such as freedom of assembly and association, opinion and expression, any restrictions must be prescribed by law, necessary and proportionate in the circumstances. Restrictions should remain the

---

334   *Ibid,* para. 25.
335   HR Committee, *CCPR General Comment No. 25 Article 25 (Participation in Public Affairs and the Right to Vote),* 12 July 1996, CCPR/C/21/Rev.1/Add.7, paras. 8 and 25.
336   *Ibid,* para. 25.
337   *Ibid,* para. 4.

exception rather than the rule and these limitations should never impair the essence of the right at issue.[338]

Right to equality and freedom from discrimination

International human rights law requires that States ensure that the rights and freedoms that they are bound to respect, protect and fulfill are enjoyed by all persons within their territories and subject to their jurisdiction, without distinction of any kind.[339]

This means that States must take additional measures to protect and facilitate the equal exercise by all persons, without discrimination, of the rights to freedom of expression, freedom of assembly and association and freedom to participate in public affairs.

The term "discrimination" as used in the *ICCPR* implies "any distinction, exclusion, restriction or preference which is based on any ground such as race, colour, sex, language, religion, political or other opinion, national or social origin, property, birth or other status, and which has the purpose or effect of nullifying or impairing the recognition, enjoyment or exercise by all persons, on an equal footing, of all rights and freedoms".[340] The HR Committee has established that sexual orientation and gender identity also constitute prohibited grounds for discrimination under *ICCPR* Article 2.[341]

Particular attention should be paid to ensure equal and effective protection of the rights of groups or individuals who have historically experienced discrimination. This includes women, children and young people, persons with disabilities, non-nationals (including asylum seekers and refugees), members of ethnic and religious minorities, displaced persons, persons with albinism, indigenous peoples and individuals who have been discriminated

---

338   UN, HRC, *Report of the United Nations High Commissioner for Human Rights on factors that impede equal political participation and steps to overcome those challenges*, A/HRC/27/29 (30 June 2014), para. 31. See also UN General Assembly, *Report of the Special Rapporteur on the promotion and protection of the right to freedom of opinion and expression, Frank La Rue*, A/66/290 (10 August 2011).

339   See, for example, *ICCPR* Article 2(1).

340   HR Committee, *CCPR General Comment No. 18: Non-discrimination*, 10 November 1989, HRI/GEN/Rev.9 (Vol.1), para. 7.

341   See, *inter alia*, HR Committee, Communication No. 488/1992, *Toonen v. Australia*, Views adopted on 31 March 1994.

against on the basis of their sexual orientation or gender identity.[342]

The OHCHR warns that discrimination and other barriers to the full realization of the rights of freedoms of peaceful assembly and association, opinion and expression and the rights to information and education will undermine efforts to ensure the equal enjoyment of other political and public participation rights.[343]

A study by the OHCHR of factors that impede equal political participation reports that:

International human rights mechanisms have observed that women, indigenous peoples, minorities, persons with disabilities, human rights defenders, non-citizens and other marginalized or excluded individuals and groups are frequently unable to fully participate in political and public affairs on an equal basis. This disadvantage is heightened where multiple or intersecting grounds of discrimination are involved.[344]

It is not sufficient for States to ensure formal participation of persons belonging to minorities; States must also ensure that the participation of minority representatives has a substantial influence on decisions that are taken, so that there is, as far as possible, a shared ownership of the decisions taken.[345]

The CESCR, in its *General Comment No. 21*, considers that *ICESCR* Article 15(1)(a) (right to participate in cultural affairs) includes, *inter alia*, the

---

342   UN HRC, *Joint report of the Special Rapporteur on the rights to freedom of peaceful assembly and of association and the Special Rapporteur on extrajudicial, summary or arbitrary executions on the proper management of assemblies*, 4 February 2016, A/HRC/31/66, para. 16. See also UN HRC, *Report of the Special Rapporteur on the rights to freedom of peaceful assembly and of association, Maina Kiai*, 14 April 2014, A/HRC/26/29.
343   UN, HRC, *Report of the United Nations High Commissioner for Human Rights on factors that impede equal political participation and steps to overcome those challenges*, A/HRC/27/29 (30 June 2014), para. 22.
344   *Ibid*, para. 4. See also UN HRC, *Report of the independent expert on minority issues, Gay McDougall*, 7 January 2010, A/HRC/13/23, para. 56; CEDAW, *General Recommendation No. 28 on the Core Obligations of States Parties under Article 2 of the Convention on the Elimination of All Forms of Discrimination against Women*, 16 December 2010, para. 18; CERD, *General Recommendation No. 25 on gender-related dimensions of racial discrimination (2000)*.
345   UN HRC, *Report of the independent expert on minority issues, Gay McDougall*, 7 January 2010, A/HRC/13/23, para. 53.

following obligation:

> To allow and encourage the participation of persons belonging to minority groups, indigenous peoples or to other communities in the design and implementation of laws and policies that affect them.[346]

The application of restrictions to rights must not be discriminatory

In *General Comment No. 27*, on the right to freedom of movement, the HR Committee states that the application of restrictions permissible under *ICCPR* Article 12 (the right to freedom of movement) – to protect national security, public order (ordre public), public health or morals and the rights and freedoms of others – must be consistent with other rights guaranteed in the *ICCPR* and the fundamental principles of equality and non-discrimination. The HR Committee finds:

> Thus, it would be a clear violation of the [*ICCPR*] if the rights enshrined in article 12, paragraphs 1 and 2, were restricted by making distinctions of any kind, such as on the basis of race, colour, sex, language, religion, political or other opinion, national or social origin, property, birth or other status.[347]

Any limitations imposed on freedom of expression must allow for changes in the content of "public morals" and not be applied so as to perpetuate prejudice or promote intolerance.[348]

The CERD states, in its *General Recommendation No. 20* on *CERD* Article 5 (enjoyment of civil, political, economic, social and cultural rights and freedoms without racial discrimination), that whenever a State imposes a restriction upon one of the rights listed in CERD Article 5 that applies ostensibly to all within its jurisdiction, it must ensure that the restriction is not discriminatory in its purpose or effect.[349]

---

346   UN Committee on Economic, Social and Cultural Rights, *General Comment No. 21: Article 15(1)(a), Right of everyone to take part in cultural life*, 21 December 2009, E/C.12/GC/21, para. 55(e).

347   UN HRC Committee, *CCPR General Comment No. 27 (1999): Article 12, Freedom of movement*, para. 18.

348   HR Committee, *Leo Hertzberg et al. v. Finland*, Communication No. 61/1979, Appendix.

349   CERD, *General Recommendation no. 20, Non-discriminatory implementation of rights*

The Committee on the Rights of Persons with Disabilities, in its *General Comment No. 1*, on the *CRPD*, Article 12 (equal recognition before the law), states:

> In order to fully realize the equal recognition of legal capacity in all aspects of life, it is important to recognize the legal capacity of persons with disabilities in public and political life (art. 29). This means that a person's decision-making ability cannot be a justification for any exclusion of persons with disabilities from exercising their political rights, including the right to vote, the right to stand for election and the right to serve as a member of a jury.[350]

The OSCE Guidelines provide that, in regulating freedom of assembly, authorities must not discriminate against any individual or group on any grounds:

> The freedom to organize and participate in public assemblies must be guaranteed to individuals, groups, unregistered associations, legal entities and corporate bodies; to members of minority ethnic, national, sexual and religious groups; to nationals and non-nationals (including stateless persons, refugees, foreign nationals, asylum seekers, migrants and tourists); to children, women and men; to law-enforcement personnel; and to persons without full legal capacity, including persons with mental illnesses.[351]

Equality before the law and equal protection of the law implies that decisions by authorities concerning the exercise of the right must not have a discriminatory impact, and so both direct and indirect discrimination are prohibited.[352] Law enforcement officials have a duty to investigate whether discrimination may have been a contributing factor to any criminal conduct that occurred during an assembly.[353]

---

and freedoms (Art. 5), 15 March 1996, para. 2.

350   UN Committee on the Rights of Persons with Disabilities (CRPD), *General Recommendation No. 1: Article 12, Equal Recognition before the law*, 11 April 2014, CRPD/C/GC/1, para. 48.

351   *OSCE Guidelines*, para. 2.5.

352   *OSCE Guidelines*, para. 50.

353   ECtHR, *Case of Nachova and Others v. Bulgaria*, App. nos. 43577/98 and 43579/98, Judgment of 6 July 2005, para. 161.

Right to privacy

States must respect, protect and fulfill the privacy rights of all individuals in the exercise of their rights to freedom of expression, freedom of peaceful assembly and association and freedom to participate in public affairs.

Under *ICCPR* Article 17(1), no one shall be subjected to "arbitrary or unlawful interference with his privacy, family, home or correspondence, nor to unlawful attacks on his honour and reputation". *ICCPR* Article 17(2) provides that everyone "has the right to the protection of the law against such interference or attacks".

This right must be guaranteed against all such interferences and attacks whether they emanate from State authorities or from natural or legal persons.[354] The term "unlawful" means that no interference can take place except in cases envisaged by the law. Interference authorized by States can take place only on the basis of law, which itself must comply with the provisions, aims and objectives of the *ICCPR*.[355] According to the HR Committee, the expression "arbitrary interference" is also relevant to the protection of the right provided for in *ICCPR* Article 17 and can extend to interference provided for under law:

> The introduction of the concept of arbitrariness is intended to guarantee that even interference provided for by law should be in accordance with the provisions, aims and objectives of the [*ICCPR*] and should be, in any event, reasonable in the particular circumstances.[356]

Even with regard to interferences that conform to the *ICCPR*, legislation must specify in detail the precise circumstances in which such interferences may be permitted. A decision to make use of such authorized interference must be made only by the authority designated under the law, and on a case-by-case basis.[357] *ICCPR* Article 17 "requires that the integrity and confidentiality of correspondence should be guaranteed de jure and de

---

354   HR Committee, *CCPR General Comment No. 16: Article 17 (Right to Privacy), The Right to Respect of Privacy, Family, Home and Correspondence, and Protection of Honour and Reputation*, 8 April 1988, HRI/GEN/1/Rev.9 (Vol. I), para. 1.

355   *Ibid*, para. 3.

356   *Ibid*, para. 4.

357   *Ibid*, para. 8.

facto". Surveillance should be prohibited.[358]

In *Case of Pfeifer v. Austria*,[359] the ECtHR commented on the content of *ECHR* Article 8 (respect for private and family life):

> As to the applicability of [*ECHR*] Article 8, the Court reiterates that "private life" extends to aspects relating to personal identity, such as a person's name or picture, and furthermore includes a person's physical and psychological integrity; the guarantee afforded by Article 8 of the [*ECHR*] is primarily intended to ensure the development, without outside interference, of the personality of each individual in his relations with other human beings. There is therefore a zone of interaction of a person with others, even in a public context, which may fall within the scope of "private life".[360]

In relation to the exercise of freedom of association, authorities should not be entitled to impose conditions on any decisions and activities of an association; reverse the election of board members; require the presence of a government representative at a board meeting or request that an internal decision be withdrawn; request associations to submit annual reports in advance; or enter an association's premises without advance notice.[361] Procedures to provide for the examination by independent bodies of an association's records to ensure transparency and accountability "should not be arbitrary and must respect the principle of non-discrimination and the right to privacy as it would otherwise put the independence of associations and the safety of their members at risk".[362]

The ACHPR found that the right to freedom of association had been violated when the Government of Nigeria provided the Nigerian Bar Association with a new governing body and stipulated that 97 of the 128 members constituting this body would be appointed by the government.[363]

---

358   *Ibid.*
359   ECtHR, *Case of Pfeifer v. Austria*, App. no. 12556/03, Judgment of 15 February 2008 (final).
360   *Ibid*, para. 33.
361   UN HRC, *Report of the Special Rapporteur on the rights to freedom of peaceful assembly and of association, Maina Kiai*, 21 May 2012, A/HRC/20/27, para. 65.
362   *Ibid.*
363   UN General Assembly, *Report of the Special Rapporteur on the situation of human rights defenders*, 4 August 2009, A/64/226, para. 34.

" Freedom of assembly and the right to express one's views through it are among the paramount values of a democratic society. The essence of democracy is its capacity to resolve problems through open debate. Sweeping measures of a preventive nature to suppress freedom of assembly and expression other than in cases of incitement to violence or rejection of democratic principles – however shocking and unacceptable certain views or words used may appear to the authorities, and however illegitimate the demands made may be – do a disservice to democracy and often even endanger it.

European Court of Human Rights, Case of Stankov and the United Macedonian Organisation Ilinden v. Bulgaria, para. 97 (App. nos. 29221/95 and 29225/95, 2 January 2002)

Similarly, the collection and processing of personal information by authorities in the proper management of assemblies must comply with protections against arbitrary or unlawful interference with privacy.[364] Recording peaceful assembly participants in a context and manner that intimidates or harasses them is an impermissible interference with rights, including privacy, freedom of assembly, association and expression.[365]

Right to life, liberty and security of the person

Everyone has the right to life, liberty and security of the person. These fundamental human rights are reflected in *UDHR* Article 3, and in all of the major international and regional human rights treaties. These rights must be respected, protected and fulfilled by States at all times. Persons exercising their rights to dissent and protest are at a heightened risk of having their rights to life, liberty and security of the person infringed, particularly when authorities use excessive force in policing assemblies or fail to protect individuals from violence by others, or individuals are detained by authorities.

The HR Committee has elaborated on the content of the right to liberty and security of the person contained in *ICCPR* Article 9:

> Liberty of person concerns freedom from confinement of the body, not a general freedom of action. Security of person concerns freedom from injury to the body and the mind, or bodily and mental integrity... [CCPR] Article 9 guarantees these rights to everyone. "Everyone" includes, among others, girls and boys, soldiers, persons with disabilities, lesbian, gay, bisexual and transgender persons, aliens, refugees and asylum seekers, stateless persons, migrant workers, persons convicted of crime, and persons who have engaged in terrorist activity.
>
> ...
>
> The right to security of person protects individuals against intentional infliction of bodily or mental injury, regardless of whether the victim is detained or non-detained...The right to personal security also

---

364   UN HRC, *Joint report of the Special Rapporteur on the rights to freedom of peaceful assembly and of association and the Special Rapporteur on extrajudicial, summary or arbitrary executions on the proper management of assemblies, 4 February 2016*, A/HRC/31/66, para. 73.
365   *Ibid*, para. 76.

obliges States parties to take appropriate measures in response to death threats against persons in the public sphere, and more generally to protect individuals from foreseeable threats to life or bodily integrity proceeding from any governmental or private actors. States parties must take both prospective measures to prevent future injury and retrospective measures such as enforcement of criminal laws in response to past injury...They should also prevent and redress unjustifiable use of force in law enforcement, and protect their populations against abuses by private security forces, and against the risks posed by excessive availability of firearms. The right to security of person does not address all risks to physical or mental health, and is not implicated in the indirect health impact of being the target of a civil or criminal proceedings.[366]

The right to life and the right to be free from torture or cruel, inhuman or degrading treatment or punishment should be the overarching principles governing the policing of public assemblies.[367]

SCOPE OF THE RIGHT TO PEACEFUL PROTEST

Introduction

The guarantee of the right to dissent and to participate in peaceful protest is not found in a single formulated right in international law, but rather is firmly anchored in a number of distinct but interconnected and mutually enforcing fundamental human rights, which include the right to freedom of expression, the rights to freedom of association and peaceful assembly and the right to participate in public affairs. The UN and regional bodies have also passed numerous resolutions, declarations and guidelines specifically aimed at the protection of the right to peaceful protest.[368] A violation of the

---

366   HR Committee, *CCPR General Comment No. 35, Article 9: Liberty and security of person,* 16 December 2014, CCPR/C/GC/35, paras. 3 and 9 [footnotes omitted].
367   UN HRC, *Report of the Special Rapporteur on the rights to freedom of peaceful assembly and of association, Maina Kiai,* 21 May 2012, A/HRC/20/27, para. 35.
368   See, for example, HRC resolutions 25/38, 22/10, 19/35; for the protection of human rights defenders, see HRC resolutions 24/24, 31/32 and 22/6; for the protection of journalists, see HRC resolution 21/12. See also ARTICLE 19, *The Right to Protest: Principles*

" The right to protest is an essential element of the right to participation in any democratic dispensation and restrictions imposed on this right must be closely scrutinized with respect to their necessity and reasonableness.

United Nations, Report on Human Rights Defenders report submitted by the Special Representative of the Secretary-General on Human Rights Defenders, Hina Jilani, 5 September 2006 (A/61/312, para. 56)

"Protecting the right to protest in the context of freedom of assembly entails both negative and positive obligations.

The negative obligation on the part of the State not to interfere with peaceful protests is to be combined with the positive obligation to protect rights holders in the exercise of this right, particularly when persons protesting hold unpopular or controversial views, or belong to minorities or other groups exposed to higher risks of victimization, attacks and other forms of intolerance.

Report of the Special Representative of the Secretary-General on human rights defenders, 13 August 2007 (A/62/225 para. 97)

right to dissent and protest, therefore, may constitute a violation of any or all of these fundamental rights and may also involve interference with other freedoms, such as rights to equality and non-discrimination, dignity, privacy and the rights to life, liberty and security of the person. (See previous section for an analysis of the content and scope of the individual rights that make up the right to dissent and peaceful protest.)

UN Special Representative of the Secretary-General on the situation of human rights defenders Hina Jilani writes that

> [t]he right to protest is a fully fledged right and entails the enjoyment of a set of rights internationally recognized and reiterated in the Declaration on Human Rights Defenders. These rights include freedom of expression and opinion, freedom of association, freedom of peaceful assembly and trade union rights, including the right to strike.[369]

The scope of the rights to dissent and to peaceful protest is informed, then, by the broad scope of the fundamental human rights involved, which may be restricted under international law only in certain limited and narrow circumstances. Even if participants in an assembly are not peaceful and as a result forfeit their right to peaceful assembly, they retain all their other rights, subject to the normal limitations. No assembly should thus be considered unprotected.[370]

State obligation to respect, protect and fulfill the rights to dissent and protest

on protection of human rights in protests (Policy Brief, 2015). Although not an authoritative source, this document draws on existing international human rights standards to propose a useful set of principles applicable to the right to protest. The principles were launched at a meeting of the UN HRC on June 19, 2015. The establishment in 2010 of the mandate of the UN SR on the right to peaceful assembly and of association is also significant in the move towards the effective protection of peaceful protest in the framework of international human rights law.

369   UN General Assembly, *Report of the Special Representative of the Secretary-General on human rights defenders*, A/62/225, 13 August 2007, para. 96.

370   UN HRC, *Joint report of the Special Rapporteur on the rights to freedom of peaceful assembly and of association and the Special Rapporteur on extrajudicial, summary or arbitrary executions on the proper management of assemblies*, 4 February 2016, A/HRC/31/66, para. 9.

Under international law, States are legally bound to respect, protect and fulfill the rights to dissent and peaceful protest. As summarized by UN SR on the rights to peaceful assembly and of association Maina Kiai, States are obligated:

(a) to refrain from committing violations, including through the use of excessive force, against individuals exercising their rights to peaceful assembly, expression and association;

(b) to protect individuals exercising these rights from abuses committed by non-State actors; and

(c) to fulfil these rights by taking positive measures to prevent any violations from occurring, and to ensure that everyone could freely and effectively exercise such rights.[371]

When violations occur, States have an obligation to thoroughly investigate such acts and provide effective remedy to victims.

States must respect the rights to dissent and protest by refraining from interfering with or curtailing the enjoyment of these rights, except to the extent allowed by international human rights law. States must respect the presumption in favour of allowing peaceful protests and the right of individuals and groups to choose the cause or issue of protest and its form, timing and location.

States must ensure that the rights to dissent and protest are subject to restrictions only on grounds specified in international and regional human rights instruments. In particular, no restriction on the rights to freedom of expression, assembly and association and privacy may be imposed unless the restriction is "prescribed by law"; pursues a "legitimate aim" identified in the relevant treaty provision; and is both "necessary" and "proportionate" in pursuance of that aim.

Based on the fundamental freedoms of expression, peaceful assembly and association, the right to dissent and protest embraces conduct or expression that may annoy or give offence to people who are opposed to the ideas

---

371   Maina Kiai, "Summary of the Human Rights Council panel discussion on the promotion and protection of human rights in the context of peaceful protests prepared by the Office of the United Nations High Commissioner for Human Rights", UN doc. A/HRC/19/40, 19 December 2011, para. 14.

or claims that a protest is seeking to promote, or conduct that temporarily hinders, impedes, or obstructs the activities of third parties.[372]

Under the obligation to protect rights, States must take steps to adequately protect individuals and groups against abuse of their right to engage in dissent and protest. States must ensure that the protection of all internationally guaranteed human rights apply during all protests, including the right to freedom of expression; the right to life and the right to be free from torture, inhuman or degrading treatment; rights to equality and freedom from discrimination; and the right to privacy.

The obligation of States to fulfill human rights means that States must take positive action to facilitate the enjoyment of the rights to dissent and protest, including providing effective remedies for violations.

The duty of States to facilitate the right to dissent and peaceful protest includes obligations to:

- create an enabling environment, including facilitating access to public spaces;

- protect participants from violence; and

- protect participants from external interference that might disrupt the expression of dissent or peaceful protest.

The use of force by law enforcement authorities in the context of protests must comply with binding international and regional human rights instruments, including *ICCPR* and *CAT*. Relevant soft law international instruments include the *Code of Conduct for Law Enforcement Officials* and *UN Basic Principles on the Use of Force and Firearms by Law Enforcement Officials* ("UN Basic Principles").

The *UN Basic Principles* provide:

12. As everyone is allowed to participate in lawful and peaceful assemblies, in accordance with the principles embodied in the Universal Declaration of Human Rights and the International Covenant on Civil and Political Rights, Governments and law enforcement agencies and

---

372   ARTICLE 19, *The Right to Protest: Principles on protection of human rights in protests* (Policy Brief, 2015), p. 22.

officials shall recognize that force and firearms may be used only in accordance with principles 13 and 14.

13. In the dispersal of assemblies that are unlawful but non-violent, law enforcement officials shall avoid the use of force or, where that is not practicable, shall restrict such force to the minimum extent necessary.

14. In the dispersal of violent assemblies, law enforcement officials may use firearms only when less dangerous means are not practicable and only to the minimum extent necessary. Law enforcement officials shall not use firearms in such cases, except under the conditions stipulated in principle 9.[373]

Under the *UN Code of Conduct for Law Enforcement Officials*, paragraphs 2 and 3, "law enforcement officials shall respect and protect human dignity and maintain and uphold the human rights of all persons" and "may use force only when strictly necessary and to the extent required for the performance of their duty".

The *Joint Declaration on violence against journalists and media workers in the context of protests*,[374] adopted in 2013, establishes that the rights of freedom of assembly and freedom of expression

are fundamental, and guaranteeing them is a vital condition to the existence and proper functioning of a democratic society. A State may impose reasonable limitations on demonstrations for purposes of ensuring that they are conducted peacefully, or to disperse those that turn violent, provided that such limits are governed by the principles of legality, necessity, and proportionality. In addition, the breaking-up of a demonstration must be warranted by the duty to protect individuals,

---

373   Principle 9 states: "[l]aw enforcement officials shall not use firearms against persons except in self-defence or defence of others against the imminent threat of death or serious injury, to prevent the perpetration of a particularly serious crime involving grave threat to life, to arrest a person presenting such a danger and resisting their authority, or to prevent his or her escape, and only when less extreme means are insufficient to achieve these objectives. In any event, intentional lethal use of firearms may only be made when strictly unavoidable in order to protect life".

374   UN SR on the Protection and Promotion of the Right to Freedom of Opinion and Expression and SR for Freedom of Expression of the OAS IACHR, *Joint declaration on violence against journalists and media workers in the context of protests*, September 13, 2013.

and authorities must use the measures that are safest and least harmful to the demonstrators. The use of force at public demonstrations must be an exception, used under strictly necessary circumstances consistent with internationally recognized principles.

Interpretation

This section examines jurisprudence and observations of the human rights courts and treaty bodies as they relate specifically to the exercise of rights to dissent and protest. This analysis should be read together with the jurisprudence discussed above under each of the individual rights protected in the right to dissent – freedom of expression and opinion, freedom of association and assembly, freedom to participate in the conduct of public affairs, right to privacy, right to equality and freedom from discrimination, and right to life, liberty and security of the person.

Freedom to choose cause or issue

The right under freedom of expression to seek, receive and impart information and ideas of all kinds, regardless of frontiers, means that everyone has the freedom to express dissent and engage in protest on any topic, without interference by the State, subject only to limited restrictions permitted by international human rights law.

As discussed above, the State has a duty to guarantee that, in principle, there are no persons, groups, ideas or means of expression excluded a priori from public debate. The State's primary duty of content-neutrality creates a presumption in favour of all types of speech, including speech that is offensive, shocking, unsettling, unpleasant or disturbing to the State or to any segment of the population.[375]

Restrictions on the content of assemblies may be imposed only in conformity with the legitimate limitations on rights outlined above, for example, where the message advocates national, racial or religious hatred that constitutes incitement to discrimination, hostility or violence. Where

---

375   See, for example, Office of the SR for Freedom of Expression of the IACHR, "The Inter-American Legal Framework regarding the Right to Freedom of Expression", OEA Ser.L/V/II, December 30, 2009, paras. 30-31.

a content-based restriction is justified, authorities should take the least intrusive and restrictive measures to address the issue.[376]

Regulation of a public protest based upon the content of the message protesters seek to communicate was at issue in *Hyde Park and Others v. Moldova*.[377] The ECtHR found that rejecting an application to hold a protest demonstration on the grounds that "the protest was unwelcome and unfounded" was incompatible with *ECHR* Article 11, holding that "[t]he guarantee of the right to freedom of assembly cannot be left to the whim of the authorities and their perception of what is or is not deserving of authorization".[378]

The ECtHR remarked, in *Stankov v. Bulgaria*, that

> [o]ne of the principal characteristics of democracy is the possibility it offers of resolving a country's problems through dialogue, without recourse to violence, even when those problems are irksome. Democracy thrives on freedom of expression. From that point of view, there can be no justification for hindering a group solely because it seeks to debate in public the situation of part of the State's population and to find, according to democratic rules, solutions capable of satisfying everyone concerned.[379]

Nor, as noted above, should criticism of the government or a state official *per se* constitute a sufficient ground for imposing restrictions on the right to dissent and protest.[380]

According to the IACHR, in order for limitations to respect the standards for the protection of freedom of expression and freedom of assembly, "they must not depend on the content of what is to be expressed in the

---

376   UN HRC, *Joint report of the Special Rapporteur on the rights to freedom of peaceful assembly and of association and the Special Rapporteur on extrajudicial, summary or arbitrary executions on the proper management of assemblies*, 4 February 2016, A/HRC/31/66, para. 33.
377   ECtHR, *Hyde Park and Others v. Moldova*, App. no. 33482/06, Judgment of 30 June 2009 (Final).
378   *Ibid*, para. 30.
379   ECtHR, *Case of Stankov and the United Macedonian Organisation Ilinden v. Bulgaria*, App. nos. 29221/95 and 29225/95, Judgment of 2 January 2002 (Final), para. 88.
380   See, for example, ECtHR, *Incal v. Turkey*, App. no. 41/1997/825/1031, Judgment of 9 June 1998, para. 54.

demonstration, they must serve a public interest, and they must leave open alternative channels of communication".[381]

Freedom to choose form of dissent and protest

The guarantees under international law of freedom to use all forms and means of expression mean that the right to express dissent and protest can take any form, such as speech, images or actions, and may be expressed through any means, including audio-visual as well as electronic and internet-based modes of expression.

The IACtHR has ruled that as the expression and dissemination of thoughts and ideas are indivisible, "a restriction to the possibilities of spreading information directly represents, in the same measure, a limit to the right to express oneself freely".[382]

Role of digital technologies in exercising right to dissent and protest

As Frank La Rue, UN SR on the promotion and protection of the right to freedom of opinion and expression, notes, the internet has become "a key means by which individuals can exercise their right to freedom of opinion and expression".[383] Given that the right to freedom of opinion and expression is as much a fundamental right on its own accord as it is an "enabler" of other rights, including civil and political rights and the rights to freedom of association and assembly, the internet facilitates the realization of a range of other human rights by acting as a catalyst for the exercise of the right to freedom of opinion and expression.[384]

Indeed, the use of digital technologies in dissent and protest is becoming

---

381   OAS, IACHR, *Annual Report of the Inter-American Commission on Human Rights 2005, Vol. III: Report of The Office of the Special Rapporteur for Freedom of Expression*, OEA/Ser.L/V/II.124, Doc. 7, 27 February 2006, p. 141.
382   IACtHR, *Case of López-Álvarez v. Honduras*, Judgment of February 1, 2006, (Merits, Reparations and Costs), para. 164.
383   UN General Assembly, *Report of the Special Rapporteur on the promotion and protection of the right to freedom of opinion and expression, Frank La Rue*, 16 May 2011, A/HRC/17/27, para. 20.
384   *Ibid*, para. 22.

increasingly important, as both a medium in protests – enabling protests to take place in physical space – and also as a platform.[385] Digital developments have also blurred the boundaries between who is a journalist and who is a protester.[386]

UN SR Frank La Rue calls on all States to ensure that internet access is maintained at all times, including during times of political unrest,[387] and that "[a]ny determination on what [website] content should be blocked must be undertaken by a competent judicial authority or a body which is independent of any political, commercial, or other unwarranted influences".[388]

Role of the media in promoting exercise of right to peaceful protest

The media play a key role during peaceful protests in promoting the full and effective exercise of the right to freedom of peaceful assembly. The UN High Commissioner for Human Rights has recommended that media coverage be recognized as an element of protection of human rights in the context of peaceful protests.[389] In a case involving an attack on a video journalist who was attempting to film a demonstration, the IACtHR concluded that dissemination of information about the protest was of public interest and "enabled those who saw it to observe and verify whether, during the demonstration, the members of the armed forces were performing their duties correctly, with an appropriate use of force".[390]

---

385   ARTICLE 19, *The Right to Protest: Background paper* (ARTICLE 19: London), p. 4, online <https://right-to-protest.org/wp-content/uploads/2015/06/Right-to-Protest-Background-paper-EN.pdf>.

386   *Ibid*, p. 17.

387   UN General Assembly, *Report of the Special Rapporteur on the promotion and protection of the right to freedom of opinion and expression, Frank La Rue*, 16 May 2011, A/HRC/17/27, para. 79.

388   *Ibid*, para. 70.

389   UN HRC, *Report of the United Nations High Commissioner for Human Rights on Effective measures and best practices to ensure the promotion and protection of human rights in the context of peaceful protests*, 21 January 2013, A/HRC/22/28, para. 68.

390   IACtHR, *Case of Vélez Restrepo and Family v. Colombia, Preliminary objection, merits, reparations and costs*, Judgment of 3 September 2012, para. 145.

Right to access to information

The HR Committee has found that the right to freedom of expression under *ICCPR* Article 19(2) embraces a right of access to information held by public bodies. Such information includes records held by a public body, regardless of the form in which the information is stored, its source and the date of production.[391]

In their joint report on the proper management of assemblies, the UN SRs elaborate on the right of everyone to access information related to assemblies:

79. The ability to access information is essential to enabling individuals to exercise their rights in the context of assemblies and to ensuring accountability. Information includes records held by a public body at any level or by private bodies performing public functions.

80. The public should have easy, prompt, effective and practical access to such information, through proactive disclosure and the enactment of legislation to facilitate public access to information. Legislation facilitating such access should be based on the principle of maximum disclosure, establishing a presumption that information is accessible, subject only to a narrow system of exceptions.

81. Exceptions to the right to information should be carefully tailored to protect overriding public and private interests, including privacy. Exceptions should apply only where there is a risk of substantial harm to the protected interest and where that harm is greater than the overall public interest in having access to the information. The onus should be on the public authority to demonstrate that the information falls within the scope of an exception. Its decisions must be subject to oversight and review.

82. Practical recommendations:

(a) States should proactively disseminate key information relating to the management of assemblies. Such information should include: laws and regulations relating to the management of assemblies; information

---

391   HR Committee, *CCPR General Comment No. 34, Article 19: Freedoms of opinion and expression,* 12 September 2011, CCPR/C/GC/34, para. 18.

regarding the responsibilities and procedures of agencies and bodies that manage assemblies; standard operating procedures and policies, including codes of conduct, governing the policing of assemblies; the types of equipment routinely used in policing assemblies; information on the training of law enforcement officers; and information on how to access accountability processes;

(b) States should enact comprehensive legislation, for example freedom of information acts, to facilitate public access to information, based upon the principle of maximum disclosure. States should manage information so that it is comprehensive and easily retrieved, and should respond promptly and fully to all requests for information;

(c) States should establish an effective oversight mechanism that has, inter alia, the power to receive and investigate complaints and to make binding orders for the release of information where it finds in favour of the applicant or complainant.[392]

In *Vélez Restrepo and family v. Colombia*, the IACtHR concluded that attacks against journalists limit the freedom of expression of all citizens because they have an intimidating effect on the free flow of information.[393]

Freedom to choose location of protest and to have access to public space

Everyone should have the freedom to choose the location of a protest, and the chosen location should be considered integral to its expressive purpose.[394]

Even if protests may cause a certain degree of disruption to daily life, the State must be tolerant and regard them as equally legitimate uses of public

---

392   UN HRC, *Joint report of the Special Rapporteur on the rights to freedom of peaceful assembly and of association and the Special Rapporteur on extrajudicial, summary or arbitrary executions on the proper management of assemblies*, 4 February 2016, A/HRC/31/66, paras. 79-82 [footnotes omitted].

393   IACtHR, *Case of Vélez Restrepo and Family v. Colombia, Preliminary objection, merits, reparations and costs*, Judgment of 3 September 2012, para. 146.

394   ARTICLE 19, *The Right to Protest: Principles on protection of human rights in protests* (Policy Brief, 2015), Principle 8, p. 20.

space as other, more routine activities.[395]

The IACHR observes that, "[i]n a democratic society, 'the urban space is not only an area for circulation, but also a space for participation.'"[396] States must guarantee and not obstruct the right of demonstrators to meet freely both in private and in public spaces and workplaces. With regard to the use of private space, the right should not be obstructed if it is exercised with the consent of the owners. In public space, States should ensure that any restrictions do not invalidate the exercise of the right.[397]

Presumption in favor of allowing peaceful protests

Consistent with the presumption in favour of allowing peaceful assembly is the presumption in favour of allowing peaceful protests.

The HRC has stressed that peaceful protests should not be viewed as a threat, and therefore encourages all States to engage in an open, inclusive and meaningful dialogue when dealing with peaceful protests and their causes.[398]

As discussed above, the only type of event that is not protected as a "peaceful assembly" is that in which the organizers and participants intend to use violence. The ECtHR has clarified that "the possibility of extremists with violent intentions, not members of the organizing association, joining the demonstration cannot as such take away [the right under *ECHR* Article 11]".[399] The ECtHR has ruled, moreover, that the conduct of the individual must be assessed separately from that of the crowd. An individual does not cease to enjoy the right to peaceful assembly as a result of sporadic violence or other punishable acts committed by others in the course of the demonstration if the individual in question remains peaceful in his or her

---

395   See, for example, ECtHR, *Case of Patyi and Others v. Hungary,* App. no. 5529/05, Judgment of 7 January 2009 (Final), paras. 42-43; ECtHR, *Case of Balçik and Others v. Turkey,* App. no. 25/02, Judgment of 29 February 2008 (Final), para. 52; ECtHR, *Case of Ashughyan v. Armenia,* App. no. 33268/03, Judgment of 1 December 2008 (Final), para. 90.

396   IACHR, *Second Report on the Situation of Human Rights Defenders in the Americas,* OEA/Ser.L/V/II. Doc. 66, 31 December 2011, p. 52.

397   *Ibid.*

398   HRC resolution 22/10, Preamble.

399   ECtHR, *Primov and Others v. Russia,* App. no. 17391/06, Judgment of 13 October 2014 (Final), para. 155.

own intentions or behavior.[400]

The burden of proving demonstrators' violent intentions or actions lies with the authorities.[401] Moreover, while violent protesters lose their protection under the right to peaceful assembly, they retain all their other rights, including the right to bodily integrity and not to be tortured or subjected to excessive force.[402]

---

400   ECtHR, *Case of Ziliberg v. Moldova,* App. no. 61821/00 (Admissibility decision) Judgment of 4 May 2004. See also UN HRC, *Report of the Special Rapporteur on the rights to freedom of peaceful assembly and of association, Maina Kiai,* 21 May 2012, A/HRC/20/27, para. 25.

401   ECtHR, *Case of Christian Democratic People's Party v. Moldova (No. 2),* App. no. 25196/04, Judgment of 2 May 2010 (Final), para. 23.

402   UN, *Statement by the United Nations Special Rapporteur on the Rights to Freedom of Peaceful Assembly and of Association at the conclusion of his visit to the Republic of Korea,* 29 January 2016.

Limited scope of restrictions on the right to dissent and protest

The right to freedom of peaceful assembly is one of the foundations of a democratic society and should not be interpreted restrictively.[403] As the ECtHR has stated, "[i]t goes without saying that any demonstration in a public place may cause a certain level of disruption to ordinary life and encounter hostility".[404] Public authorities must, however, "show a certain degree of tolerance towards peaceful gatherings if the freedom of assembly... is not to be deprived of all substance".[405]

The OAS SR for Freedom of Expression warns that in regulating freedom of expression and freedom of assembly in order to protect the rights of others, "it should be borne in mind that the right to freedom of expression is not just another right, but one of the primary and most important foundations of any democratic structure: the undermining of freedom of expression directly affects the central nerve of the democratic system".[406] Similarly, "governments may not invoke one of the lawful restrictions of freedom of expression, such as the maintenance of 'public order,' as a means to deny a right guaranteed by the [ACHR] or to impair it of its true content".[407] The right of assembly and demonstration cannot be considered as synonymous with public disorder for the purpose of restricting it per se.[408]

In *Bączkowski and Others v. Poland*, the ECtHR found that a decision to deny permission to hold a peaceful march against homophobia may have been influenced by the mayor's public opinions and, as a result, impinged on the applicants' right to freedom of assembly in a discriminatory manner.[409]

---

403   ECHR, *Case of M.C. v. the Federal Republic of Germany*, App. no. 13079/87, 6 March 1989 (Admissibility decision).
404   ECtHR, *Case of Oya Ataman v. Turkey*, App. no. 74552/01, Judgment of 5 March 2007 (Final), para. 38.
405   *Ibid*, para. 42.
406   OAS, IACHR, *Annual Report of the Inter-American Commission on Human Rights 2005, Vol. III: Report of The Office of the Special Rapporteur for Freedom of Expression*, OEA/Ser.L/V/II.124, Doc. 7, 27 February 2006, p. 141.
407   *Ibid*.
408   *Ibid*.
409   ECtHR, *Case of Bączkowski and Others v. Poland*, App. no. 1543/06, Judgment of 24 September 2007 (Final), para. 100. See also ECtHR, *Alekseyev v. Russia*, App. Nos. 4916/07,

In *Ezelin v. France*,[410] where a lawyer who attended a protest that then turned violent was reprimanded for breach of discretion by his professional body, the ECtHR held that the sanction, however minimal, was disproportionate, as it would result in advocates being discouraged, for fear of disciplinary sanctions, from making clear their beliefs on such occasions.[411]

Regulation of the right to peaceful protest must respect international human rights law. In *International Pen and Others v. Nigeria*, the complainant argued that many hundreds of people, including the President of the Movement for the Survival of the Ogoni Peoples (MOSOP), who were arrested and put on trial for the murders of four Ogoni leaders during a riot that broke out at a public meeting organized by MOSOP, had been convicted and sentenced to death for the peaceful expression of their views. The ACHPR found that the victims had been disseminating information and opinions on the rights of the people who live in the oil-producing area of Ogoniland and that the State had therefore violated Articles 10 and 11 and, implicitly, Article 9 of the *Banjul Charter*.[412]

CCPR General Comment 29 on *ICCPR* Article 4 (States of Emergency) provides that the rights to freedom of peaceful assembly and of association shall not be derogated during a state of emergency, since "the possibility of restricting certain [*ICCPR*] rights under the terms of, for instance ... freedom of assembly is generally sufficient during such situations and no derogation from the provisions in question would be justified by the exigencies of the situation".[413]

The OAS SR for Freedom of Expression observes that "societal participation through public demonstrations is important for the consolidation of democratic life of societies" and of "crucial social interest" as an exercise of freedom of expression and assembly.[414] This leaves the State with a

---

25924/08 and 14599/09, Judgment of 21 October 2010; ECtHR, *Case of Patyi and Others v. Hungary,* App. no. 5529/05, Judgment of 7 January 2009 (Final).

410   ECtHR, *Case of Ezelin v. France,* App. no. 11800/85, Judgment of 26 April 1991.

411   *Ibid,* paras. 52-53.

412   ACHPR, *International Pen and Others v. Nigeria,* Communication Nos. 137/94, 139/94, 154/96 and 161/97 (1998).

413   HR Committee, *CCPR General Comment No. 29, Article 4: States of Emergency,* U.N. Doc. CCPR/C/21/Rev.1/Add.11 (2001), para. 5.

414   OAS, IACHR, *Annual Report of the Inter-American Commission on Human Rights*

very narrow margin to justify restrictions on this right. In this respect, "the purpose of the regulation of the right to assembly cannot be that of establishing grounds for prohibiting meetings or demonstrations".[415]

The OAS SR reviewed four types of regulation that States commonly impose on the exercise of freedom of assembly:

- legislative regulation;

- administrative regulation;

- interference on the part of the judiciary; and

- restrictions imposed by officers in the exercise of police power.[416]

Each type of restriction requires specific safeguards to avoid unduly infringing the right. Legislative regulation that restricts the time, place or manner in which a demonstration may be held "must not depend on the content of what is to be expressed in the demonstration... must serve a public interest, and...must leave open alternative channels of communication".[417]

Administrative regulation includes requirements for prior notification. The OAS SR warns that restrictions, including administrative restrictions, on the right of assembly "must be intended exclusively to prevent serious and imminent dangers; the general possibility of future danger is insufficient".[418]

In terms of interference by the judiciary, the OAS SR notes that, "in principle, criminalization per se of demonstrations in public thoroughfares is inadmissible when they are carried out in exercise of the rights to freedom of expression and to freedom of assembly".[419] It must be examined whether the application of criminal sanctions "satisfies a pressing public interest necessary for the operation of a democratic society".[420] It is also necessary to examine "whether the imposition of criminal sanctions is the least harmful means to restrict the freedom of expression, exercised through the right of

---

2005, Vol. III: Report of The Office of the Special Rapporteur for Freedom of Expression, OEA/Ser.L/V/II.124, Doc. 7, 27 February 2006, p. 140.

415   *Ibid.*

416   *Ibid*, pp. 140-144.

417   *Ibid*, p. 141.

418   *Ibid*, p. 142.

419   *Ibid*, p. 143.

420   *Ibid.*

assembly, in turn exercised through a demonstration on a thoroughfare or in a public space".[421] States must also be cognizant of the intimidating effect criminalization could have on "this form of participatory expression among those sectors of society that lack access to other channels of complaint or petition, such as the traditional press or the right of petition within the state body from which the object of the claim arose". The OAS SR warns that

> [e]ngaging in intimidating actions against free speech by imprisoning those who make use of this means of expression has a dissuading effect on those sectors of society that express their points of view or criticisms of government actions as a way of influencing the decision-making processes and state policies that directly affect them.[422]

Finally, reasonable restrictions may be placed upon demonstrators by police to ensure that demonstrators are peaceful or to restrain those that are violent, as well as to disperse demonstrations that turn violent or obstructive. However, any such restrictions must be for the purpose of protecting, rather than discouraging the right to peaceful protest. Hence, "the dispersing of a demonstration should be justified by the duty to protect the people".[423] According to the OAS SR, police may not arrest persons who are protesting peacefully and legally. "It is only if otherwise lawful conduct gives rise to a reasonable apprehension that it will, by interfering with the rights or liberties of others, provoke violence, that a police officer is empowered to take steps to prevent it; mere disorder is not enough".[424]

In *Sir Dawda K. Jawara v. the Gambia*,[425] the ACHPR found that a ban on political parties and of Ministers of the former civilian government from taking part in any political activity violated rights under the *Banjul Charter*, including rights to freedom of expression (Article 9), freedom of association (Article 10), freedom of assembly (Article 11) and the right to participate freely in government (Article 13).[426]

---

421   *Ibid.*
422   *Ibid.*
423   *Ibid.*
424   *Ibid*, p. 144.
425   ACHPR, *Sir Dawda K. Jawara v. the Gambia,* Communication nos. 147/95 and 149/96 (2000).
426   *Ibid,* paras. 65-70.

States must ensure that the rights to dissent and protest are subject to restrictions only on grounds specified in international law. No restriction on the rights to freedom of expression, assembly, association and privacy may be imposed unless the restriction is "prescribed by law"; pursues a "legitimate aim" identified in the relevant treaty provision; and is both "necessary" and "proportionate" in pursuance of that aim (see above for detailed discussion on limited ability to restrict rights to freedom of expression, freedom of assembly and association and the right to participate in public affairs).

Freedom to hold and participate in peaceful protests is to be considered the rule, and limitations thereto considered the exception. The OHCHR states that, "[i]n this regard, the protection of the rights and freedoms of others should not be used as an excuse to limit the exercise of peaceful protests. Complete prohibition involving blanket bans on time and location does not comply with human rights in the context of peaceful protests, unless it is a measure of last resort, adopted to protect lives".[427] The mere existence of a risk, however, is insufficient for prohibiting an assembly.[428]

UN SRs have stated that where the risk of violent clashes between participants within or between assemblies exists, the least restrictive measures must be taken to ensure the safety and security of participants and others.[429]

OAS SR for Freedom of Expression Edison Lanza reports that, in keeping with Principle 2 of the OAS Declaration of Principles on Freedom of Expression,

> During protests and situations of heightened social unrest, States must adhere to the strictest international standards on freedom of expression in order to fully guarantee this right, without improper interventions against individuals...

---

427   UN HRC, *Report of the United Nations High Commissioner for Human Rights on Effective measures and best practices to ensure the promotion and protection of human rights in the context of peaceful protests,* 21 January 2013, A/HRC/22/28, para. 12.

428   ECtHR, *Alekseyev v. Russia,* App. Nos. 4916/07, 25924/08 and 14599/09, Judgment of 11 April 2011 (Final), para. 75.

429   UN HRC, *Joint report of the Special Rapporteur on the rights to freedom of peaceful assembly and of association and the Special Rapporteur on extrajudicial, summary or arbitrary executions on the proper management of assemblies,* 4 February 2016, A/HRC/31/66, para. 25.

The IACHR has reiterated that social protest is a fundamental tool for defending human rights and it is essential for expressing social and political criticism on the activities of the authorities. The Commission has stated that "in principle, criminalization per se of demonstrations in public thoroughfares is inadmissible when they are carried out in exercise of the rights to freedom of expression and to freedom of assembly" and that "the exercise of the right of assembly through social protest must not be subject to authorization on the part of the authorities or to excessive requirements that make such protests difficult to carry out.⁴³⁰

In the Case of *Sergey Kuznetsov v. Russia*, the ECtHR reiterated that

> any measures interfering with the freedom of assembly and expression other than in cases of incitement to violence or rejection of democratic principles – however shocking and unacceptable certain views or words used may appear to the authorities – do a disservice to democracy and often even endanger it. In a democratic society based on the rule of law, the ideas which challenge the existing order must be afforded a proper opportunity of expression through the exercise of the right of assembly as well as by other lawful means.⁴³¹

The ECtHR has ruled that States must not only safeguard the right to dissent and peaceful protest, but they must also refrain from applying unreasonable indirect restrictions upon that right.⁴³²

While it is the duty of Contracting States to take reasonable and appropriate measures to enable lawful demonstrations to proceed peacefully, they cannot guarantee this absolutely and they have a wide discretion in the choice of the means to be used.⁴³³ In this respect, the duty to guarantee the right of assembly is an obligation as to means (measures to be taken) and

---

430   OAS, IACHR, *Annual Report of the Inter-American Commission on Human Rights 2015, Vol. II: Annual Report of the Office of the Special Rapporteur for Freedom of Expression*, OEA/Ser.L/V/II. Doc. 48/15, 31 December 2015, pp. 47-48 [footnotes omitted].
431   ECtHR, *Case of Sergey Kuznetsov v. Russia*, App. no. 10877/04, Judgment of 23 January 2009 (Final), para. 45.
432   ECtHR, *Case of Oya Ataman v. Turkey*, App. no. 74552/01, Judgment of 5 March 2007 (Final), para. 36.
433   ECtHR, *Case of Plattform "Ärzte Für Das Leben" v. Austria*, App. no. 10126/82, Judgment of 21 June 1988, para. 34.

not as to results to be achieved.[434]

Protests should not be subject to prior authorization

The organization of a protest should not be subject to prior authorization from the administrative authorities of the State, but at the most to a prior notification procedure, the rationale for which is to facilitate the exercise of the right to peaceful protest.[435]

In *Kivenmaa v. Finland*,[436] the HR Committee found that a requirement to notify police of an intended demonstration in a public place six hours before its commencement may be compatible with *ICCPR* Article 21, provided it is for reasons of national security or public safety, public order, the protection of public health or morals or the protection of the rights and freedoms of others. However, a gathering of several individuals displaying a banner in that instance did not constitute a demonstration.[437]

An assembly that, in the absence of notification, is unlawful does not justify an infringement of freedom of assembly, nor a disproportionate use of force by police.[438]

The IACHR states that the requirement of prior notification should not become a demand that permission be granted beforehand by an officer with unlimited discretional authority.[439]

Where a regime of authorization is in place, administrative officials in charge of issuing authorizations should be subject to oversight on a regular basis to

---

434   *Ibid.*
435   UN HRC, *Report of the United Nations High Commissioner for Human Rights on Effective measures and best practices to ensure the promotion and protection of human rights in the context of peaceful protests,* 21 January 2013, A/HRC/22/28, para. 11.
436   HR Committee, *Communication No. 412/1990, Kivenmaa v. Finland,* Views adopted on 31 March 1994.
437   *Ibid,* para. 9.2.
438   ECtHR, *Case of Oya Ataman v. Turkey,* App. no. 74552/01, Judgment of 5 March 2007 (Final), paras. 38-44. See also, ECtHR, *Case of Bukta and Others v. Hungary,* App. no. 25691/04, Judgment of 17 October 2007 (Final).
439   OAS, IACHR, *Annual Report of the Inter-American Commission on Human Rights 2005, Vol. III: Report of The Office of the Special Rapporteur for Freedom of Expression,* OEA/Ser.L/V/II.124, Doc. 7, 27 February 2006, p. 142.

ensure against arbitrary denial of requests to hold public assemblies.[440]

Simultaneous protests and counter-demonstrations

Simultaneous protests (at the same place and time) should be allowed, protected and facilitated, whenever possible.[441] Assemblies, including spontaneous assemblies and counter-protests, should, as far as possible, be facilitated to take place within sight and sound of their target.[442]

In the case of counter-demonstrations, "which aim at expressing discontent with the message of other assemblies", UN SR Maina Kiai writes, "such demonstrations should take place, but should not dissuade participants of the other assemblies from exercising their right to freedom of peaceful assembly. In this respect, the role of law enforcement authorities in protecting and facilitating the events is crucial".[443]

The ECtHR has ruled that "[i]n a democracy the right to counter-demonstrate cannot extend to inhibiting the exercise of the right to demonstrate".[444] Where a counter-demonstration has been organized with the intention of interfering with the rights of others to lawfully assemble, the counter-demonstration loses its protection under *ICCPR* Article 21.[445]

---

440   UN HRC, *Report of the Special Rapporteur on the rights to freedom of peaceful assembly and of association, Maina Kiai*, 21 May 2012, A/HRC/20/27, para. 44.
441   *Ibid*, para. 30.
442   UN HRC, *Joint report of the Special Rapporteur on the rights to freedom of peaceful assembly and of association and the Special Rapporteur on extrajudicial, summary or arbitrary executions on the proper management of assemblies, 4 February 2016*, A/HRC/31/66, para. 24.
443   UN HRC, *Report of the Special Rapporteur on the rights to freedom of peaceful assembly and of association, Maina Kiai*, 21 May 2012, A/HRC/20/27, para. 30.
444   ECtHR, *Case of Plattform "Ärzte Für Das Leben" v. Austria*, App. no. 10126/82, Judgment of 21 June 1988, para. 32.
445   UN HRC, *Joint report of the Special Rapporteur on the rights to freedom of peaceful assembly and of association and the Special Rapporteur on extrajudicial, summary or arbitrary executions on the proper management of assemblies, 4 February 2016*, A/HRC/31/66, at footnote 14.

Limitations must be based on legitimate grounds and narrowly applied

The permitted grounds for restriction under the *ICCPR* – necessary for the respect or reputations of others; the protection of national security or of public order, or of public health or morals – may not be invoked as a justification for the muzzling of any advocacy or multi-party democracy, democratic tenets or human rights.[446]

The application of overbroad legislation restricting the right to freedom of assembly is not a restriction permitted by *ICCPR* Article 21.[447]

In the Case of *Norin Catriman and Others (leaders, members and activists of the Mapuche Indigenous People) v. Chile*,[448] the ACtHR referred to "the intimidating effect on the exercise of freedom of expression that may result from the fear of being subject to a civil or criminal sanction that is unnecessary or disproportionate in a democratic society, and that may lead to the self-censorship of the person on whom the punishment is imposed, and on other members of society". In that case, the ACtHR found that the criminalization by authorities of demonstrations and social protests by the Mapuche indigenous people "could have instilled a reasonable fear in other members of this people involved in actions related to the social protest and the claim for their territorial rights, or who would eventually want to participate in this".[449]

---

446   HR Committee, *CCPR General Comment No. 34, Article 19: Freedoms of opinion and expression,* 12 September 2011, CCPR/C/GC/34, para. 23. See also HR Committee, Communication No. 458/91, *Mukong v. Cameroon,* Views adopted on 21 July 1994.

447   See, for example, HR Committee, Communication No. 412/1990, *Kivenmaa v. Finland,* Views adopted on 31 March 1994; ECtHR, *Case of Bączkowski and Others v. Poland,* App. no. 1543/06, Judgment of 24 September 2007 (Final).

448   IACtHR, *Case of Norín Catrimán et al. (Leaders, Members And Activist of the Mapuche Indigenous People) v. Chile,* Judgment of May 29, 2014 (Merits, Reparations And Costs).

449   *Ibid,* para. 376.

State duty to facilitate exercise of right to dissent and to peaceful protest

In addition to the negative duty on States to refrain from applying unreasonable restrictions on the rights to dissent and peaceful protest, States have a positive duty to enable effective exercise of these rights and to protect protesters from violence and external interference by others.

Special Representative of the UN Secretary-General on the situation of human rights defenders Hina Jilani states that the

negative obligation on the part of the State not to interfere with peaceful protests is to be combined with the positive obligation to protect rights holders in the exercise of this right, particularly when persons protesting hold unpopular or controversial views, or belong to minorities or other groups exposed to higher risks of victimization, attacks and other forms of intolerance.[450]

The ECtHR explained the basis of the positive duty on States in the *Case of Plattform "Ärzte Für Das Leben" v. Austria*:

A demonstration may annoy or give offence to persons opposed to the ideas or claims that it is seeking to promote. The participants must, however, be able to hold the demonstration without having to fear that they will be subjected to physical violence by their opponents; such a fear would be liable to deter associations or other groups supporting common ideas or interests from openly expressing their opinions on highly controversial issues affecting the community. In a democracy the right to counter-demonstrate cannot extend to inhibiting the exercise of the right to demonstrate.

Genuine, effective freedom of peaceful assembly cannot, therefore, be reduced to a mere duty on the part of the State not to interfere: a purely negative conception would not be compatible with the object and purpose of [*ECHR*] Article 11. Like [*ECHR*] Article 8, [*ECHR*] Article 11 sometimes requires positive measures to be taken, even in the

---

450   UN General Assembly, *Report of the Special Representative of the Secretary-General on human rights defenders*, A/62/225, 13 August 2007, para. 97.

sphere of relations between individuals, if need be...[451]

The IACHR has said the rights to freedom of assembly and of association are "fundamental to the existence and functioning of a democratic society" and the "protection of such rights may entail not only the obligation of a state not to interfere with the exercise of the right of assembly and of association, but in certain circumstances may require positive measures on the part of the state to secure the effective exercise of the freedom, for example by protecting participants in a demonstration from physical violence by individuals who may hold opposite views".[452]

The UN Special Representative of the Secretary-General on human rights defenders argues that "respecting and fulfilling the right to protest entails the obligation on the part of States to take deliberate, concrete and targeted steps to build, maintain and strengthen pluralism, tolerance and an open attitude to the expression of dissent in society".[453]

The obligation not to obstruct and to adopt positive measures to guarantee the exercise of the right to peaceful protest begins from the time administrative authorities are notified of the wish to hold a demonstration and continues during the demonstration itself, to protect the rights of the participants and any third parties who may be involved, as well as after the demonstration, to investigate and punish any person, including agents of the State, who commits acts of violence against the life or physical integrity of demonstrators or third parties.[454]

In the view of the IACHR, States must adopt regulatory and administrative measures, designing appropriate operational plans and procedures to facilitate and not obstruct the exercise of the right of assembly. Such measures involve, for example, setting application requirements for

---

451   ECtHR, *Case of Plattform "Ärzte Für Das Leben" v. Austria*, App. no. 10126/82, Judgment of 21 June 1988, para. 32. See also ECtHR, *Case of Oya Ataman v. Turkey*, App. no. 74552/01, Judgment of 5 December 2006, para. 36; ECtHR, *Djavit An v. Turkey*, App. No. 20652/92, Judgment of 9 July 2003 (Final), para. 57.
452   IACHR, *Report on terrorism and human rights*, OEA/Ser.L/V/II.116 Doc. 5, rev. 1 cor., 22 October 2002, para. 359.
453   UN General Assembly, *Report of the Special Representative of the Secretary-General on human rights defenders*, A/62/225, 13 August 2007, Summary.
454   IACHR, *Second Report on the Situation of Human Rights Defenders in the Americas*, OEA/Ser.L/V/II. Doc. 66, 31 December 2011, p. 51.

demonstrations, rerouting pedestrian and vehicular traffic and escorting participants in the demonstration to ensure their safety and effective participation.[455]

The OAS SR for Freedom of Expression states that the right to freedom of expression does not merely require that the State avoid imposing censorship, but rather demands much more: "it requires, for example, that the State become involved in keeping public spaces open and in guaranteeing a 'right to access to public fora' for all".[456]

State obligation to protect against external interference

The duty to facilitate peaceful protests implies that protests are not per se a threat to public order. Instead, police have the duty to remove violent individuals from the crowd in order to allow protesters to exercise their basic rights to assemble and express themselves peacefully.[457]

A "distinctive feature of the right of assembly [under the ACHR]...is that it be exercised peaceably and without arms" and "State authorities have an obligation to prevent and, where necessary, control any form of violent behavior that violates the rights of any other person subject to that State's jurisdiction".[458]

States must also ensure that anyone monitoring and reporting on violations and abuses occurring during peaceful protests, including journalists, community media workers, other media professionals and bloggers, do so without fear of intimidation, legal and physical harassment and violence. In this regard, the State has an obligation to protect them.[459]

---

455   *Ibid.*
456   OAS, IACHR, *Annual Report of the Inter-American Commission on Human Rights 2005, Vol. III: Report of The Office of the Special Rapporteur for Freedom of Expression*, OEA/Ser.L/V/II.124, Doc. 7, 27 February 2006, p. 145.
457   UN HRC, *Report of the United Nations High Commissioner for Human Rights on Effective measures and best practices to ensure the promotion and protection of human rights in the context of peaceful protests*, 21 January 2013, A/HRC/22/28, para. 10.
458   OAS, IACHR, *Report on Citizen Security and Human Rights (2009)*, OEA/Ser.L/V/II. Doc. 57, para. 198.
459   UN HRC, *Report of the United Nations High Commissioner for Human Rights on Effective measures and best practices to ensure the promotion and protection of human rights in the context of peaceful protests*, 21 January 2013, A/HRC/22/28, para. 16

The responsibility of States to protect peaceful demonstrators from individuals or groups, including those belonging to the State apparatus, who aim at disrupting or dispersing such assemblies should always be explicitly stated in domestic legislation.[460]

The OHCHR recommends that groups that could provide a safe haven for peaceful protesters, as well as those monitoring peaceful protest, should be promoted and strengthened. Such groups include human rights defenders coalitions; national, regional and international networks for communication of information; monitoring groups; and support groups.[461]

States should create and maintain an enabling environment

The courts and treaty bodies recommend that States put in place an enabling environment for associations to operate safely and for peaceful protests to take place free from undue restrictions.

States should put in place a legal framework for facilitating peaceful assemblies

International law obliges States to take the necessary steps to adopt such laws or other measures as may be necessary to give effect to the right to dissent and peaceful protest.[462] An adequate legal framework designed to facilitate the full enjoyment of the right to dissent and peaceful protest is a critical element of an enabling environment for the right to assembly.

As UN SR on the situation of human rights defenders Margaret Sekaggya has noted,

> [o]ne of the key elements of a safe and enabling environment for defenders is the existence of laws and provisions at all levels, including administrative provisions, that protect, support and empower defenders, and are in compliance with international human rights law

---

460　UN HRC, *Report of the Special Rapporteur on the rights to freedom of peaceful assembly and of association, Maina Kiai,* 21 May 2012, A/HRC/20/27, para. 33.
461　UN HRC, *Report of the United Nations High Commissioner for Human Rights on Effective measures and best practices to ensure the promotion and protection of human rights in the context of peaceful protests,* 21 January 2013, A/HRC/22/28, para. 18.
462　See, for example, *ICCPR* Article 2(2).

and standards.[463]

The ACHPR recommends that national constitutions guarantee the right to freedom of assembly, "which must be understood in a broad manner consistent with international human rights law; where a constitution states that the essence of this right shall be defined by law, this should in no way be interpreted to allow improper limitation of the right".[464]

The HR Committee's Concluding Observations on a periodic report[465] identified a lack of a domestic legal framework regulating peaceful events and the application by domestic courts of outdated regulations that are not in line with international standards and severely restrict the right to freedom of assembly. The HR Committee recommended that the State adopt a law regulating the freedom of assembly, imposing only restrictions that are in compliance with the strict requirements of *ICCPR* Article 21.[466]

States should prepare and plan for assemblies

It is suggested that authorities should prepare and plan for assemblies with a view to ensuring the best possible conditions for the exercise of the right to peaceful assembly, and with a view to preventing and avoiding situations where authorities might need to resort to the use of force.

In the view of UN SRs, the proper planning for and facilitation of assemblies involves the collection and analysis of information; anticipation of different scenarios and proper risk assessments; transparent decision-making; contingency plans and precautionary measures; continuous monitoring of activities; and adaptability to changing circumstances.[467]

---

463   UN HRC, *Report of the Special Rapporteur on the situation of human rights defenders, Margaret Sekaggya*, A/HRC/25/55, 23 December 2013, para. 62. The International Service for Human rights has launched a "Model Law" that countries will be able to use to create or improve their own legal protections for human rights defenders. Details are available online: <https://www.ishr.ch/news/groundbreaking-model-law-recognise-and-protect-human-rights-defenders>.
464   AU, ACHPR, *Report of the Study Group on Freedom of Association and Assembly in Africa, (ACHPR 2014)*, p.60.
465   UN HR Committee, *Concluding observations on the seventh periodic report of Ukraine*, 22 August 2013, CCPR/C/UKR/CO/7.
466   *Ibid*, para. 21.
467   UN HRC, *Joint report of the Special Rapporteur on the rights to freedom of peaceful assembly and of association and the Special Rapporteur on extrajudicial, summary or*

In the Oya Ataman group of cases,[468] the ECtHR observed under *ECHR* Article 46 (binding force and execution of judgments) that violations of the right to freedom of peaceful assembly and the ill-treatment of the applicants on account of excessive force used to disperse peaceful demonstrations were systemic, and that, therefore, the State had to adopt general measures to prevent similar violations in the future. Those measures should include, among others, clearer rules on the use of tear gas (or pepper spray) and tear gas grenades, adequate training of law enforcement officers and their control and supervision during demonstrations.[469]

Need for effective communication and collaboration with organizers

The proper facilitation of assemblies also benefits from effective communication and collaboration among all relevant parties.[470] In *Frumkin v. Russia*,[471] the ECtHR found that the authorities "did not comply with even the minimum requirements in their duty to communicate with the assembly leaders, which was an essential part of their positive obligation to ensure the peaceful conduct of the assembly, to prevent disorder and to secure the safety of all the citizens involved".[472]

Communication is not limited to verbal communication, and law enforcement officials must be trained on the possible impact of any indirect communication that may be perceived by organizers and participants as intimidation, such as, for example, the presence or use of certain equipment

---

arbitrary executions on the proper management of assemblies, 4 February 2016, A/ HRC/31/66, para. 37.

468   COE, Council of Ministers, *Oya Ataman group against Turkey - 46 cases concerning the excessive use of force to break up unlawful but peaceful demonstrations*, 1222nd meeting (March 2015).

469   COE, Committee on Legal Affairs and Human Rights, *Report on the urgent need to prevent human rights violations during peaceful protests*, Doc. 14060, 10 May 2016, para. 33.

470   UN HRC, *Joint report of the Special Rapporteur on the rights to freedom of peaceful assembly and of association and the Special Rapporteur on extrajudicial, summary or arbitrary executions on the proper management of assemblies, 4 February 2016*, A/ HRC/31/66, para. 38.

471   ECtHR, *Case of Frumkin v. Russia*, App. no. 74568/12, Judgment of 6 June 2016 (Final).

472   *Ibid*, para. 129.

and the body language of officials.[473]

As effective communication depends on a relationship of trust between law enforcement agencies and the communities they serve, the demographic makeup of law enforcement agencies should be representative of the whole community and there should be a free flow of information.[474]

State responsibility to provide basic services

It is the responsibility of the State to provide basic services to facilitate the exercise of right to protest, including adequate security and safety (including traffic and crowd management), medical assistance and clean-up services.[475] Organizers should not be held responsible for the provision of such services, nor should they be required to contribute to the cost of their provision.[476]

Adequate training of officials in relation to right to peaceful protest

States should ensure that administrative and law enforcement officials are adequately trained in relation to the respect of the right to freedom of peaceful assembly. Training should include proper knowledge of the legal framework governing assemblies, techniques of crowd facilitation and management, human rights in the context of assemblies and the important role assemblies play in a democratic order.[477] Training must also include effective communication, negotiation and mediation skills to enable law enforcement officials to avoid escalation of violence and to minimize

---

473   UN HRC, *Joint report of the Special Rapporteur on the rights to freedom of peaceful assembly and of association and the Special Rapporteur on extrajudicial, summary or arbitrary executions on the proper management of assemblies, 4 February 2016*, A/ HRC/31/66, para. 38.

474   *Ibid*, para. 39.

475   *OSCE Guidelines*, para. 32; UN HRC, *Joint report of the Special Rapporteur on the rights to freedom of peaceful assembly and of association and the Special Rapporteur on extrajudicial, summary or arbitrary executions on the proper management of assemblies, 4 February 2016*, A/HRC/31/66, para. 40. See also *Basic Principles on the Use of Force and Firearms by Law Enforcement Officials*, Principle 5.

476   *OSCE Guidelines*, paras. 5.2 and 32; UN HRC, *Joint report of the Special Rapporteur on the rights to freedom of peaceful assembly and of association and the Special Rapporteur on extrajudicial, summary or arbitrary executions on the proper management of assemblies, 4 February 2016*, A/HRC/31/66, para. 40.

477   *Ibid*, para. 42.

conflict.[478]

In the Case of Vélez Restrepo and Family v. Colombia, the ACtHR noted that the state has "the obligation to adopt special measures of prevention and protection for journalists subject to special risk owing to the exercise of their profession"[479] and ordered, among other reparation measures, that the State incorporate into its human rights education programs for the armed forces a special module on the protection of the right to freedom of thought and expression and on the work of journalists and media workers.[480]

State duty to adopt a human rights approach to policing peaceful protests

States and their law enforcement agencies and officials are obligated under international law to respect and protect, without discrimination, the rights of all those who participate in assemblies, as well as monitors and bystanders. In doing so, States have a duty to adopt a human rights approach. The normative framework governing the use of force includes the principles of legality, precaution, necessity, proportionality and accountability.[481]

The OSCE Guidelines provide:

The policing of assemblies must be guided by the human rights principles of legality, necessity, proportionality and non-discrimination and must adhere to applicable human rights standards. In particular, the state has a positive duty to take reasonable and appropriate measures to enable peaceful assemblies to take place without participants fearing physical violence. Law enforcement officials must also protect participants of a peaceful assembly from any person or group (including agents provocateurs and counter-demonstrators) that

---

478   Ibid. See also *Basic Principles on the Use of Force and Firearms by Law Enforcement Officials*, Principles 18-20; *OSCE Guidelines*, para. 147.

479   IACtHR, *Case of Vélez Restrepo and Family v. Colombia, Preliminary objection, merits, reparations and costs*, Judgment of 3 September 2012, para. 194.

480   Ibid, para. 277.

481   UN HRC, *Joint report of the Special Rapporteur on the rights to freedom of peaceful assembly and of association and the Special Rapporteur on extrajudicial, summary or arbitrary executions on the proper management of assemblies*, 4 February 2016, A/HRC/31/66, para. 50.

attempt to disrupt or inhibit the assembly in any way.[482]

The COE Committee on Legal Affairs and Human Rights notes that peaceful protests, whether authorized or not, "play a vital role in a democratic society and should not be sacrificed on the altar of security and anti-terrorism measures".[483] COE Rapporteur Ms. Ermira Mehmeti Devaja observes that

[i]n any democratic society, law enforcement officers have a duty to restrict the use of force to the minimum extent necessary, facilitate peaceful protests and protect protesters while maintaining public order. Any abuse by law enforcement agencies is therefore a "serious threat to the rule of law".[484]

In its identification of effective measures and best practices to ensure the promotion and protection of human rights in the context of peaceful protests, the OHCHR discussed a so-called "negotiated management" approach to policing assemblies, according to which "the task of the police is to protect rights and facilitate, rather than frustrate, demonstrations; they should help to diffuse tension and prevent a dangerous escalation of the situation".[485] The OHCHR also encouraged formalization of the role of the "so-called 'safety triangle' during demonstrations, based on continuous communication and interaction between the organizers of the protest, the local or State authorities and the police, aimed at averting risks and ensuring smooth management of the assembly".[486]

Limitations on the use of force

As the actions of State agents should be to protect, rather than discourage, the right of assembly, the rationale for dispersing a demonstration must

---

482   OSCE Guidelines, para. 5.3. See also ECtHR, *Case of Plattform "Ärzte Für Das Leben"* v. *Austria*, App. no. 10126/82, Judgment of 21 June 1988, para. 32.
483   COE, Committee on Legal Affairs and Human Rights, *Report on the urgent need to prevent human rights violations during peaceful protests*, Doc. 14060, 10 May 2016, summary.
484   COE, Committee on Legal Affairs and Human Rights, *Report on the urgent need to prevent human rights violations during peaceful protests*, Doc. 14060, 10 May 2016, p.5.
485   UN HRC, *Report of the United Nations High Commissioner for Human Rights on Effective measures and best practices to ensure the promotion and protection of human rights in the context of peaceful protests*, 21 January 2013, A/HRC/22/28, para. 24.
486   *Ibid.*

be informed by the duty to protect the people demonstrating, and a law enforcement officer charged with dispersing demonstrators must be prepared to use the methods that are safest and cause the least harm to demonstrators.[487] The dispersal of assemblies should only be a measure of last resort. Law enforcement authorities should not resort to force during peaceful assemblies, and they should ensure that force is used only on an exceptional basis.[488]

The IACHR has held that States should establish administrative controls to ensure that, in public protests, force is used only on an exceptional basis and that measures for planning, prevention and investigation of cases in which abuse of force may have occurred should be adopted.[489] Among others, the proposed administrative controls include: "(a) implementation of mechanisms to prohibit, in an effective manner, the use of lethal force as recourse in public demonstrations; (b) implementation of an ammunition registration and control system; (c) implementation of a communications records system to monitor operational orders, those responsible for them, and those carrying them out".[490]

In 2012, the UN SR on the promotion and protection of the right to freedom of opinion and expression and the UN SR on the rights to freedom of peaceful assembly and of association issued a joint press release in which they expressed concern over demonstrations in Quebec, Canada, which reportedly involved serious acts of violence and the detention of up to 700 protesters.[491]

UN SR on torture and other cruel, inhuman or degrading treatment or punishment has criticized the excessive use of force by Moroccan officials

---

487   OAS, IACHR, *Report on Citizen Security and Human Rights (2009)*, OEA/Ser.L/V/II. Doc. 57, para. 200.
488   UN HRC, *Report of the United Nations High Commissioner for Human Rights on Effective measures and best practices to ensure the promotion and protection of human rights in the context of peaceful protests*, 21 January 2013, A/HRC/22/28, para. 13.
489   IACHR, *Report on the Situation of Human Rights Defenders in the Americas*, OEA/Ser.L/V.II.124, Doc. 5 rev. 1, 7 March 2006, para. 68.
490   *Ibid.*
491   See UN General Assembly, *Report of the Special Rapporteur on the promotion and protection of the right to freedom of opinion and expression, Frank La Rue*, A/67/357, 7 September 2012, para. 15.

during protests and also the intimidation and punishment of protesters after an assembly had taken place.[492]

The HR Committee, in its *Concluding observations on the initial report of Indonesia*,[493] expressed concern over undue restrictions of the freedom of assembly and expression by protesters in West Papua and increased reports of excessive use of force and extra-judicial killings by the police and the military during protests, including reports that the State Party uses its security apparatus to punish political dissidents and human rights defenders. The HR Committee recommended, *inter alia*, that the State

> should take concrete steps to prevent the excessive use of force by law enforcement officers by ensuring that they comply with the 1990 United Nations' Basic Principles on the Use of Force and Firearms by Law Enforcement Officials. It should also take appropriate measures to strengthen the National Police Commission to ensure that it can effectively deal with reported cases of alleged misconduct by law enforcement personnel. Furthermore, the State party should take practical steps to put an end to impunity by its security personnel regarding arbitrary and extrajudicial killings, and should take appropriate measures to protect the rights of political dissidents and human rights defenders. The State party should systematically and effectively investigate, and prosecute cases of extra-judicial killings and, if convicted, punish those responsible; and provide adequate compensation to the victims' families.[494]

States must have a domestic legal framework for use of force

The principle of **legality** requires that States develop a domestic legal framework for the use of force, especially potentially lethal force, that complies with international standards.[495] The normative framework should

---

492   UN, HRC, *Report of the Special Rapporteur on torture and other cruel, inhuman or degrading treatment or punishment, Juan E. Méndez: Mission to Morocco*, A/HRC/22/53/Add.2, 28 February 2013, paras. 20, 21, 23, 62 and 63.

493   UN HR Committee, *Concluding observations on the initial report of Indonesia*, CCPR/C/IDN/CO/1, 21 August 2013.

494   *Ibid*, para. 16.

495   UN HRC, *Joint report of the Special Rapporteur on the rights to freedom of peaceful assembly and of association and the Special Rapporteur on extrajudicial, summary or arbitrary executions on the proper management of assemblies*, 4 February 2016, A/

specifically restrict the use of weapons and tactics during assemblies, including protests, and include a formal approval and deployment process for weaponry and equipment.[496] The laws in question must also be published and be accessible to the public.[497]

States must use precaution to minimize harm

The principle of **precaution** "requires that all feasible steps be taken in planning, preparing, and conducting an operation related to an assembly to avoid the use of force or, where force is unavoidable, to minimize its harmful consequences".[498]

The use of force must be the minimum necessary in the circumstances

The use of force by law enforcement officials should be exceptional and assemblies should ordinarily be managed with no resort to force. The **necessity** requirement restricts the kind and degree of force used to the minimum necessary in the circumstances (the least harmful means available).[499] Any force used should be targeted at individuals using violence or to avert an imminent threat.[500]

The *UN Basic Principles* provide:

> 9. Law enforcement officials shall not use firearms against persons except in self-defence or defence of others against the imminent threat of death or serious injury, to prevent the perpetration of a particularly

---

HRC/31/66, para. 51. See also UN HRC, *Report of the Special Rapporteur on extrajudicial, summary or arbitrary executions, Christof Heyns,* A/HRC/26/36, 1 April 2014, para. 56.

496   UN HRC, *Joint report of the Special Rapporteur on the rights to freedom of peaceful assembly and of association and the Special Rapporteur on extrajudicial, summary or arbitrary executions on the proper management of assemblies, 4 February 2016,* A/ HRC/31/66, para. 51.

497   UN HRC, *Report of the Special Rapporteur on extrajudicial, summary or arbitrary executions, Christof Heyns,* A/HRC/26/36, 1 April 2014, para. 57. See also ECtHR, *Case of Nachova and Others v. Bulgaria,* App. nos. 43577/98 and 43579/98, Judgment of 6 July 2005, para. 102.

498   UN HRC, *Joint report of the Special Rapporteur on the rights to freedom of peaceful assembly and of association and the Special Rapporteur on extrajudicial, summary or arbitrary executions on the proper management of assemblies, 4 February 2016,* A/ HRC/31/66, para. 52.

499   *Ibid,* para. 57.

500   *Ibid.*

serious crime involving grave threat to life, to arrest a person presenting such a danger and resisting their authority, or to prevent his or her escape, and only when less extreme means are insufficient to achieve these objectives. In any event, intentional lethal use of firearms may only be made when strictly unavoidable in order to protect life.

...

12. As everyone is allowed to participate in lawful and peaceful assemblies, in accordance with the principles embodied in the Universal Declaration of Human Rights and the International Covenant on Civil and Political Rights, Governments and law enforcement agencies and officials shall recognize that force and firearms may be used only in accordance with principles 13 and 14.

13. In the dispersal of assemblies that are unlawful but non-violent, law enforcement officials shall avoid the use of force or, where that is not practicable, shall restrict such force to the minimum extent necessary.

14. In the dispersal of violent assemblies, law enforcement officials may use firearms only when less dangerous means are not practicable and only to the minimum extent necessary. Law enforcement officials shall not use firearms in such cases, except under the conditions stipulated in principle 9.

The use of force must be proportionate to the expected benefit

The proportionality requirement sets a ceiling on the use of force based on the threat posed by the person targeted. The harm that might result from the use of force must be proportionate and justifiable in relation to the expected benefit.[501]

The principles of necessity and proportionality apply to the use of all force, including potentially lethal force. Intentional lethal use of force is only lawful where it is strictly unavoidable to protect another life from an imminent threat; this is sometimes referred to as the "protect life" principle.[502]

Firearms may be used only against an imminent threat to protect life

---

501   *Ibid*, para. 58.
502   *Ibid*, para. 60; UN HRC, *Report of the Special Rapporteur on extrajudicial, summary or arbitrary executions, Christof Heyns*, A/HRC/26/36, 1 April 2014, para. 70.

Specific rules apply to the use of firearms for law enforcement, also during assemblies.[503] Firearms may be used only against an imminent threat either to protect life or to prevent life-threatening injuries, and there must be no other feasible option.[504] Firearms should never be used simply to disperse an assembly; indiscriminate firing into a crowd is always unlawful.[505]

According to UN SR on extrajudicial, summary or arbitrary executions Christof Heyns, "the only circumstances warranting the use of firearms, including during demonstrations, is the imminent threat of death or serious injury".[506]

With regard to the use of tear gas, UN SR on the rights to freedom of peaceful assembly and of association Maina Kiai warns that "gas does not discriminate between demonstrators and non-demonstrators, healthy people and people with health conditions".[507] The SR also warns against "any modification of the chemical composition of the gas for the sole purpose of inflicting severe pain on protestors and, indirectly, bystanders".[508]

Accountability in policing assemblies

States should have in place processes and procedures to minimize the use of force in assemblies and to ensure accountability for unlawful acts or omissions by law enforcement officers.

The UN SRs state that these preventive and accountability measures include: a clear and transparent command structure; effective reporting and review procedures to address any incident in relation to an assembly in which a potentially unlawful use of force occurs; proper record keeping of decisions

---

503   Basic Principles on the Use of Force and Firearms by Law Enforcement Officials, Principle 9.
504   UN HRC, Joint report of the Special Rapporteur on the rights to freedom of peaceful assembly and of association and the Special Rapporteur on extrajudicial, summary or arbitrary executions on the proper management of assemblies, 4 February 2016, A/HRC/31/66, para. 59.
505   UN HRC, Report of the Special Rapporteur on extrajudicial, summary or arbitrary executions, Christof Heyns, A/HRC/26/36, 1 April 2014, para. 75.
506   UN HRC, Report of the Special Rapporteur on extrajudicial, summary or arbitrary executions, 23 May 2011, A/HRC/17/28, para. 60.
507   UN HRC, Report of the Special Rapporteur on the rights to freedom of peaceful assembly and of association, Maina Kiai, 21 May 2012, A/HRC/20/27, para. 35.
508   Ibid.

made by command officers; requirements that law enforcement officials must be clearly and individually identifiable; and the avoidance of the use of military in policing assemblies, except in exceptional circumstances where it is necessary, in which case the military should be subordinate to civilian authorities and be fully trained in, adopt and be bound by international human rights law and principles.[509]

It is important that law enforcement officers policing assemblies wear visible identification numbers on their uniforms.[510]

The UN SRs suggest that, with adequate safeguards to ensure privacy rights, the appropriate use of body-worn cameras by law enforcement personnel in the context of assemblies could assist the work of internal investigations or civilian oversight mechanisms.[511]

Additional measures for ensuring accountability of law enforcement officers in relation to peaceful assemblies identified by the UN SRs include:

(a) States should ensure in law and practice that law enforcement officials do not have immunity from criminal or civil liability for cases of misconduct;

(b) States should establish and fund additional levels of non-judicial oversight, including an effective internal investigations process and a statutory independent oversight body. Where there is reason to believe a crime has been committed, the matter should be immediately referred to the prosecuting authority for proper and full investigation;

(c) A law enforcement officer who is under investigation, external or internal, should not be redeployed into the field until the investigation

---

509   UN HRC, *Joint report of the Special Rapporteur on the rights to freedom of peaceful assembly and of association and the Special Rapporteur on extrajudicial, summary or arbitrary executions on the proper management of assemblies, 4 February 2016*, A/HRC/31/66, paras. 64-66. See also *UN Basic Principles*, Principle 22; *Code of Conduct for Law Enforcement Officials*, Article 8, with commentary.
510   UN HRC, *Report of the Special Rapporteur on the rights to freedom of peaceful assembly and of association, Maina Kiai, 21 May 2012*, A/HRC/20/27, para. 79.
511   UN HRC, *Joint report of the Special Rapporteur on the rights to freedom of peaceful assembly and of association and the Special Rapporteur on extrajudicial, summary or arbitrary executions on the proper management of assemblies, 4 February 2016*, A/HRC/31/66, para. 92.

is complete and the officer is cleared of wrongdoing;

(d) States should grant a broad mandate to an independent oversight body that possesses all competence and powers for effective protection of rights in the context of assemblies. The mandate should allow the body to investigate complaints from the public, to accept referrals from police and to initiate investigations itself where it is in the public interest to do so. The body should investigate all cases of use of force by law enforcement. The oversight body should have full investigative powers, and complaints should be dealt with in an objective, fair and prompt fashion, according to clear criteria;

(e) States should encourage and facilitate law enforcement agencies to conduct ongoing non-adversarial peer review of policing operations, if possible by another law enforcement agency. Such reviews should be conducted in addition to and do not exclude the State's obligation to establish independent judicial review mechanisms for the investigation and sanctioning of human rights violations;

(f) States should consider the potential of information and communication technologies, such as body-worn cameras, in contributing towards accountability for violations by law enforcement personnel in the context of assemblies.[512]

UN SR Maina Kiai recommends that States enact legislation that provides for criminal and disciplinary sanctions against those who interfere with or violently disperse public assemblies through excessive use of force.[513]

Dispersal of an assembly permitted only when strictly unavoidable

International law allows for dispersal of a peaceful assembly only in rare cases. Dispersal of a protest may only be resorted to when such an action is strictly unavoidable in the face of imminent threats to bodily safety or property and where law enforcement officials have taken all reasonable measures to facilitate the assembly and to protect participants from harm.[514] Before countenancing dispersal, law enforcement agencies should

---

512   Ibid, para. 96.
513   UN HRC, *Report of the Special Rapporteur on the rights to freedom of peaceful assembly and of association, Maina Kiai*, 21 May 2012, A/HRC/20/27, para. 78.
514   UN HRC, *Joint report of the Special Rapporteur on the rights to freedom of peaceful*

seek to identity and isolate any violent individuals from others who are protesting peacefully.

A peaceful assembly that incites discrimination, hostility or violence, in contravention of *ICCPR* Article 20, may warrant dispersal if less intrusive and discriminatory means of managing the situation have failed.[515] Similarly, where a demonstration prevents access to essential services or where interference with traffic or the economy is "serious and sustained", dispersal may be justified.[516]

An order to disperse an assembly should only be made by governmental authorities or high-ranking officers with "sufficient and accurate information of the situation unfolding on the ground".[517] If dispersal is deemed necessary, the assembly and participants should be clearly and audibly informed and should be allowed reasonable time to disperse voluntarily before any intervention by law enforcement officials.[518]

In *Movement burkinabé des droits de l'homme et des peuples v. Burkina Faso,*[519] the complainant alleged that several human rights violations against members of the Burkinabé Movement occurred during student strikes and that a few individuals who were in the streets during the protests had died. While the ACHPR did not find a violation of the rights to freedom of expression or assembly, it deplored the abusive use of means of State violence against demonstrators even when the demonstrations are not authorized by the competent administrative authorities. The ACHPR held that "the public authorities possess adequate means to disperse crowds, and that those responsible for public order must make an effort in these types of operations to cause only the barest minimum of damage and violation of physical integrity, to respect and preserve human life".[520]

---

assembly and of association and the Special Rapporteur on extrajudicial, summary or arbitrary executions on the proper management of assemblies, 4 February 2016, A/ HRC/31/66, para. 61.

515   *Ibid,* para. 62.

516   *Ibid.*

517   *Ibid,* para. 63.

518   *Ibid; OSCE Guidelines,* para. 168.

519   ACHPR, *Movement burkinabé des droits de l'homme et des peuples v. Burkina Faso,* Communication no. 204/97 (2001).

520   *Ibid,* para. 43.

Right to independently monitor and report on protests

All persons have the right to observe and monitor assemblies

All persons enjoy the right to observe, and by extension monitor, assemblies. This right is derived from the right to seek and receive information, which is protected under *ICCPR* Article 19 (2). The concept of monitoring encapsulates not only the act of observing an assembly, but also the active collection, verification and immediate use of information to address human rights problems.[521]

According to Special Representative of the UN Secretary-General on the situation of human rights defenders Hina Jilani, monitoring of assemblies can provide an impartial and objective account of what takes place, including a factual record of the conduct of both participants and law enforcement officials.[522] In Ms. Jilani's opinion, "this is a valuable contribution to the effective enjoyment of the right to peaceful assembly. The very presence of human rights monitors during demonstrations can deter human rights violations. It is therefore important to allow human rights defenders to operate freely in the context of freedom of assembly".[523]

A monitor is generally defined as any non-participant third-party individual or group whose primary aim is to observe and record the actions and activities taking place at public assemblies.[524] National human rights institutions, ombudsmen, intergovernmental entities and civil society organizations all commonly act as monitors. Journalists, including citizen journalists, play an important role.[525]

---

521 UN HRC, *Joint report of the Special Rapporteur on the rights to freedom of peaceful assembly and of association and the Special Rapporteur on extrajudicial, summary or arbitrary executions on the proper management of assemblies, 4 February 2016*, A/HRC/31/66, para. 68.
522 UN General Assembly, *Report of the Special Representative of the Secretary-General on human rights defenders*, A/62/225, 13 August 2007, para. 91.
523 *Ibid.*
524 *OSCE Guidelines*, para. 201.
525 UN HRC, *Joint report of the Special Rapporteur on the rights to freedom of peaceful assembly and of association and the Special Rapporteur on extrajudicial, summary or arbitrary executions on the proper management of assemblies, 4 February 2016*, A/HRC/31/66, para. 69.

State duty to protect the rights of assembly monitors

States have an obligation to protect the rights of assembly monitors. This includes respecting and facilitating the right to observe and monitor all aspects of an assembly, subject to the narrow permissible restrictions outlined in *ICCPR* Article 19(3). States must fully investigate any human rights violations or abuse against persons monitoring assemblies, pursue prosecution of violations and ensure an adequate remedy. The protections afforded to monitors apply irrespective of whether an assembly is peaceful.[526]

Every person has the right to record an assembly

The State is obligated to protect the right of everyone — whether a participant, monitor or observer — to record an assembly.[527] The right to record an assembly includes the right to record the law enforcement operation and any interaction in which he or she is being recorded by a State agent.[528] Confiscation, seizure and/or destruction of notes and visual or audio recording equipment without due process should be prohibited and punished.[529]

The OAS SR stresses that journalists and camera operators doing their job in a public demonstration "should not be bothered, detained, relocated, or made to suffer any other restriction of their rights due to their being engaged in the practice of their profession. Moreover, their work implements should not be confiscated. To the contrary, any action intended to obstruct their work should be prevented, as long as they do not place the rights of others at risk."[530]

Recording of an assembly by law enforcement officials, on the other hand, may have a chilling effect on the exercise of the right to peaceful protest. Recording peaceful assembly participants in a context and manner that

---

526   *Ibid*, para. 70.
527   *Ibid*, para. 71.
528   *Ibid*.
529   *Ibid*.
530   OAS, IACHR, *Annual Report of the Inter-American Commission on Human Rights 2005, Vol. III: Report of The Office of the Special Rapporteur for Freedom of Expression*, OEA/Ser.L/V/II.124, Doc. 7, 27 February 2006, p. 145.

intimidates or harasses is an impermissible interference with these rights.[531]

State obligation to protect rights to equality and freedom from discrimination

States must ensure that all persons can effectively enjoy the rights to engage in criticism, opposition and dissent without distinction of any kind, such as race, colour, sex, sexual orientation, language, religion, political or other opinion, gender identity, national or social origin, property, birth or other status. These rights apply to women, children, indigenous peoples, persons with disabilities, persons belonging to minority groups or groups at risk of marginalization or exclusion, including those victims of discrimination because of their sexual orientation and gender identity, non-nationals, including stateless persons, refugees or migrants, as well as associations, including unregistered groups.

Decisions by the authorities concerning the right to protest should not have a discriminatory impact and must be free of both direct and indirect discrimination.

Historical and persistent structural inequalities in power relations and discrimination against women require that States address the specific needs of women to ensure their equal participation in public affairs. In a 2013 resolution on women human rights defenders, members of the UN General Assembly expressed their deep concern that

> women human rights defenders are at risk of and suffer from violations and abuses, including systematic violations and abuses of their fundamental rights to life, liberty and security of person, to psychological and physical integrity, to privacy and respect for private and family life and to freedom of opinion and expression, association and peaceful assembly, and in addition can experience gender-based violence, rape and other forms of sexual violence, harassment and verbal abuse and attacks on reputation, online and offline, by State actors, including law enforcement personnel and security forces, and

---

531   UN HRC, *Joint report of the Special Rapporteur on the rights to freedom of peaceful assembly and of association and the Special Rapporteur on extrajudicial, summary or arbitrary executions on the proper management of assemblies, 4 February 2016*, A/ HRC/31/66, para. 76.

non-State actors, such as those related to family and community, in both public and private spheres.[532]

The resolution called on States to, *inter alia*, "take all measures necessary" to ensure the protection of all human rights defenders, including women human rights defenders, and "to integrate a gender perspective into their efforts to create a safe and enabling environment for the defence of human rights",[533] including "their important role in the context of peaceful protests".[534]

UN SR Maina Kiai recommends that States develop specific training materials in relation to the right to peaceful assembly and association, with a view to preventing discriminatory treatment and measures against women, minors, persons with disabilities, indigenous peoples, individuals and groups of individuals belonging to minorities and other marginalized groups.[535]

In the *Case of Identoba and Others v. Georgia*,[536] the ECtHR found that Georgian authorities failed to protect a 2012 march for the rights of LGBT persons in Tbilisi from violent attacks of counter-demonstrators. The ECtHR ruled that "the authorities knew or should have known of the risk of tensions associated with the applicant organisation's street march to mark the International Day Against Homophobia" and "were thus under an obligation to use any means possible...to advocate, without any ambiguity, a tolerant, conciliatory stance...as well as to warn potential law-breakers of the nature of possible sanctions" and to ensure the availability of adequate police manpower.[537]

On a country visit, UN SR Maina Kiai, having been informed of allegations

---

532 UN General Assembly resolution, *Promotion of the Declaration on the Right and Responsibility of Individuals, Groups and Organs of Society to Promote and Protect Universally Recognized Human Rights and Fundamental Freedoms: protecting women human rights defenders*, A/RES/68/181 (30 January 2014), preamble.

533 *Ibid*, para. 5.

534 *Ibid*, para. 8.

535 UN HRC, *Report of the Special Rapporteur on the rights to freedom of peaceful assembly and of association, Maina Kiai*, 21 May 2012, A/HRC/20/27, para. 47.

536 ECtHR, *Case of Identoba and Others v. Georgia*, App. no. 73235/12, Judgment of 12 August 2015 (Final).

537 *Ibid*, paras. 99-100.

by persons with disabilities who reported that their unique circumstances are not accommodated by police during the management of assemblies, urged the authorities "to exercise great caution in interacting with disabled individuals and their assistive devices, which are integral to their lives".[538]

State obligation to protect children and vulnerable groups

Children and groups at risk may require additional protections to ensure their rights to participate in dissent and protest.

State obligation to protect rights to privacy

States must ensure that the rights to privacy of persons exercising rights to dissent and peaceful protest are respected and protected.

The obligation to respect, protect and fulfil rights to privacy is even more critical in today's world, where changing attitudes towards privacy and technological developments threaten traditional notions of privacy and challenge the adequacy of existing protections. As Joseph A. Cannataci, the new (first-ever) UN SR on the right to privacy, noted:

> For the passage of time and the impact of technology, taken together with the different rate of economic development and technology deployment in different geographical locations means that legal principles established fifty years ago (*ICCPR*) or even thirty-five years ago (e.g. the European Convention on Data Protection) let alone seventy years ago (*UDHR*) may need to be re-visited, further developed and possibly supplemented and complemented to make them more relevant and useful to the realities of 2016.[539]

In Resolution 68/167,[540] The UN General Assembly recognized the power of new technologies to both advance and threaten human rights:

---

538   UN, *Statement by the United Nations Special Rapporteur on the Rights to Freedom of Peaceful Assembly and of Association at the conclusion of his visit to the Republic of Korea*, 29 January 2016.

539   UN HRC, *Report of the Special Rapporteur on the right to privacy, Joseph A. Cannataci*, A/HRC/31/64, 8 March 2016, para. 22.

540   UN General Assembly, *Resolution 68/167. The right to privacy in the digital age*, 18 December 2013, A/RES/68/167.

the rapid pace of technological development enables individuals all over the world to use new information and communication technologies and at the same time enhances the capacity of governments, companies and individuals to undertake surveillance, interception and data collection, which may violate or abuse human rights, in particular the right to privacy, as set out in article 12 of the Universal Declaration of Human Rights and article 17 of the International Covenant on Civil and Political Rights, and is therefore an issue of increasing concern,...[541]

Recognizing the "global and open nature of the Internet and the rapid advancement in information and communications technologies as a driving force in accelerating progress towards development in its various forms" and affirming that "the same rights that people have offline must also be protected online, including the right to privacy", the UN General Assembly called on States:

(a) To respect and protect the right to privacy, including in the context of digital communication;

(b) To take measures to put an end to violations of those rights and to create the conditions to prevent such violations, including by ensuring that relevant national legislation complies with their obligations under international human rights law;

(c) To review their procedures, practices and legislation regarding the surveillance of communications, their interception and the collection of personal data, including mass surveillance, interception and collection, with a view to upholding the right to privacy by ensuring the full and effective implementation of all their obligations under international human rights law;...[542]

In a country visit, UN SR Maina Kiai found that accounts of hacked e-mail and social media accounts and of civil society activists who were repeatedly summonsed to meet with intelligence officers, who had detailed knowledge of their movements and activities, not only infringed the right to privacy but also had the effect of "chilling" social interaction and political activity.[543]

---

541   *Ibid,* preamble.
542   *Ibid,* paras. 2-4.
543   UN HRC, *Report of the Special Rapporteur on the rights to freedom of peaceful*

The IACHR observes that,

[i]f they are to do their work freely, human rights defenders need adequate protection from the state authorities to guarantee they will not be victims of arbitrary meddling in their private lives, or of attacks on their honor and dignity. This right includes state protection from harassment and intimidation, assaults, surveillance, interference with correspondence and telephone and electronic communications, and illegal intelligence activities.[544]

The right to "private life" under *ECHR* Article 8(1) covers the physical and moral integrity of the person.[545] The right to privacy does not merely compel the State to abstain from arbitrary interference in one's private or family life, but also imposes positive obligations on the State to secure respect for private life even in the sphere of the relations of individuals between themselves.

The right to privacy is not an absolute right, and thus not every restriction in and of itself is incompatible with international law. For an interference not to be arbitrary, it must be established by law; have a legitimate purpose; and it must be appropriate, necessary, and proportionate.

In their joint report on the proper management of assemblies, the UN SRs warn that States must guard against arbitrary or unlawful interferences with privacy in the collection and processing of personal information in relation to assemblies:

Legislation and policies regulating the collection and processing of information relating to assemblies or their organizers and participants must incorporate legality, necessity and proportionality tests. Given the intrusiveness of such methods, the threshold for these tests is especially high. Where they interfere with the exercise of rights, data collection and processing may represent a violation of the rights to

---

assembly and of association, Maina Kiai: Mission to Oman, A/HRC/29/25/Add.1, 27 April 2015, para. 19(d).

544　IACHR, *Report on the Situation of Human Rights Defenders in the Americas*, OEA/Ser.L/V.II.124, Doc. 5 rev. 1, 7 March 2006, para. 94.

545　ECtHR, *X and Y v. The Netherlands*, App. no. 8978/80, Judgment of 26 March 1985, para. 22.

freedom of peaceful assembly and expression.[546]

The SRs also highlighted the need to ensure that arrest powers are exercised consistently with international human rights standards, including those relating to the rights to privacy, liberty, and due process.[547]

State obligation to protect rights to life, liberty and security of the person

The right to life and the right to be free from torture or cruel, inhuman or degrading treatment or punishment must be guaranteed by States to all individuals under all circumstances and at all times. States must ensure there are no interferences with these rights in the context of the exercise of freedom of dissent and peaceful protest.

No one should be criminalized or subjected to any threats or acts of violence, harassment, persecution, intimidation or reprisals for addressing human rights issues through peaceful protest or for reporting on human rights violations and abuses committed in the context of peaceful protests. The protection of women, especially women human rights defenders, must be guaranteed. Instances of gender-based violence occurring during demonstrations should be investigated and prosecuted as a matter of priority.[548]

The OHCHR notes that, according to *ICCPR* Article 4(2),

> the right to life and the prohibition of torture and other cruel, inhuman or degrading treatment or punishment are non-derogable rights. As such, it is imperative that States ensure prompt and adequate medical care for any person injured during a peaceful protest and that the injured person as well as his or her relatives are protected from any threat of reprisal. It is imperative that States ensure prompt and

---

546   UN HRC, *Joint report of the Special Rapporteur on the rights to freedom of peaceful assembly and of association and the Special Rapporteur on extrajudicial, summary or arbitrary executions on the proper management of assemblies*, 4 February 2016, A/HRC/31/66, para. 74.

547   *Ibid*, para. 44.

548   UN HRC, *Report of the United Nations High Commissioner for Human Rights on Effective measures and best practices to ensure the promotion and protection of human rights in the context of peaceful protests*, 21 January 2013, A/HRC/22/28, para. 15.

adequate medical care for any person injured during a peaceful protest and that the injured person as well as his or her relatives are protected from any threat of reprisal.[549]

Rashida Manjoo, the UN SR on violence against women, its causes and consequences, noted in a report on women's incarceration that in Egypt, in 2011, 20 female prisoners were arrested in a peaceful public protest and 17 were subjected to forced virginity testing in a military prison. It is alleged that the purpose was to humiliate them and deter other women from protesting.[550]

In its consideration of a periodic report of Chile, the CEDAW Committee found a "disproportionate use of violence by the police, including sexual abuse, against female students during social protests and against women during Mapuche protests" and the "absence of prosecution of perpetrators and the failure of the State party to provide access to justice to women victims of such violence".[551]

The "pretext of maintenance of public security cannot be invoked to violate the right to life".[552]

The UN SRs caution that the use of "stop-and-search" tactics by law enforcement against individuals organizing or participating in an assembly may affect the rights to liberty and bodily security, as well as privacy.[553] Stop-and-search must not be arbitrary and must meet the tests of legality, necessity and proportionality. The mere fact that an individual is participating in a peaceful assembly does not constitute reasonable grounds for conducting a search.

---

549   *Ibid*, para. 14.
550   UN General Assembly, *Report of the Special Rapporteur on violence against women, its causes and consequences: Pathways to, conditions and consequences of incarceration for women*, A/68/340, 21 August 2013, para. 36.
551   CEDAW, *Concluding observations of the Committee on the Elimination of Discrimination against Women: Chile*, CEDAW/C/CHL/CO/5-6, 24 October 2012, para. 20.
552   IACtHR, *Case of Caracazo v. Venezuela, Judgment of August 29, 2002, (Reparations and Costs)*, para. 127.
553   UN HRC, *Joint report of the Special Rapporteur on the rights to freedom of peaceful assembly and of association and the Special Rapporteur on extrajudicial, summary or arbitrary executions on the proper management of assemblies*, 4 February 2016, A/HRC/31/66, para. 43.

Powers of arrest must be exercised consistently with international human rights standards, including those relating to the rights to privacy, liberty, and due-process rights. The SRs reiterate that

> [n]o one may be subject to arbitrary arrest or detention. In the context of assemblies this has particular import for the criminalization of assemblies and dissent. Arrest of protestors to prevent or punish the exercise of their right to freedom of peaceful assembly, for example on charges that are spurious, unreasonable or lack proportionality, may violate these protections. Similarly, intrusive pre-emptive measures should not be used unless a clear and present danger of imminent violence actually exists. "Mass arrest" of assembly participants often amounts to indiscriminate and arbitrary arrests.[554]

Where an arrest takes place, detention conditions must meet minimum standards. This applies to any location or situation in which an individual has been deprived of his or her liberty, including jails, holding cells, public spaces and vehicles used to transfer detainees, and any other location in which detainees are held. Detainees must be treated in a humane manner and with respect for their dignity.[555]

According to the UN SRs, the issue of proportionality is particularly relevant to administrative sanctions imposed in the context of assemblies: "Any penalty must not be excessive — for example, a disproportionately large fine. Such penalties raise due-process concerns, and may have a chilling effect more broadly on the exercise of the right to freedom of peaceful assembly".[556]

In *Schwabe and M.G. v. Germany*, the ECtHR found that the use of preventative detention for almost six days to prevent the applicants from inciting others to liberate prisoners by force during demonstrations against the G8 summit did not fall within any of the permissible grounds for deprivation of liberty under *ECHR* Article 5(1) and had a chilling effect on the expression of opinion on matters of public interest, namely the effects of globalization on people's lives, and restricted the public debate on that

---

554   *Ibid*, para. 45.
555   *Ibid*, para. 46.
556   *Ibid*, para. 48.

issue.[557]

---

557   ECtHR, *Case of Schwabe and M.G. v. Germany,* App. nos. 8080/08 and 8577/08, Judgment of 1 March 2012 (Final), paras. 114 and 116.

" Everyone has the right to an effective remedy by the competent national tribunals for acts violating the fundamental rights granted him by the constitution or by law.

Universal Declaration of Human Rights, article 8

RIGHT TO AN EFFECTIVE REMEDY FOR VIOLATION OF RIGHT TO DISSENT

Right to an adequate, effective and prompt remedy

Under international law, everyone is entitled to an adequate, effective and prompt remedy determined by a competent authority having the power to enforce remedies for a violation of their human rights. The right to a remedy is guaranteed notwithstanding that the violation may have been caused by persons acting in an official capacity, and is available equally to all persons, without discrimination. The right to a remedy includes the right to equal and effective access to justice; adequate, effective and prompt reparation for harm suffered; and access to relevant information concerning violations and reparation mechanisms.[558]

ICCPR Article 3 states:

3. Each State Party to the present Covenant undertakes:

(a) To ensure that any person whose rights or freedoms as herein recognized are violated shall have an effective remedy, notwithstanding that the violation has been committed by persons acting in an official capacity;

(b) To ensure that any person claiming such a remedy shall have his right thereto determined by competent judicial, administrative or legislative authorities, or by any other competent authority provided for by the legal system of the State, and to develop the possibilities of judicial remedy;

(c) To ensure that the competent authorities shall enforce such remedies when granted.

Duty of States to investigate violations

States are required to investigate violations effectively, promptly, thoroughly and impartially and, where appropriate, take actions against those allegedly

---

558   *Ibid,* para. 89.

responsible in accordance with domestic and international law.

A failure by a State Party to investigate allegations of violations could in and of itself give rise to a separate breach of the *ICCPR*. Cessation of an ongoing violation is an essential element of the right to an effective remedy.[559] As with failure to investigate, failure to bring to justice perpetrators of *ICCPR* violations could in and of itself give rise to a separate breach of the *ICCPR*.[560] States must also take measures to prevent a recurrence of a violation of the *ICCPR*.[561]

Right to reparation

States must make reparation to individuals whose *ICCPR* rights have been violated. Reparation generally entails appropriate compensation, and can, where appropriate, involve restitution, rehabilitation and measures of satisfaction, such as public apologies, public memorials, guarantees of non-repetition and changes in relevant laws and practices, as well as bringing to justice the perpetrators of human rights violations.[562]

Under the *UN Basic Principles and Guidelines on the Right to a Remedy and Reparation for Victims of Gross Violations of International Human Rights Law and Serious Violations of International Humanitarian Law,*

> 2. If they have not already done so, States shall, as required under international law, ensure that their domestic law is consistent with their international legal obligations by:
>
> > (a) Incorporating norms of international human rights law and international humanitarian law into their domestic law, or otherwise implementing them in their domestic legal system;
> >
> > (b) Adopting appropriate and effective legislative and administrative procedures and other appropriate measures that provide fair, effective and prompt access to justice;

---

559   UN, HR Committee, *CCPR General Comment No. 31, Article 2 (The Nature of the General Legal Obligation Imposed on States Parties to the Covenant)*, 29 March 2004, CCPR/C/21/Rev.1/Add.13, para. 15.

560   *Ibid*, para. 18.

561   *Ibid*, para. 17.

562   *Ibid*, para. 16.

(c) Making available adequate, effective, prompt and appropriate remedies, including reparation, as defined below;

(d) Ensuring that their domestic law provides at least the same level of protection for victims as that required by their international obligations.

Comparable provisions to *ICCPR* Article 3 are contained in other international as well as regional human rights instruments.

Under the *UN Basic Principles*,

23. Persons affected by the use of force and firearms or their legal representatives shall have access to an independent process, including a judicial process. In the event of the death of such persons, this provision shall apply to their dependants accordingly.

24. Governments and law enforcement agencies shall ensure that superior officers are held responsible if they know, or should have known, that law enforcement officials under their command are resorting, or have resorted, to the unlawful use of force and firearms, and they did not take all measures in their power to prevent, suppress or report such use.

25. Governments and law enforcement agencies shall ensure that no criminal or disciplinary sanction is imposed on law enforcement officials who, in compliance with the Code of Conduct for Law Enforcement Officials and these basic principles, refuse to carry out an order to use force and firearms, or who report such use by other officials.

26. Obedience to superior orders shall be no defence if law enforcement officials knew that an order to use force and firearms resulting in the death or serious injury of a person was manifestly unlawful and had a reasonable opportunity to refuse to follow it. In any case, responsibility also rests on the superiors who gave the unlawful orders.

Human Rights Council resolution 25/38, para. 19, urges States to

ensure accountability for human rights violations and abuses through judicial or other national mechanisms, based on law in conformity with their international human rights obligations and commitments, and to provide victims with access to a remedy and redress, including in the context of peaceful protests.

Interpretation

In order to ensure accountability in respecting, protecting and fulfilling the right to dissent and protest, States should ensure accessible and transparent decision-making, including the provision of timely and fulsome notice of, and the reasons for, any restrictions imposed on the exercise of the right, and information concerning the right to appeal decisions in a timely manner. States must establish accessible and effective complaints mechanisms that are able to independently, promptly and thoroughly investigate allegations of human rights violations or abuses in order to hold those responsible accountable and to ensure that the violation will not be repeated in the future. Specific attention must be paid to members of groups at risk.[563]

Right to transparent decision-making

States should ensure that any decision-making processes by public authorities related to the exercise of the right to dissent and protest are transparent, accessible and comply with international due process standards.[564] The process should enable the fair and objective assessment of all available information.[565]

Right to reasons for any restrictions on right to dissent and peaceful protest

Regulatory authorities must provide assembly organizers with timely and fulsome reasons for the imposition of any restrictions imposed on the right to peaceful assembly and the possibility of an expedited appeal procedure.[566]

The OSCE Guidelines state that restrictions placed on an assembly must be communicated in writing to organizers of the event, with a brief explanation

---

563   UN HRC, *Report of the Special Rapporteur on the rights to freedom of peaceful assembly and of association, Maina Kiai,* 21 May 2012, A/HRC/20/27, para. 77.
564   ARTICLE 19, *The Right to Protest: Principles on protection of human rights in protests* (Policy Brief, 2015), Principle 17(1).
565   *OSCE Guidelines,* para. 4.5.
566   UN HRC, *Report of the Special Rapporteur on the rights to freedom of peaceful assembly and of association, Maina Kiai,* 21 May 2012, A/HRC/20/27, para. 42.

of the reason for each restriction, which reason must correspond with the permissible grounds set out in international human rights law, and as interpreted by the courts and tribunals. Decisions should be communicated sufficiently in advance of the date of a proposed event to be appealed to an independent tribunal or court before the date provided in the notification for the event.[567] Regulatory decisions should be published so that the public has access to reliable information about events taking place in the public domain.[568]

Right to appeal restriction or prohibitions on right to dissent and peaceful protest

If a restriction is imposed on the right to peaceful protest, there should be an option for organizers to seek judicial review and, where relevant, administrative review, that is prompt, competent, independent and impartial.[569] Any administrative review procedures must be sufficiently prompt to enable judicial review to take place once administrative remedies have been exhausted, prior to the date of the assembly provided in the notification.[570]

The OSCE Guidelines provide that where an administrative review fails to satisfy the applicant, there should be an appeal in a prompt and timely manner to an independent court. A final ruling, or injunctive relief, should be given prior to the date for the assembly provided in the notification.[571]

State duty to ensure accountability

The UN SRs recommend that, in addition to guaranteeing accountability through judicial processes, States should implement additional levels of non-judicial oversight, including an effective internal investigations process and

---

567 *OSCE Guidelines*, para. 135.
568 *OSCE Guidelines*, para. 136.
569 UN HRC, *Joint report of the Special Rapporteur on the rights to freedom of peaceful assembly and of association and the Special Rapporteur on extrajudicial, summary or arbitrary executions on the proper management of assemblies*, 4 February 2016, A/HRC/31/66, para. 35; UN HRC, *Report of the Special Rapporteur on the rights to freedom of peaceful assembly and of association, Maina Kiai*, 21 May 2012, A/HRC/20/27, para. 42.
570 *OSCE Guidelines*, para. 137.
571 *OSCE Guidelines*, para. 4.6.

an independent oversight body.[572] These systems should operate in addition to, and not as an alternative to, criminal, public and private legal remedies for police misconduct. The role of such a body may be complemented by the work of a national human rights institution or ombudsman.[573]

State duty to promptly investigate allegations of rights violations

States must investigate any allegations of violations of internationally protected rights promptly and effectively, through bodies that are independent and impartial. A failure to investigate allegations of violations of the *ICCPR* could in and of itself give rise to a separate breach of the *ICCPR*.[574]

In addition, the procedural component of the right to life requires States to investigate any alleged unlawful or arbitrary killing. The failure of a State to properly investigate suspected unlawful or arbitrary killing is a violation of the right to life itself.[575]

In cases of gross violations of international human rights law and serious violations of international humanitarian law constituting crimes under international law, States have the duty to investigate and, if there is sufficient evidence, the duty to submit to prosecution the person allegedly responsible for the violations and, if found guilty, the duty to punish her

---

572   UN HRC, *Joint report of the Special Rapporteur on the rights to freedom of peaceful assembly and of association and the Special Rapporteur on extrajudicial, summary or arbitrary executions on the proper management of assemblies, 4 February 2016,* A/HRC/31/66, para. 94.

573   *Ibid.*

574   UN, HR Committee, *CCPR General Comment No. 31, Article 2 (The Nature of the General Legal Obligation Imposed on States Parties to the Covenant),* 29 March 2004, CCPR/C/21/Rev.1/Add.13, para. 15.

575   UN General Assembly, *Report of the Special Rapporteur on extrajudicial, summary or arbitrary executions, Christof Heyns, on extrajudicial, summary or arbitrary executions,* A/70/304, 7 August 2015. See, for example, HR Committee, *Bautista de Arellana v. Colombia,* Communication No. 563/1993, Views adopted on 11 October 1994, para. 8.6; ECtHR, *McKerr v. the United Kingdom,* App. no. 28883/95, Judgment of 4 August 2001 (Final), para. 111; IACtHR, *Case of the Ituango Massacres v. Colombia, Judgment of 1 July 2006 (Preliminary Objections, Merits, Reparations and Costs),* paras. 131, 297, 300, 399.

or him.[576] Moreover, in these cases, States should, in accordance with international law, cooperate with one another and assist international judicial organs competent in the investigation and prosecution of these violations.

Effective investigation includes the following factors: an official investigation initiated by the State; independence from those implicated; capability of determining whether the act was justified in the circumstances; a level of promptness and reasonable expedition; and a level of public scrutiny.[577]

In the *Case of Şandru v. Romania*,[578] the ECtHR reiterated that the obligation of the State to protect the right to life under *ECHR* Article 2 required by implication that there should be some form of effective official investigation following the violent repression of the December 1989 anti-communist demonstrations in Timişoara, when the use of lethal force against an individual during the demonstrations had placed the latter's life in danger.[579]

State responsibility for violations by non-State actors

A State can incur responsibility for violations of human rights by non-State actors if it:

- approves, supports or acquiesces in those acts;
- fails to exercise due diligence to prevent the violation; or
- fails to ensure proper investigation and accountability.[580]

---

576   *Basic Principles and Guidelines on the Right to a Remedy and Reparation for Victims of Gross Violations of International Human Rights Law and Serious Violations of International Humanitarian Law*, para. 4.

577   ECtHR, *Case of Isayeva v. Russia*, App. no. 57950/00, Judgment of 24 February 2005, paras. 211-214. See also UN HRC, *Report of the Special Rapporteur on extrajudicial, summary or arbitrary executions, Christof Heyns*, A/HRC/26/36, 1 April 2014, para. 80; UN, HRC, *Joint report of the Special Rapporteur on the rights to freedom of rights to freedom of peaceful assembly and of association and the Special Rapporteur on extrajudicial, summary or arbitrary executions on the proper management of assemblies*, 4 February 2016, A/HRC/31/66, para. 90.

578   CtHR, *Case of Şandru v. Romania*, App. no. 22465/03, Judgment of 10 May 2010 (Final).

579   *Ibid*, para. 80.

580   UN HRC, *Joint report of the Special Rapporteur on the rights to freedom of peaceful assembly and of association and the Special Rapporteur on extrajudicial, summary or*

States also have a duty to take appropriate measures to prevent, investigate and provide effective remedies for relevant misconduct by business enterprises, and to hold to account private parties that are responsible for causing or contributing to an arbitrary deprivation of life in the State's territory or jurisdiction.[581]

State duty to carry out prosecutions impartially and without discrimination

Prosecutors should carry out their functions impartially and without discrimination, and should give due attention to prosecuting crimes committed by public officials. The *UN Guidelines on the Role of Prosecutors* provide:

> 12. Prosecutors shall, in accordance with the law, perform their duties fairly, consistently and expeditiously, and respect and protect human dignity and uphold human rights, thus contributing to ensuring due process and the smooth functioning of the criminal justice system.

> 13. In the performance of their duties, prosecutors shall:

> (a) Carry out their functions impartially and avoid all political, social, religious, racial, cultural, sexual or any other kind of discrimination;

> 15. Prosecutors shall give due attention to the prosecution of crimes committed by public officials, particularly corruption, abuse of power, grave violations of human rights and other crimes recognized by international law and, where authorized by law or consistent with local practice, the investigation of such offences.

When law enforcement officials are prosecuted, the judiciary shall decide matters impartially. Under the *UN Basic Principles on the Independence of the Judiciary*, Principle 2,

> 2. The judiciary shall decide matters before them impartially, on the basis of facts and in accordance with the law, without any restrictions,

arbitrary executions on the proper management of assemblies, 4 February 2016, A/ HRC/31/66, para. 87.
581   Ibid.

improper influences, inducements, pressures, threats or interferences, direct or indirect, from any quarter or for any reason.

Defendants should be brought before an ordinary court or tribunal, and shall be availed of the fair trial protections guaranteed under international law.[582]

The HR Committee observes, in *CCPR General Comment No. 31* on the nature of the general legal obligation on States Parties to the *ICCPR*, that remedies for violations of the *ICCPR* should be appropriately adapted so as to take account of the special vulnerability of certain categories of person, including in particular children.[583]

State obligation to apply criminal and/or civil sanctions

Where appropriate, criminal and/or civil sanctions must be applied. Liability should extend to officers with command and control where they have failed to exercise that command and control effectively. Where superior officers knew, or should have known, that law enforcement officials under their command resorted to the unlawful use of force or firearms, and they did not take all measures in their power to prevent, suppress or report such use, they should also be held responsible.[584]

State obligation to provide reparation

States may also have an obligation to provide adequate reparation for violations of internationally protected human rights. In *Kimel v. Argentina*, the IACtHR reiterated:

---

582   UN HRC, *Joint report of the Special Rapporteur on the rights to freedom of peaceful assembly and of association and the Special Rapporteur on extrajudicial, summary or arbitrary executions on the proper management of assemblies*, 4 February 2016, A/HRC/31/66, para. 93.

583   UN, HR Committee, *CCPR General Comment No. 31, Article 2 (The Nature of the General Legal Obligation Imposed on States Parties to the Covenant)*, 29 March 2004, CCPR/C/21/Rev.1/Add.13, para. 15.

584   UN HRC, *Joint report of the Special Rapporteur on the rights to freedom of peaceful assembly and of association and the Special Rapporteur on extrajudicial, summary or arbitrary executions on the proper management of assemblies*, 4 February 2016, A/HRC/31/66, para. 91. See also *Basic Principles on the Use of Force and Firearms by Law Enforcement Officials*, Principle 24.

It is an International Law rule that any violation of an international obligation that has caused damage entails the duty to provide adequate reparation.[585]

The State has a duty to provide adequate, effective and prompt reparation to victims for acts or omissions that can be attributed to the State and constitute gross violations of international human rights law or serious violations of international humanitarian law.[586] Reparation should be proportional to the gravity of the violation and the harm suffered, and should include elements of restitution, compensation, rehabilitation, satisfaction and guarantees of non-repetition,[587] as well as access to relevant information concerning violations and reparation mechanisms.[588]

In *Kimel v. Argentina*, a journalist was charged and convicted for defamation for publishing a book in which he had criticized the conduct of a criminal judge in charge of investigating a massacre. In finding that the punishment was disproportionate and violated the victim's right to freedom of expression, the IACtHR ordered the State to, among other things, provide the victim with reparations and reform its criminal legislation on the protection of honour and reputation to comply with the requirements of legal certainty so that, consequently, they do not affect the exercise of the right to freedom of thought and expression.[589]

---

585   IACtHR, *Case of Kimel v. Argentina, Merits, Reparations and Costs,* Judgment of 2 May 2008, para. 98.

586   *Basic Principles and Guidelines on the Right to a Remedy and Reparation for Victims of Gross Violations of International Human Rights Law and Serious Violations of International Humanitarian Law,* para. 15.

587   *Ibid,* para. 18.

588   *Ibid,* para. 24.

589   IACtHR, *Case of Kimel v. Argentina, Merits, Reparations and Costs,* Judgment of 2 May 2008, para. 128.

APPENDIX A: INTERNATIONAL STANDARDS

UN Instruments

UNIVERSAL DECLARATION OF HUMAN RIGHTS (*UDHR*)

2.	Everyone is entitled to all the rights and freedoms set forth in this Declaration, without distinction of any kind, such as race, colour, sex, language, religion, political or other opinion, national or social origin, property, birth or other status. Furthermore, no distinction shall be made on the basis of the political, jurisdictional or international status of the country or territory to which a person belongs, whether it be independent, trust, non-self-governing or under any other limitation of sovereignty.
3.	Everyone has the right to life, liberty and security of person.
7.	All are equal before the law and are entitled without any discrimination to equal protection of the law. All are entitled to equal protection against any discrimination in violation of this Declaration and against any incitement to such discrimination.
8.	Everyone has the right to an effective remedy by the competent national tribunals for acts violating the fundamental rights granted him by the constitution or by law.
12.	No one shall be subjected to arbitrary interference with his privacy, family, home or correspondence, nor to attacks upon his honour and reputation. Everyone has the right to the protection of the law against such interference or attacks.
18.	Everyone has the right to freedom of thought, conscience and religion; this right includes freedom to change his religion or belief, and freedom, either alone or in community with others and in public or private, to manifest his religion or belief in teaching, practice, worship and observance.
19.	Everyone has the right to freedom of opinion and expression; this right includes freedom to hold opinions without interference and to seek, receive and impart information and ideas through any media and regardless of frontiers.
20.	1. Everyone has the right to freedom of peaceful assembly and association.

21.	1. Everyone has the right to take part in the government of his country, directly or through freely chosen representatives.
	2. Everyone has the right of equal access to public service in his country.
	3. The will of the people shall be the basis of the authority of government; this will shall be expressed in periodic and genuine elections which shall be by universal and equal suffrage and shall be held by secret vote or by equivalent free voting procedures.

INTERNATIONAL COVENANT ON CIVIL AND POLITICAL RIGHTS (*ICCPR*)

2.	1. Each State Party to the present Covenant undertakes to respect and to ensure to all individuals within its territory and subject to its jurisdiction the rights recognized in the present Covenant, without distinction of any kind, such as race, colour, sex, language, religion, political or other opinion, national or social origin, property, birth or other status.
2.	3. Each State Party to the present Covenant undertakes:
	(a) To ensure that any person whose rights or freedoms as herein recognized are violated shall have an effective remedy, notwithstanding that the violation has been committed by persons acting in an official capacity;
	(b) To ensure that any person claiming such a remedy shall have his right thereto determined by competent judicial, administrative or legislative authorities, or by any other competent authority provided for by the legal system of the State, and to develop the possibilities of judicial remedy;
	(c) To ensure that the competent authorities shall enforce such remedies when granted.
3.	The States Parties to the present Covenant undertake to ensure the equal right of men and women to the enjoyment of all civil and political rights set forth in the present Covenant.

9.	1. Everyone has the right to liberty and security of person. No one shall be subjected to arbitrary arrest or detention. No one shall be deprived of his liberty except on such grounds and in accordance with such procedure as are established by law.
17.	1. No one shall be subjected to arbitrary or unlawful interference with his privacy, family, home or correspondence, nor to unlawful attacks on his honour and reputation.
	2. Everyone has the right to the protection of the law against such interference or attacks.
19.	1. Everyone shall have the right to hold opinions without interference.
	2. Everyone shall have the right to freedom of expression; this right shall include freedom to seek, receive and impart information and ideas of all kinds, regardless of frontiers, either orally, in writing or in print, in the form of art, or through any other media of his choice.
	3. The exercise of the rights provided for in paragraph 2 of this article carries with it special duties and responsibilities. It may therefore be subject to certain restrictions, but these shall only be such as are provided by law and are necessary:
	(a) For respect of the rights or reputations of others;
	(b) For the protection of national security or of public order (ordre public), or of public health or morals.
20.	1. Any propaganda for war shall be prohibited by law.
	2. Any advocacy of national, racial or religious hatred that constitutes incitement to discrimination, hostility or violence shall be prohibited by law.
21.	The right of peaceful assembly shall be recognized. No restrictions may be placed on the exercise of this right other than those imposed in conformity with the law and which are necessary in a democratic society in the interests of national security or public safety, public order (ordre public), the protection of public health or morals or the protection of the rights and freedoms of others.

22.	1. Everyone shall have the right to freedom of association with others, including the right to form and join trade unions for the protection of his interests.
	2. No restrictions may be placed on the exercise of this right other than those which are prescribed by law and which are necessary in a democratic society in the interests of national security or public safety, public order (ordre public), the protection of public health or morals or the protection of the rights and freedoms of others. This article shall not prevent the imposition of lawful restrictions on members of the armed forces and of the police in their exercise of this right.
24.	1. Every child shall have, without any discrimination as to race, colour, sex, language, religion, national or social origin, property or birth, the right to such measures of protection as are required by his status as a minor, on the part of his family, society and the State.
25.	Every citizen shall have the right and the opportunity, without any of the distinctions mentioned in article 2 and without unreasonable restrictions:
	(a) To take part in the conduct of public affairs, directly or through freely chosen representatives;
26.	All persons are equal before the law and are entitled without any discrimination to the equal protection of the law. In this respect, the law shall prohibit any discrimination and guarantee to all persons equal and effective protection against discrimination on any ground such as race, colour, sex, language, religion, political or other opinion, national or social origin, property, birth or other status.

INTERNATIONAL COVENANT ON ECONOMIC, SOCIAL AND CULTURAL RIGHTS (*ICESCR*)

| 2. | 1. Each State Party to the present Covenant undertakes to take steps, individually and through international assistance and co-operation, especially economic and technical, to the maximum of its available resources, with a view to achieving progressively the full realization of the rights recognized in the present Covenant by all appropriate means, including particularly the adoption of legislative measures. |

2. The States Parties to the present Covenant undertake to guarantee that the rights enunciated in the present Covenant will be exercised without discrimination of any kind as to race, colour, sex, language, religion, political or other opinion, national or social origin, property, birth or other status.

3. Developing countries, with due regard to human rights and their national economy, may determine to what extent they would guarantee the economic rights recognized in the present Covenant to nonnationals.

3.

The States Parties to the present Covenant undertake to ensure the equal right of men and women to the enjoyment of all economic, social and cultural rights set forth in the present Covenant.

8.

1.   The States Parties to the present Covenant undertake to ensure:

(a) The right of everyone to form trade unions and join the trade union of his choice, subject only to the rules of the organization concerned, for the promotion and protection of his economic and social interests. No restrictions may be placed on the exercise of this right other than those prescribed by law and which are necessary in a democratic society in the interests of national security or public order or for the protection of the rights and freedoms of others;...

(c) The right of trade unions to function freely subject to no limitations other than those prescribed by law and which are necessary in a democratic society in the interests of national security or public order or for the protection of the rights and freedoms of others;

15.

1. The States Parties to the present Covenant recognize the right of everyone:

(a) To take part in cultural life;

OPTIONAL PROTOCOL TO THE INTERNATIONAL COVENANT ON ECONOMIC, SOCIAL AND CULTURAL RIGHTS

13.   A State Party shall take all appropriate measures to ensure that individuals under its jurisdiction are not subjected to any form of ill-treatment or intimidation as a consequence of communicating with the Committee pursuant to the present Protocol.

CONVENTION ON THE ELIMINATION OF ALL FORMS OF DISCRIMINATION AGAINST WOMEN (CEDAW)

1.   For the purposes of the present Convention, the term "discrimination against women" shall mean any distinction, exclusion or restriction made on the basis of sex which has the effect or purpose of impairing or nullifying the recognition, enjoyment or exercise by women, irrespective of their marital status, on a basis of equality of men and women, of human rights and fundamental freedoms in the political, economic, social, cultural, civil or any other field.

2.   States Parties condemn discrimination against women in all its forms, agree to pursue by all appropriate means and without delay a policy of eliminating discrimination against women and, to this end, undertake:

(a) To embody the principle of the equality of men and women in their national constitutions or other appropriate legislation if not yet incorporated therein and to ensure, through law and other appropriate means, the practical realization of this principle;

(b) To adopt appropriate legislative and other measures, including sanctions where appropriate, prohibiting all discrimination against women;

(c) To establish legal protection of the rights of women on an equal basis with men and to ensure through competent national tribunals and other public institutions the effective protection of women against any act of discrimination;

(d) To refrain from engaging in any act or practice of discrimination against women and to ensure that public authorities and institutions shall act in conformity with this obligation;

(e) To take all appropriate measures to eliminate discrimination against women by any person, organization or enterprise;

(f) To take all appropriate measures, including legislation, to modify or abolish existing laws, regulations, customs and practices which constitute discrimination against women;

(g) To repeal all national penal provisions which constitute discrimination against women.

3.   States Parties shall take in all fields, in particular in the political, social, economic and cultural fields, all appropriate measures, including legislation, to en sure the full development and advancement of women , for the purpose of guaranteeing them the exercise and enjoyment of human rights and fundamental freedoms on a basis of equality with men.

7.   States Parties shall take all appropriate measures to eliminate discrimination against women in the political and public life of the country and, in particular, shall ensure to women, on equal terms with men, the right:…

(b) To participate in the formulation of government policy and the implementation thereof and to hold public office and perform all public functions at all levels of government;

(c) To participate in non-governmental organizations and associations concerned with the public and political life of the country.

8.   States Parties shall take all appropriate measures to ensure to women, on equal terms with men and without any discrimination, the opportunity to represent their Governments at the international level and to participate in the work of international organizations.

OPTIONAL PROTOCOL TO THE CONVENTION ON THE ELIMINATION OF ALL FORMS OF DISCRIMINATION AGAINST WOMEN

11.   A State Party shall take all appropriate steps to ensure that individuals under its jurisdiction are not subjected to ill treatment or intimidation as a consequence of communicating with the Committee pursuant to the present Protocol.

INTERNATIONAL CONVENTION ON THE ELIMINATION OF ALL FORMS OF RACIAL DISCRIMINATION (*ICERD*)

5.   In compliance with the fundamental obligations laid down in article 2 of this Convention, States Parties undertake to prohibit and to eliminate racial discrimination in all its forms and to guarantee the right of everyone, without distinction as to race, colour, or national or ethnic origin, to equality before the law, notably in the enjoyment of the following rights:

         (a) The right to equal treatment before the tribunals and all other organs administering justice;

         (b) The right to security of person and protection by the State against violence or bodily harm, whether inflicted by government officials or by any individual group or institution;

         (c) Political rights, in particular the right to participate in elections-to vote and to stand for election-on the basis of universal and equal suffrage, to take part in the Government as well as in the conduct of public affairs at any level and to have equal access to public service;

         (d) Other civil rights, in particular:...

         (viii) The right to freedom of opinion and expression;

         (ix) The right to freedom of peaceful assembly and association;...

         (f) The right of access to any place or service intended for use by the general public, such as transport hotels, restaurants, cafes, theatres and parks.

6.   States Parties shall assure to everyone within their jurisdiction effective protection and remedies, through the competent national tribunals and other State institutions, against any acts of racial discrimination which violate his human rights and fundamental freedoms contrary to this Convention, as well as the right to seek from such tribunals just and adequate reparation or satisfaction for any damage suffered as a result of such discrimination.

INTERNATIONAL CONVENTION ON THE PROTECTION OF THE RIGHTS OF ALL MIGRANT WORKERS AND MEMBERS OF THEIR FAMILIES	
7.	States Parties undertake, in accordance with the international instruments concerning human rights, to respect and to ensure to all migrant workers and members of their families within their territory or subject to their jurisdiction the rights provided for in the present Convention without distinction of any kind such as to sex, race, colour, language, religion or conviction, political or other opinion, national, ethnic or social origin, nationality, age, economic position, property, marital status, birth or other status.
13.	2. Migrant workers and members of their families shall have the right to freedom of expression; this right shall include freedom to seek, receive and impart information and ideas of all kinds, regardless of frontiers, either orally, in writing or in print, in the form of art or through any other media of their choice.
13.	3. The exercise of the right provided for in paragraph 2 of the present article carries with it special duties and responsibilities. It may therefore be subject to certain restrictions, but these shall only be such as are provided by law and are necessary: (a) For respect of the rights or reputation of others; (b) For the protection of the national security of the States concerned or of public order (ordre public) or of public health or morals; (c) For the purpose of preventing any propaganda for war; (d) For the purpose of preventing any advocacy of national, racial or religious hatred that constitutes incitement to discrimination, hostility or violence.
16.	1. Migrant workers and members of their families shall have the right to liberty and security of person. 2. Migrant workers and members of their families shall be entitled to effective protection by the State against violence, physical injury, threats and intimidation, whether by public officials or by private individuals, groups or institutions.

26.	1. States Parties recognize the right of migrant workers and members of their families:
	(a) To take part in meetings and activities of trade unions and of any other associations established in accordance with law, with a view to protecting their economic, social, cultural and other interests, subject only to the rules of the organization concerned;
	(b) To join freely any trade union and any such association as aforesaid, subject only to the rules of the organization concerned;...
	2. No restrictions may be placed on the exercise of these rights other than those that are prescribed by law and which are necessary in a democratic society in the interests of national security, public order (ordre public) or the protection of the rights and freedoms of others.
40.	1. Migrant workers and members of their families shall have the right to form associations and trade unions in the State of employment for the promotion and protection of their economic, social, cultural and other interests.
	2. No restrictions may be placed on the exercise of this right other than those that are prescribed by law and are necessary in a democratic society in the interests of national security, public order (ordre public) or the protection of the rights and freedoms of others.
41.	1. Migrant workers and members of their families shall have the right to participate in public affairs of their State of origin and to vote and to be elected at elections of that State, in accordance with its legislation.
	2. The States concerned shall, as appropriate and in accordance with their legislation, facilitate the exercise of these rights.

42.	2. States of employment shall facilitate, in accordance with their national legislation, the consultation or participation of migrant workers and members of their families in decisions concerning the life and administration of local communities.
	3. Migrant workers may enjoy political rights in the State of employment if that State, in the exercise of its sovereignty, grants them such rights.
83.	Each State Party to the present Convention undertakes:

(a) To ensure that any person whose rights or freedoms as herein recognized are violated shall have an effective remedy, notwithstanding that the violation has been committed by persons acting in an official capacity;

(b) To ensure that any persons seeking such a remedy shall have his or her claim reviewed and decided by competent judicial, administrative or legislative authorities, or by any other competent authority provided for by the legal system of the State, and to develop the possibilities of judicial remedy;

(c) To ensure that the competent authorities shall enforce such remedies when granted.

UN CONVENTION ON THE RIGHTS OF THE CHILD (CRC)

| 2. | 1. States Parties shall respect and ensure the rights set forth in the present Convention to each child within their jurisdiction without discrimination of any kind, irrespective of the child's or his or her parent's or legal guardian's race, colour, sex, language, religion, political or other opinion, national, ethnic or social origin, property, disability, birth or other status. |
| | 2. States Parties shall take all appropriate measures to ensure that the child is protected against all forms of discrimination or punishment on the basis of the status, activities, expressed opinions, or beliefs of the child's parents, legal guardians, or family members. |

12.	1. States Parties shall assure to the child who is capable of forming his or her own views the right to express those views freely in all matters affecting the child, the views of the child being given due weight in accordance with the age and maturity of the child.
13.	1. The child shall have the right to freedom of expression; this right shall include freedom to seek, receive and impart information and ideas of all kinds, regardless of frontiers, either orally, in writing or in print, in the form of art, or through any other media of the child's choice.

2. The exercise of this right may be subject to certain restrictions, but these shall only be such as are provided by law and are necessary:

(a) For respect of the rights or reputations of others; or

(b) For the protection of national security or of public order (ordre public), or of public health or morals.

15.	1. States Parties recognize the rights of the child to freedom of association and to freedom of peaceful assembly.

2. No restrictions may be placed on the exercise of these rights other than those imposed in conformity with the law and which are necessary in a democratic society in the interests of national security or public safety, public order (ordre public), the protection of public health or morals or the protection of the rights and freedoms of others.

OPTIONAL PROTOCOL TO THE CONVENTION ON THE RIGHTS OF THE CHILD ON A COMMUNICATIONS PROCEDURE

4.	1. A State party shall take all appropriate steps to ensure that individuals under its jurisdiction are not subjected to any human rights violation, ill-treatment or intimidation as a consequence of communications or cooperation with the Committee pursuant to the present Protocol.

UN CONVENTION RELATING TO THE STATUS OF REFUGEES

15.   As regards non-political and non-profit-making associations and trade unions the Contracting States shall accord to refugees lawfully staying in their territory the most favourable treatment accorded to nationals of a foreign country, in the same circumstances.

UN CONVENTION FOR THE PROTECTION OF ALL PERSONS FROM ENFORCED DISAPPEARANCE

24.   7. Each State Party shall guarantee the right to form and participate freely in organizations and associations concerned with attempting to establish the circumstances of enforced disappearances and the fate of disappeared persons, and to assist victims of enforced disappearance.

UN CONVENTION ON THE RIGHTS OF PERSONS WITH DISABILITIES

4.   1. States Parties undertake to ensure and promote the full realization of all human rights and fundamental freedoms for all persons with disabilities without discrimination of any kind on the basis of disability...

21.   States Parties shall take all appropriate measures to ensure that persons with disabilities can exercise the right to freedom of expression and opinion, including the freedom to seek, receive and impart information and ideas on an equal basis with others and through all forms of communication of their choice, as defined in article 2 of the present Convention, including by:

a)   Providing information intended for the general public to persons with disabilities in accessible formats and technologies appropriate to different kinds of disabilities in a timely manner and without additional cost;

b)   Accepting and facilitating the use of sign languages, Braille, augmentative and alternative communication, and all other accessible means, modes and formats of communication of their choice by persons with disabilities in official interactions;

c)   Urging private entities that provide services to the general public, including through the Internet, to provide information and services in accessible and usable formats for persons with disabilities;

d)   Encouraging the mass media, including providers of information through the Internet, to make their services accessible to persons with disabilities;

e)   Recognizing and promoting the use of sign languages.

29.   States Parties shall guarantee to persons with disabilities political rights and the opportunity to enjoy them on an equal basis with others, and shall undertake to:

(a) Ensure that persons with disabilities can effectively and fully participate in political and public life on an equal basis with others, directly or through freely chosen representatives, including the right and opportunity for persons with disabilities to vote and be elected...

(b) Promote actively an environment in which persons with disabilities can effectively and fully participate in the conduct of public affairs, without discrimination and on an equal basis with others, and encourage their participation in public affairs, including:

(i) Participation in non-governmental organizations and associations concerned with the public and political life of the country, and in the activities and administration of political parties;

(ii) Forming and joining organizations of persons with disabilities to represent persons with disabilities at international, national, regional and local levels.

30.	1. States Parties recognize the right of persons with disabilities to take part on an equal basis with others in cultural life, and shall take all appropriate measures to ensure that persons with disabilities:

a) Enjoy access to cultural materials in accessible formats;

b) Enjoy access to television programmes, films, theatre and other cultural activities, in accessible formats;

c) Enjoy access to places for cultural performances or services, such as theatres, museums, cinemas, libraries and tourism services, and, as far as possible, enjoy access to monuments and sites of national cultural importance.

ILO CONVENTION 87, FREEDOM OF ASSOCIATION AND PROTECTION OF THE RIGHT TO ORGANISE CONVENTION

2.	Workers and employers, without distinction whatsoever, shall have the right to establish and, subject only to the rules of the organisation concerned, to join organisations of their own choosing without previous authorisation.
3.	(2) The public authorities shall refrain from any interference which would restrict this right or impede the lawful exercise thereof.

UN DECLARATION ON THE RIGHT AND RESPONSIBILITY OF INDIVIDUALS, GROUPS AND ORGANS OF SOCIETY TO PROMOTE AND PROTECT UNIVERSALLY RECOGNIZED HUMAN RIGHTS AND FUNDAMENTAL FREEDOMS

1.	Everyone has the right, individually and in association with others, to promote and to strive for the protection and realization of human rights and fundamental freedoms at the national and international levels.
5.	For the purpose of promoting and protecting human rights and fundamental freedoms, everyone has the right, individually and in association with others, at the national and international levels:

(a) To meet or assemble peacefully;

(b) To form, join and participate in non-governmental organizations, associations or groups;

(c) To communicate with non-governmental or intergovernmental organizations.

6.   Everyone has the right, individually and in association with others:

(a) To know, seek, obtain, receive and hold information about all human rights and fundamental freedoms, including having access to information as to how those rights and freedoms are given effect in domestic legislative, judicial or administrative systems;

(b) As provided for in human rights and other applicable international instruments, freely to publish, impart or disseminate to others views, information and knowledge on all human rights and fundamental freedoms;

(c) To study, discuss, form and hold opinions on the observance, both in law and in practice, of all human rights and fundamental freedoms and, through these and other appropriate means, to draw public attention to those matters.

8.   1. Everyone has the right, individually and in association with others, to have effective access, on a non-discriminatory basis, to participation in the government of his or her country and in the conduct of public affairs.

2. This includes, inter alia, the right, individually and in association with others, to submit to governmental bodies and agencies and organizations concerned with public affairs criticism and proposals for improving their functioning and to draw attention to any aspect of their work that may hinder or impede the promotion, protection and realization of human rights and fundamental freedoms.

9.   1. In the exercise of human rights and fundamental freedoms, including the promotion and protection of human rights as referred to in the present Declaration, everyone has the right, individually and in association with others, to benefit from an effective remedy and to be protected in the event of the violation of those rights.

2. To this end, everyone whose rights or freedoms are allegedly violated has the right, either in person or through legally authorized representation, to complain to and have that complaint promptly reviewed in a public hearing before an independent, impartial and competent judicial or other authority established by law and to obtain from such an authority a decision, in accordance with law, providing redress, including any compensation due, where there has been a violation of that person's rights or freedoms, as well as enforcement of the eventual decision and award, all without undue delay.

3. To the same end, everyone has the right, individually and in association with others, inter alia:

(a) To complain about the policies and actions of individual officials and governmental bodies with regard to violations of human rights and fundamental freedoms, by petition or other appropriate means, to competent domestic judicial, administrative or legislative authorities or any other competent authority provided for by the legal system of the State, which should render their decision on the complaint without undue delay;

(b) To attend public hearings, proceedings and trials so as to form an opinion on their compliance with national law and applicable international obligations and commitments;

(c) To offer and provide professionally qualified legal assistance or other relevant advice and assistance in defending human rights and fundamental freedoms.

4. To the same end, and in accordance with applicable international instruments and procedures, everyone has the right, individually and in association with others, to unhindered access to and communication with international bodies with general or special competence to receive and consider communications on matters of human rights and fundamental freedoms.

5. The State shall conduct a prompt and impartial investigation or ensure that an inquiry takes place whenever there is reasonable ground to believe that a violation of human rights and fundamental freedoms has occurred in any territory under its jurisdiction.

12.	1. Everyone has the right, individually and in association with others, to participate in peaceful activities against violations of human rights and fundamental freedoms.
	2. The State shall take all necessary measures to ensure the protection by the competent authorities of everyone, individually and in association with others, against any violence, threats, retaliation, de facto or de jure adverse discrimination, pressure or any other arbitrary action as a consequence of his or her legitimate exercise of the rights referred to in the present Declaration.
	3. In this connection, everyone is entitled, individually and in association with others, to be protected effectively under national law in reacting against or opposing, through peaceful means, activities and acts, including those by omission, attributable to States that result in violations of human rights and fundamental freedoms, as well as acts of violence perpetrated by groups or individuals that affect the enjoyment of human rights and fundamental freedoms.

UN DECLARATION ON THE ELIMINATION OF ALL FORMS OF INTOLERANCE AND OF DISCRIMINATION BASED ON RELIGION OR BELIEF

6.	In accordance with article 1 of the present Declaration, and subject to the provisions of article 1, paragraph 3, the right to freedom of thought, conscience, religion or belief shall include, inter alia, the following freedoms:...
	(a) To worship or assemble in connexion with a religion or belief, and to establish and maintain places for these purposes;
7.	The rights and freedoms set forth in the present Declaration shall be accorded in national legislation in such a manner that everyone shall be able to avail himself of such rights and freedoms in practice.

UN DECLARATION ON THE RIGHTS OF PERSONS BELONGING TO NATIONAL OR ETHNIC, RELIGIOUS AND LINGUISTIC MINORITIES

2.	2. Persons belonging to minorities have the right to participate effectively in cultural, religious, social, economic and public life.
	3. Persons belonging to minorities have the right to participate effectively in decisions on the national and, where appropriate, regional level concerning the minority to which they belong or the regions in which they live, in a manner not incompatible with national legislation.
	4. Persons belonging to minorities have the right to establish and maintain their own associations.
	5. Persons belonging to minorities have the right to establish and maintain, without any discrimination, free and peaceful contacts with other members of their group and with persons belonging to other minorities, as well as contacts across frontiers with citizens of other States to whom they are related by national or ethnic, religious or linguistic ties.
3.	1. Persons belonging to minorities may exercise their rights, including those set forth in the present Declaration, individually as well as in community with other members of their group, without any discrimination.
4.	1. States shall take measures where required to ensure that persons belonging to minorities may exercise fully and effectively all their human rights and fundamental freedoms without any discrimination and in full equality before the law.

UN DECLARATION ON THE RIGHTS OF INDIGENOUS PEOPLES

1.	Indigenous peoples have the right to the full enjoyment, as a collective or as individuals, of all human rights and fundamental freedoms as recognized in the Charter of the United Nations, the Universal Declaration of Human Rights and international human rights law.
2.	Indigenous peoples and individuals are free and equal to all other peoples and individuals and have the right to be free from any kind of discrimination, in the exercise of their rights, in particular that based on their indigenous origin or identity.

5.	Indigenous peoples have the right to maintain and strengthen their distinct political, legal, economic, social and cultural institutions, while retaining their right to participate fully, if they so choose, in the political, economic, social and cultural life of the State.
18.	Indigenous peoples have the right to participate in decision-making in matters which would affect their rights, through representatives chosen by themselves in accordance with their own procedures, as well as to maintain and develop their own indigenous decision-making institutions.

DURBAN DECLARATION ON RACISM, RACIAL DISCRIMINATION, XENOPHOBIA AND RELATED INTOLERANCE

22.	We express our concern that in some States political and legal structures or institutions, some of which were inherited and persist today, do not correspond to the multi-ethnic, pluricultural and plurilingual characteristics of the population and, in many cases, constitute an important factor of discrimination in the exclusion of indigenous peoples;
34.	We recognize that people of African descent have for centuries been victims of racism, racial discrimination and enslavement and of the denial by history of many of their rights, and assert that they should be treated with fairness and respect for their dignity and should not suffer discrimination of any kind. Recognition should therefore be given to their rights to culture and their own identity; to participate freely and in equal conditions in political, social, economic and cultural life; to development in the context of their own aspirations and customs; to keep, maintain and foster their own forms of organization, their mode of life, culture, traditions and religious expressions; to maintain and use their own languages; to the protection of their traditional knowledge and their cultural and artistic heritage; to the use, enjoyment and conservation of the natural renewable resources of their habitat and to active participation in the design, implementation and development of educational systems and programmes, including those of a specific and characteristic nature; and where applicable to their ancestrally inhabited land;

42.	We emphasize that, in order for indigenous peoples freely to express their own identity and exercise their rights, they should be free from all forms of discrimination, which necessarily entails respect for their human rights and fundamental freedoms. Efforts are now being made to secure universal recognition for those rights in the negotiations on the draft declaration on the rights of indigenous peoples, including the following: to call themselves by their own names; to participate freely and on an equal footing in their country's political, economic, social and cultural development; to maintain their own forms of organization, lifestyles, cultures and traditions; to maintain and use their own languages; to maintain their own economic structures in the areas where they live; to take part in the development of their educational systems and programmes; to manage their lands and natural resources, including hunting and fishing rights; and to have access to justice on a basis of equality;

DURBAN PROGRAMME OF ACTION ON RACISM, RACIAL DISCRIMINATION, XENOPHOBIA AND RELATED INTOLERANCE

47.	Urges States to guarantee the rights of persons belonging to national or ethnic, religious and linguistic minorities, individually or in community with other members of their group, to ... participate effectively in the cultural, social, economic and political life of the country in which they live...

UN DECLARATION ON THE RIGHT TO DEVELOPMENT

1.	1. The right to development is an inalienable human right by virtue of which every human person and all peoples are entitled to participate in, contribute to, and enjoy economic, social, cultural and political development, in which all human rights and fundamental freedoms can be fully realized.

2.	1. The human person is the central subject of development and should be the active participant and beneficiary of the right to development.
	2. All human beings have a responsibility for development, individually and collectively, taking into account the need for full respect for their human rights and fundamental freedoms as well as their duties to the community, which alone can ensure the free and complete fulfilment of the human being, and they should therefore promote and protect an appropriate political, social and economic order for development.
	3. States have the right and the duty to formulate appropriate national development policies that aim at the constant improvement of the well-being of the entire population and of all individuals, on the basis of their active, free and meaningful participation in development and in the fair distribution of the benefits resulting therefrom.
8.	2. States should encourage popular participation in all spheres as an important factor in development and in the full realization of all human rights.

THE PUBLIC'S RIGHT TO KNOW: UN PRINCIPLES ON FREEDOM OF INFORMATION LEGISLATION

Principle 7	Freedom of information includes the public's right to know what the Government is doing on its behalf and to participate in decision-making processes...

UN BASIC PRINCIPLES ON THE USE OF FORCE AND FIREARMS BY LAW ENFORCEMENT OFFICIALS

4.	Law enforcement officials, in carrying out their duty, shall, as far as possible, apply non-violent means before resorting to the use of force and firearms. They may use force and firearms only if other means remain ineffective or without any promise of achieving the intended result.

5.   Whenever the lawful use of force and firearms is unavoidable, law enforcement officials shall:

(a) Exercise restraint in such use and act in proportion to the seriousness of the offence and the legitimate objective to be achieved;

(b) Minimize damage and injury, and respect and preserve human life;

(c) Ensure that assistance and medical aid are rendered to any injured or affected persons at the earliest possible moment;

(d) Ensure that relatives or close friends of the injured or affected person are notified at the earliest possible moment.

6.   Where injury or death is caused by the use of force and firearms by law enforcement officials, they shall report the incident promptly to their superiors, in accordance with principle 22.

7.   Governments shall ensure that arbitrary or abusive use of force and firearms by law enforcement officials is punished as a criminal offence under their law.

8.   Exceptional circumstances such as internal political instability or any other public emergency may not be invoked to justify any departure from these basic principles.

9.   Law enforcement officials shall not use firearms against persons except in self-defence or defence of others against the imminent threat of death or serious injury, to prevent the perpetration of a particularly serious crime involving grave threat to life, to arrest a person presenting such a danger and resisting their authority, or to prevent his or her escape, and only when less extreme means are insufficient to achieve these objectives. In any event, intentional lethal use of firearms may only be made when strictly unavoidable in order to protect life.

12.	As everyone is allowed to participate in lawful and peaceful assemblies, in accordance with the principles embodied in the Universal Declaration of Human Rights and the International Covenant on Civil and Political Rights, Governments and law enforcement agencies and officials shall recognize that force and firearms may be used only in accordance with principles 13 and 14.
13.	In the dispersal of assemblies that are unlawful but non-violent, law enforcement officials shall avoid the use of force or, where that is not practicable, shall restrict such force to the minimum extent necessary.
14.	In the dispersal of violent assemblies, law enforcement officials may use firearms only when less dangerous means are not practicable and only to the minimum extent necessary. Law enforcement officials shall not use firearms in such cases, except under the conditions stipulated in principle 9.

UN CODE OF CONDUCT FOR LAW ENFORCEMENT OFFICIALS

2.	In the performance of their duty, law enforcement officials shall respect and protect human dignity and maintain and uphold the human rights of all persons.
3.	Law enforcement officials may use force only when strictly necessary and to the extent required for the performance of their duty.
5.	No law enforcement official may inflict, instigate or tolerate any act of torture or other cruel, inhuman or degrading treatment or punishment, nor may any law enforcement official invoke superior orders or exceptional circumstances such as a state of war or a threat of war, a threat to national security, internal political instability or any other public emergency as a justification of torture or other cruel, inhuman or degrading treatment or punishment.

UN GUIDELINES FOR THE EFFECTIVE IMPLEMENTATION OF THE CODE OF CONDUCT FOR LAW ENFORCEMENT OFFICIALS	
I. A.	1. The principles embodied in the Code shall be reflected in national legislation and practice.
	4. Governments shall adopt the necessary measures to instruct, in basic training and all subsequent training and refresher courses, law enforcement officials in the provisions of national legislation connected with the Code as well as other basic texts on the issue of human rights.
II. A.	2. Governments shall disseminate the Code and all domestic laws giving effect to it so as to ensure that the principles and rights contained therein become known to the public in general.
	3. In considering measures to promote the application of the Code, Governments shall organize symposia on the role and functions of law enforcement officials in the protection of human rights and the prevention of crime.
BASIC PRINCIPLES AND GUIDELINES ON THE RIGHT TO A REMEDY AND REPARATION FOR VICTIMS OF GROSS VIOLATIONS OF INTERNATIONAL HUMAN RIGHTS LAW AND SERIOUS VIOLATIONS OF INTERNATIONAL HUMANITARIAN LAW	
2.	If they have not already done so, States shall, as required under international law, ensure that their domestic law is consistent with their international legal obligations by:
	(a) Incorporating norms of international human rights law and international humanitarian law into their domestic law, or otherwise implementing them in their domestic legal system;
	(b) Adopting appropriate and effective legislative and administrative procedures and other appropriate measures that provide fair, effective and prompt access to justice;
	(c) Making available adequate, effective, prompt and appropriate remedies, including reparation, as defined below;
	(d) Ensuring that their domestic law provides at least the same level of protection for victims as that required by their international obligations.

3.   The obligation to respect, ensure respect for and implement international human rights law and international humanitarian law as provided for under the respective bodies of law, includes, inter alia, the duty to:

(a) Take appropriate legislative and administrative and other appropriate measures to prevent violations;

(b) Investigate violations effectively, promptly, thoroughly and impartially and, where appropriate, take action against those allegedly responsible in accordance with domestic and international law;

(c) Provide those who claim to be victims of a human rights or humanitarian law violation with equal and effective access to justice, as described below, irrespective of who may ultimately be the bearer of responsibility for the violation; and

(d) Provide effective remedies to victims, including reparation, as described below.

4.   In cases of gross violations of international human rights law and serious violations of international humanitarian law constituting crimes under international law, States have the duty to investigate and, if there is sufficient evidence, the duty to submit to prosecution the person allegedly responsible for the violations and, if found guilty, the duty to punish her or him. Moreover, in these cases, States should, in accordance with international law, cooperate with one another and assist international judicial organs competent in the investigation and prosecution of these violations.

11.   Remedies for gross violations of international human rights law and serious violations of international humanitarian law include the victim's right to the following as provided for under international law:

(a) Equal and effective access to justice;

(b) Adequate, effective and prompt reparation for harm suffered;

(c) Access to relevant information concerning violations and reparation mechanisms.

| 15. | Adequate, effective and prompt reparation is intended to promote justice by redressing gross violations of international human rights law or serious violations of international humanitarian law. Reparation should be proportional to the gravity of the violations and the harm suffered. In accordance with its domestic laws and international legal obligations, a State shall provide reparation to victims for acts or omissions which can be attributed to the State and constitute gross violations of international human rights law or serious violations of international humanitarian law. In cases where a person, a legal person, or other entity is found liable for reparation to a victim, such party should provide reparation to the victim or compensate the State if the State has already provided reparation to the victim. |

UN GUIDELINES ON THE ROLE OF PROSECUTORS

11.	Prosecutors shall perform an active role in criminal proceedings, including institution of prosecution and, where authorized by law or consistent with local practice, in the investigation of crime, supervision over the legality of these investigations, supervision of the execution of court decisions and the exercise of other functions as representatives of the public interest.
12.	Prosecutors shall, in accordance with the law, perform their duties fairly, consistently and expeditiously, and respect and protect human dignity and uphold human rights, thus contributing to ensuring due process and the smooth functioning of the criminal justice system.
13.	In the performance of their duties, prosecutors shall: (a) Carry out their functions impartially and avoid all political, social, religious, racial, cultural, sexual or any other kind of discrimination;
15.	Prosecutors shall give due attention to the prosecution of crimes committed by public officials, particularly corruption, abuse of power, grave violations of human rights and other crimes recognized by international law and, where authorized by law or consistent with local practice, the investigation of such offences.

UN BASIC PRINCIPLES ON THE INDEPENDENCE OF THE JUDICIARY

2.   The judiciary shall decide matters before them impartially, on the basis of facts and in accordance with the law, without any restrictions, improper influences, inducements, pressures, threats or interferences, direct or indirect, from any quarter or for any reason.

UN GA RESOLUTION 68/181 ON THE PROMOTION OF THE DECLARATION ON THE RIGHT AND RESPONSIBILITY OF INDIVIDUALS, GROUPS AND ORGANS OF SOCIETY TO PROMOTE AND PROTECT UNIVERSALLY RECOGNIZED HUMAN RIGHTS AND FUNDAMENTAL FREEDOMS: PROTECTING WOMEN HUMAN RIGHTS DEFENDERS

1.   Calls upon all States to promote, translate and give full effect to the Declaration on the Right and Responsibility of Individuals, Groups and Organs of Society to Promote and Protect Universally Recognized Human Rights and Fundamental Freedoms, including by taking appropriate, robust and practical steps to protect women human rights defenders;...

5.   Expresses particular concern about systemic and structural discrimination and violence faced by women human rights defenders of all ages, and calls upon States to take all measures necessary to ensure their protection and to integrate a gender perspective into their efforts to create a safe and enabling environment for the defence of human rights;

6.   Reiterates strongly the right of anyone, individually and in association with others, to defend the human rights of women in all their aspects, and stresses the important role of women human rights defenders in promoting and protecting human rights and fundamental freedoms, to which everyone is entitled without distinction of any kind, including in addressing all forms of human rights violations, combating impunity, fighting poverty and discrimination and promoting access to justice, democracy, the full participation of women in society, tolerance, human dignity and the right to development, while recalling that the exercise of these rights carries duties and responsibilities set out in the Declaration; ...

8.	Calls upon States to ensure that human rights defenders, including women human rights defenders, can perform their important role in the context of peaceful protests, in accordance with national legislation consistent with the Charter of the United Nations and international human rights law, and in this regard to ensure that no one is subject to excessive or indiscriminate use of force, arbitrary arrest or detention, torture or other cruel, inhuman or degrading treatment or punishment, enforced disappearance, abuse of criminal and civil proceedings or threats of such acts;
9.	Also calls upon States to exercise due diligence in preventing violations and abuses against human rights defenders, including through practical steps to prevent threats, harassment and violence against women human rights defenders, who face particular risks, and in combating impunity by ensuring that those responsible for violations and abuses, including gender-based violence and threats against women human rights defenders, committed by State and non-State actors, including online, are promptly brought to justice through impartial investigations;
10	Further calls upon States to ensure that the promotion and protection of human rights are not criminalized or met with limitations in contravention of their obligations and commitments under international human rights law and that women human rights defenders are not prevented from enjoying universal human rights owing to their work, including by ensuring that all legal provisions, administrative measures and policies affecting women human rights defenders, including those aimed at preserving public morals, are clearly defined, determinable, non- retroactive and compatible with relevant provisions of international human rights law;...
13	Stresses that, in the exercise of the rights and freedoms referred to in the Declaration, women human rights defenders, acting individually and in association with others, shall be subject only to such limitations as are in accordance with applicable international obligations and are determined by law solely for the purpose of securing due recognition and respect for the rights and freedoms of others and of meeting the just requirements of morality, public order and the general welfare in a democratic society;

17.	Strongly calls upon States to refrain from, and ensure adequate protection from, any act of intimidation or reprisal against women human rights defenders who cooperate, have cooperated or seek to cooperate with international institutions, including their family members and associates;...
19.	Urges States to develop and put in place comprehensive, sustainable and gender-sensitive public policies and programmes that support and protect women human rights defenders, including by providing adequate resources for immediate and long-term protection and making sure that these can be mobilized in a flexible and timely manner to guarantee effective physical and psychological protection, while also extending protection measures to their relatives, including children, and otherwise to take into account the role of many women human rights defenders as the main or sole caregivers in their families;...
21.	Urges States to adopt and implement policies and programmes that provide women human rights defenders with access to effective remedies...

HRC RESOLUTION 30/9 ON THE EQUAL PARTICIPATION IN POLITICAL AND PUBLIC AFFAIRS

1.	Expresses concern that, despite progress made towards the full implementation of the right to participate in public affairs worldwide, many people continue to face obstacles, including discrimination, in the enjoyment of their right to participate in the public affairs of their countries as well as in the enjoyment of other human rights that enable it;
2.	Recognizes that women, persons belonging to marginalized groups or minorities, and persons in vulnerable situations are among those who are most affected by discrimination in participation in political and public affairs;
3.	Reaffirms the obligation of States to take all appropriate measures to ensure that every citizen has an effective right and opportunity to equal participation in public affairs;
4.	Notes the emergence of new forms of participation and grass-roots engagement, in particular through new information and communications technology and social media, and the challenges to established forms of political participation in some States;...

7.	Urges all States to ensure the full, effective and equal participation of all citizens in political and public affairs, including by, inter alia:...

(i) Ensuring the rights of everyone to freedom of expression, peaceful assembly and freedom of association, education and development, and facilitating equal and effective access to information, media and communications technology in order to enable pluralistic debates fostering inclusive and effective participation in political and public affairs;

(j) Creating a safe and enabling environment for human rights defenders and civil society organizations, which together with other actors play a key role in the effective promotion and protection of all human rights;

(k) Providing full and effective access to justice and redress mechanisms to those citizens whose right to participate in public affairs has been violated, including by developing effective, independent and pluralistic national human rights institutions, in accordance with the principles relating to the status of national institutions for the promotion and protection of human rights (Paris Principles);

HRC RESOLUTION 25/38 ON THE PROMOTION AND PROTECTION OF HUMAN RIGHTS IN THE CONTEXT OF PEACEFUL PROTESTS

3.	Calls upon States to promote a safe and enabling environment for individuals and groups to exercise their rights to freedom of peaceful assembly, of expression and of association, including by ensuring that their domestic legislation and procedures relating to the rights to freedom of peaceful assembly, of expression and of association are in conformity with their international human rights obligations and commitments, clearly and explicitly establish a presumption in favour of the exercise of these rights, and that they are effectively implemented;
4.	Urges States to facilitate peaceful protests by providing protestors with access to public space and protecting them, without discrimination, where necessary, against any form of threat and harassment, and underlines the role of local authorities in this regard;

5.	Underlines the important role that communication between protestors, local authorities and officials exercising law enforcement duties can play in the proper management of assemblies, such as peaceful protests, and calls on States to establish appropriate channels in that regard;
6.	Urges States to pay particular attention to the safety and protection of women and women human rights defenders from acts of intimidation and harassment, as well as gender-based violence, including sexual assault, in the context of peaceful protests;
7.	Reaffirms that States must take all appropriate measures for the safety and protection of children, including while they exercise their rights to freedom of peaceful assembly, expression and association, including in the context of peaceful protests;
8.	Calls upon all States to pay particular attention to the safety of journalists and media workers covering peaceful protests, taking into account their specific role, exposure and vulnerability;
9.	Urges all States to avoid using force during peaceful protests and to ensure that, where force is absolutely necessary, no one is subject to excessive or indiscriminate use of force;
10.	Calls upon States, as a matter of priority, to ensure that their domestic legislation and procedures are consistent with their international obligations and commitments in relation to the use of force in the context of law enforcement and are effectively implemented by officials exercising law enforcement duties, in particular applicable principles of law enforcement, such as the principles of necessity and proportionality, bearing in mind that lethal force may only be used as a last resort to protect against an imminent threat to life and that it may not be used merely to disperse a gathering;
11.	Affirms that nothing can ever justify the indiscriminate use of lethal force against a crowd, which is unlawful under international human rights law;
12.	Calls upon States to investigate any death or significant injury committed during protests, including those resulting from the discharge of firearms or the use of nonlethal weapons by officials exercising law enforcement duties;

13.	Also calls upon States to ensure adequate training of officials exercising law enforcement duties and, where applicable, to promote adequate training for private personnel acting on behalf of a State, including in international human rights law and, where appropriate, international humanitarian law;
14.	Encourages States to make protective equipment and non-lethal weapons available to their officials exercising law enforcement duties, while pursuing international efforts to regulate and establish protocols for the training and use of non-lethal weapons;
15.	Underlines the importance of thorough, independent and scientific testing of non-lethal weapons prior to deployment to establish their lethality and the extent of likely injury, and of monitoring appropriate training and use of such weapons;
16.	Stresses the importance of international cooperation in support of national efforts for the promotion and protection of human rights and fundamental freedoms in the context of peaceful protests, in order to raise the capacities of law enforcement agencies to deal with such protests in a manner that conforms to their international human rights obligations and commitments;
17.	Underlines the necessity to address the management of assemblies, including peaceful protests, so as to contribute to their peaceful conduct, and to prevent loss of life of and injuries to protestors, bystanders, those monitoring such protests and officials exercising law enforcement duties, as well as any human rights violation or abuse;
18.	Recognizes the importance of documenting human rights violations and abuses committed in the context of peaceful protests, and the role that can be played by national human rights institutions, civil society, including non-governmental organizations, journalists and other media workers, Internet users and human rights defenders, in this regard;
19.	Urges States to ensure accountability for human rights violations and abuses through judicial or other national mechanisms, based on law in conformity with their international human rights obligations and commitments, and to provide victims with access to a remedy and redress, including in the context of peaceful protests;

HRC RESOLUTION 22/10 ON THE PROMOTION AND PROTECTION OF HUMAN RIGHTS IN THE CONTEXT OF PEACEFUL PROTESTS

3.	Calls upon States to promote a safe and enabling environment for individuals and groups to exercise their rights to freedom of peaceful assembly, of expression and of association, including by ensuring that their domestic legislation and procedures related to the rights to freedom of peaceful assembly, of expression and of association are in conformity with their international human rights obligations and commitments;
4.	Urges States to facilitate peaceful protests by providing protestors with access to public space and protecting them, where necessary, against any forms of threats, and underlines the role of local authorities in this regard;
5.	Underlines the role that communication between protestors, local authorities and police can play in the proper management of assemblies such as peaceful protests, including protests that are spontaneous, simultaneous, unauthorized or restricted;
6.	Urges States to pay particular attention to the safety of women and their protection from gender-based violence, including sexual assault in the context of peaceful protests;
7.	Calls upon all States to avoid using force during peaceful protests, and to ensure that, where force is absolutely necessary, no one is subject to excessive or indiscriminate use of force;
8.	Calls upon States, as a matter of priority, to ensure that their domestic legislation and procedures are consistent with their international obligations and commitments in relation to the use of force by law enforcement officials, in particular applicable principles of law enforcement such as the principles of necessity and proportionality, bearing in mind that lethal force may only be used to protect against an imminent threat to life and that it may not be used merely to disperse a gathering;
9.	Also calls upon States to investigate any death or injury committed during protests, including those resulting from the discharge of firearms or the use of non-lethal weapons by law enforcement officials;

10.	Further calls upon States and, where applicable, the relevant governmental authorities to ensure adequate training of law enforcement officials and military personnel and to promote adequate training for private personnel acting on behalf of a State, including in international human rights law and, where appropriate, international humanitarian law;
11.	Encourages States to make protective equipment and non-lethal weapons available to their law enforcement officials and to refrain from using lethal force during peaceful protests, while pursuing efforts to regulate and establish protocols for the use of non-lethal weapons;
12.	Underlines the necessity to address the management of assemblies, such as peaceful protests, so as to contribute to their peaceful conduct, and to prevent loss of life of, and injuries to, protestors, bystanders, those monitoring such protests, and law enforcement officials, as well as any human rights violations or abuses;
13.	Recognizes the key role played by national human rights institutions, civil society, including non-governmental organizations, journalists, writers and other media workers, Internet users and human rights defenders, and other relevant stakeholders, in documenting human rights violations or abuses committed in the context of peaceful protests;
14.	Urges States to ensure that national mechanisms, based on law in conformity with their international human rights obligations and commitments, can ensure oversight and accountability for human rights violations and abuses, including in the context of peaceful protests;
15.	Also urges States to ensure that victims of human rights violations and abuses have, through existing national mechanisms, access to a remedy and that they obtain redress, including in the context of peaceful protests; ...

HRC RESOLUTION 19/35 ON THE PROMOTION AND PROTECTION OF HUMAN RIGHTS IN THE CONTEXT OF PEACEFUL PROTESTS

6.	Encourages all States to avoid using force wherever possible during peaceful protests, and to ensure that, where force is absolutely necessary, no one is subject to excessive or indiscriminate use of force;

| 7. | Calls upon States, and where applicable relevant governmental authorities, to ensure adequate training of law enforcement officials and military personnel and to promote adequate training for private personnel acting on behalf of a State, including in human rights and, where appropriate, international humanitarian law;... |

HRC RESOLUTION 12/16 ON FREEDOM OF OPINION AND EXPRESSION

| 1. | Reaffirms the rights contained in the International Covenant on Civil and Political Rights, in particular the right of everyone to hold opinions without interference, as well as the right to freedom of expression, including the freedom to seek, receive and impart information and ideas of all kinds, regardless of frontiers, either orally, in writing or in print, in the form of art or through any other media of their choice, and the intrinsically linked rights to freedom of thought, conscience and religion, peaceful assembly and association and the right to take part in the conduct of public affairs;... |

| 5. | Calls upon all States: |

a) To respect and ensure the respect for the rights referred to in paragraph 1 above;

b) To take all necessary measures to put an end to violations of these rights and to create the conditions to prevent such violations, including by ensuring that relevant national legislation complies with their international human rights obligations and is effectively implemented;

c) To ensure that victims of violations of the rights referred to in paragraph 1 above have an effective remedy, to investigate effectively threats and acts of violence, including terrorist acts, against journalists, including in situations of armed conflict, and to bring to justice those responsible in order to combat impunity;

d) To ensure that persons exercising the above-mentioned rights are not discriminated against, particularly in employment, housing, the justice system, social services and education, with particular attention to women;

5.

e) To facilitate the full, equal and effective participation and free communication of women at all levels of decision-making in their societies and in national, regional and international institutions, including in mechanisms for the prevention, management and resolution of conflicts;

f) To enable children to exercise their right to express their views freely, including through school curricula that encourage the development of and respect for different opinions, and to have their views taken into account in all matters affecting them, the views of the child being given due weight in accordance with the age and maturity of the child;

g) To respect freedom of expression in the media and broadcasting, in particular the editorial independence of the media;

h) To promote a pluralistic approach to information and multiple points of view by encouraging a diversity of ownership of media and of sources of information, including mass media, through, inter alia, transparent licensing systems and effective regulations on undue concentration of ownership of the media in the private sector;

i) To create and permit an enabling environment in which training and professional development of the media can be organized in order to promote and protect the right to freedom of opinion and expression and can be carried out without threat of legal, criminal or administrative sanction by the State;

j) Consistent with their human rights law obligations, to refrain from the use of imprisonment or the imposition of fines for offences relating to the media, which are disproportionate to the gravity of the offence;

k) To adopt and implement policies and programmes that aim to effectively raise awareness of, and disseminate information and education on, prevention and treatment of HIV/AIDS and other diseases through effective and equal access to information and all appropriate means, including through the media and availability of information and communication technologies, and targeted at specific vulnerable groups;

l) To adopt and implement laws and policies that provide for a general right of public access to information held by public authorities, which may be restricted only in accordance with article 19 of the International Covenant on Civil and Political Rights;

m) To facilitate equal participation in, access to and use of information and communications technology, such as the Internet, applying a gender perspective, and to encourage international cooperation aimed at the development of media and information and communication facilities in all countries;

n) To review their procedures, practices and legislation, as necessary, with a view to ensure the full and effective implementation of all their obligations under international human rights law, including to ensure that any limitations on the right to freedom of opinion and expression are only such as are provided by law and are necessary for the respect of the rights and reputations of others, or for the protection of national security or of public order (ordre public) or of public health or morals;

o) To refrain from using counter-terrorism as a pretext to restrict the right to freedom of opinion and expression in ways that are contrary to their obligations under international law;

p) While noting that article 19, paragraph 3, of the International Covenant on Civil and Political Rights provides that the exercise of the right to freedom of opinion and expression carries with it special duties and responsibilities, to refrain from imposing restrictions that are not consistent with paragraph 3 of that article, including on:

(i) Discussion of government policies and political debate; reporting on human rights, government activities and corruption in government; engaging in election campaigns, peaceful demonstrations or political activities, including for peace or democracy; and expression of opinion and dissent, religion or belief, including by persons belonging to minorities or vulnerable groups;

(ii) The free flow of information and ideas, including practices such as the banning or closing of publications or other media and the abuse of administrative measures and censorship;

(iii) Access to or use of information and communication technologies, including radio, television and the Internet;

HRC RESOLUTION 24/5 ON THE RIGHTS TO FREEDOM OF PEACEFUL ASSEMBLY AND OF ASSOCIATION

2. Reminds States of their obligation to respect and fully protect the rights of all individuals to assemble peacefully and associate freely, online as well as offline, including in the context of elections, and including persons espousing minority or dissenting views or beliefs, human rights defenders, trade unionists and others, including migrants, seeking to exercise or to promote these rights, and to take all necessary measures to ensure that any restrictions on the free exercise of the rights to freedom of peaceful assembly and of association are in accordance with their obligations under international human rights law;

HRC RESOLUTION 21/16 ON THE RIGHTS TO FREEDOM OF PEACEFUL ASSEMBLY AND OF ASSOCIATION

...Reiterating the important role of new information and communications technologies in enabling and facilitating the enjoyment of the rights to freedom of peaceful assembly and of association, and the importance for all States to promote and facilitate access to the Internet and international cooperation aimed at the development of media and information and communications facilities in all countries,...

1.   Reminds States of their obligation to respect and fully protect the rights of all individuals to assemble peacefully and associate freely, online as well as offline, including in the context of elections, and including persons espousing minority or dissenting views or beliefs, human rights defenders, trade unionists and others, including migrants, seeking to exercise or to promote these rights, and to take all necessary measures to ensure that any restrictions on the free exercise of the rights to freedom of peaceful assembly and of association are in accordance with their obligations under international human rights law;

HRC RESOLUTION 15/21 ON THE RIGHTS TO FREEDOM OF PEACEFUL ASSEMBLY AND OF ASSOCIATION

1.   Calls upon States to respect and fully protect the rights of all individuals to assemble peacefully and associate freely, including in the context of elections, and including persons espousing minority or dissenting views or beliefs, human rights defenders, trade unionists and others, including migrants, seeking to exercise or to promote these rights, and to take all necessary measures to ensure that any restrictions on the free exercise of the rights to freedom of peaceful assembly and of association are in accordance with their obligations under international human rights law;

HRC RESOLUTION 24/24 ON COOPERATION WITH THE UNITED NATIONS, ITS REPRESENTATIVES AND MECHANISMS IN THE FIELD OF HUMAN RIGHTS

1.   Reaffirms the right of everyone, individually and in association with others, to unhindered access to and communication with international bodies, in particular the United Nations, its representatives and mechanisms in the field of human rights, including the Human Rights Council, its special procedures, the universal periodic review mechanism and treaty bodies, as well as regional human rights mechanisms, bearing in mind that free and unhindered access to and communication with individuals and civil society are indeed indispensable to enable the United Nations and its mechanisms to fulfil their mandates;

HRC RESOLUTION 24/21 ON CIVIL SOCIETY SPACE: CREATING AND MAINTAINING, IN LAW AND IN PRACTICE, A SAFE AND ENABLING ENVIRONMENT

1.   Reminds States of their obligation to respect and fully protect the civil, political, economic, social and cultural rights of all individuals, inter alia the rights to freedom of expression and opinion and to assemble peacefully and associate freely, online as well as offline, including for persons espousing minority or dissenting views or beliefs, and that respect for all such rights, in relation to civil society, contributes to addressing and resolving challenges and issues that are important to society, such as addressing financial and economic crises, responding to humanitarian crises, including armed conflict, promoting the rule of law and accountability, achieving transitional justice goals, protecting the environment, realizing the right to development, empowering persons belonging to minorities and vulnerable groups, combating racism and racial discrimination, supporting crime prevention, promoting corporate social responsibility and accountability, combating human trafficking, empowering women and youth, advancing social justice and consumer protection, and the realization of all human rights;

2.   Urges States to create and maintain, in law and in practice, a safe and enabling environment in which civil society can operate free from hindrance and insecurity;

3.	Also urges States to acknowledge publicly the important and legitimate role of civil society in the promotion of human rights, democracy and the rule of law, and to engage with civil society to enable it to participate in the public debate on decisions that would contribute to the promotion and protection of human rights and the rule of law, and of any other relevant decisions;
4.	Urges all non-State actors to respect all human rights and not to undermine the capacity of civil society to operate free from hindrance and insecurity;

HRC RESOLUTION 31/32 ON PROTECTING HUMAN RIGHTS DEFENDERS, WHETHER INDIVIDUALS, GROUPS OR ORGANS OF SOCIETY, ADDRESSING ECONOMIC, SOCIAL AND CULTURAL RIGHTS

1.	Stresses that the right of everyone, individually and in association with others, to promote and strive for the protection and realization of all human rights and fundamental freedoms, in accordance with the Declaration1, without retaliation or fear thereof is an essential element in building and maintaining sustainable, open and democratic societies, and reaffirms the urgent need to respect, protect, promote and facilitate the work of those defending economic, social and cultural rights as a vital factor contributing towards the realization of those rights, including as they relate to environmental and land issues as well as development;
2.	Calls upon all States to take all measures necessary to ensure the rights and safety of human rights defenders, including those working towards the realization of economic, social and cultural rights and who, in so doing, exercise other human rights, such as the rights to freedom of opinion, expression, peaceful assembly and association, to participate in public affairs, and to seek an effective remedy;...
4.	Urges all States to acknowledge in public statements at the national and local levels, and through laws, policies or programmes, the important and legitimate role of human rights defenders, including women human rights defenders, in the promotion of human rights, democracy and the rule of law in all areas of society, in urban and rural areas, as essential components of ensuring their recognition and protection, including those promoting and defending economic, social and cultural rights;...

6.	Calls upon all States to combat impunity by investigating and pursuing accountability for all attacks and threats by State and non-State actors against any individual, group or organ of society that is defending human rights, including against family members, associates and legal representatives, and by condemning publically all cases of violence, discrimination, intimidation and reprisals against them;...
8.	Emphasizes the importance of national protection programmes for human rights defenders, and encourages States to consider, as a matter of priority, enacting relevant legislative and policy frameworks to this end, in consultation with human rights defenders, civil society and relevant stakeholders, taking into account, inter alia, the principles presented by the Special Rapporteur on the situation of human rights defenders;
9.	Continues to express particular concern about systemic and structural discrimination and violence faced by women human rights defenders of all ages, and calls upon all States to give effect to the principles and objectives established by the General Assembly in its resolution 68/181 by protecting the rights of women human rights defenders and by integrating a gender perspective into the efforts to create a safe and enabling environment for the defence of human rights, including economic, social and cultural rights;...
13.	Calls upon all States to ensure that information held by public authorities, including with respect to economic, social and cultural rights, and as related to environmental, land, natural resources and development issues, is proactively disclosed and not unnecessarily classified or otherwise withheld from the public, and also calls upon all States to adopt transparent, clear and expedient laws and policies that provide for the effective disclosure of information held by public authorities and a general right to request and receive information, for which public access should be granted, except within narrow, proportionate, necessary and clearly defined limitations;...

15.	Recognizes the important and legitimate role of individuals, groups and organs of society that are defending human rights in identifying and raising awareness of human rights impacts, the benefits and risks of development projects and business operations, including in relation to workplace health, safety and rights, and natural resource exploitation, environmental, land and development issues, by expressing their views, concerns, support, criticism or dissent regarding government policy or action or business activities, and underlines the need for Governments to take the measures necessary to safeguard space for such public dialogue and its participants;
16.	Encourages non-State actors to respect and promote the human rights and fundamental freedoms of all persons, including their economic, social and cultural rights, and to refrain from actions that undermine the capacity of human rights defenders to operate free from hindrance and insecurity, and encourages leaders in all sectors of society to express public support for the important and legitimate role of human rights defenders, including women human rights defenders;...
19.	Encourages all States to engage in initiatives to promote effective prevention, accountability, remedy and reparations with a view to protecting the human rights of everyone, including human rights defenders, including from human rights abuses by business enterprises;

HRC RESOLUTION 22/6 ON PROTECTING HUMAN RIGHTS DEFENDERS

2.	Urges States to create a safe and enabling environment in which human rights defenders can operate free from hindrance and insecurity, in the whole country and in all sectors of society, including by extending support to local human rights defenders;

3. Stresses that legislation affecting the activities of human rights defenders and its application must be consistent with international human rights law, including the International Covenant on Civil and Political Rights and the International Covenant on Economic, Social and Cultural Rights, and guided by the Declaration on the Right and Responsibility of Individuals, Groups and Organs of Society to Promote and Protect Universally Recognized Human Rights and Fundamental Freedoms, and, in this regard, condemns the imposition of any limitations on the work and activities of human rights defenders enforced in contravention of international human rights law;

4. Calls upon States to ensure that legislation designed to guarantee public safety and public order contains clearly defined provisions consistent with international human rights law, including the principle of non-discrimination, and that such legislation is not used to impede or restrict the exercise of any human right, including freedom of expression, association and peaceful assembly, which are essential for the promotion and protection of other rights;

5. Urges States to acknowledge publicly the important and legitimate role of human rights defenders in the promotion of human rights, democracy and the rule of law as an essential component of ensuring their protection, including by respecting the independence of their organizations and by avoiding the stigmatization of their work;

6. Calls upon States to ensure that human rights defenders can perform their important role in the context of peaceful protests, in accordance with national legislation consistent with the Charter of the United Nations and international human rights law and, in this regard, to ensure that no one is subject to excessive or indiscriminate use of force, arbitrary arrest or detention, torture or other cruel, inhuman or degrading treatment or punishment, enforced disappearance, abuse of criminal and civil proceedings or threats of such acts;

7.	Underlines that the access to and use of information technologies and the media of one's choice, including radio, television and the Internet, should be promoted and facilitated at the national level, between States and at the international level as an integral part of the enjoyment of the fundamental rights to freedom of opinion and expression, and also encourages international cooperation aimed at the development of media and information and communications technologies in all countries;
8.	Calls upon States to respect, protect and ensure the right to freedom of association of human rights defenders and, in this regard, to ensure, where procedures governing the registration of civil society organizations exist, that these are transparent, accessible, non-discriminatory, expeditious and inexpensive, allow for the possibility to appeal and avoid requiring re-registration, in accordance with national legislation, and are in conformity with international human rights law;
9.	Also calls upon States:
	(a) To ensure that reporting requirements placed on individuals, groups and organs of society do not inhibit functional autonomy;
	(b) To ensure that they do not discriminatorily impose restrictions on potential sources of funding aimed at supporting the work of human rights defenders in accordance with the Declaration referred to in paragraph 3 above, other than those ordinarily laid down for any other activity unrelated to human rights within the country to ensure transparency and accountability, and that no law should criminalize or delegitimize activities in defence of human rights on account of the origin of funding thereto;
10.	Further calls upon States to ensure that measures to combat terrorism and preserve national security:
	(a) Are in compliance with their obligations under international law, in particular under international human rights law, and do not hinder the work and safety of individuals, groups and organs of society engaged in promoting and defending human rights;

(b) Clearly identify which offences qualify as terrorist acts by defining transparent and foreseeable criteria, including, inter alia, considering without prejudice those formulated by the Special Rapporteur on the promotion and protection of human rights while countering terrorism;

(c) Prohibit and do not provide for, or have the effect of, subjecting persons to arbitrary detention, such as detention without due process guarantees, the deprivation of liberty that amounts to placing a detained person outside the protection of the law, or the illegal deprivation of liberty and transfer of individuals suspected of terrorist activities, nor the unlawful deprivation of the right to life or the trial of suspects without fundamental judicial guarantees;

(d) Allow appropriate access for relevant international bodies, non-governmental organizations and national human rights institutions, where such exist, to persons detained under anti-terrorism and other legislation relating to national security, and to ensure that human rights defenders are not harassed or prosecuted for providing legal assistance to persons detained and charged under legislation relating to national security;

11.   Calls upon States to ensure that all legal provisions and their application affecting human rights defenders are clearly defined, determinable and non-retroactive in order to avoid potential abuse to the detriment of fundamental freedoms and human rights, and specifically to ensure that:

(a) The promotion and the protection of human rights are not criminalized, and that human rights defenders are not prevented from enjoying universal human rights owing to their work, whether they operate individually or in association with others, while emphasizing that everyone shall respect the human rights of others;

(b) The judiciary is independent, impartial and competent to review effectively legislation and its application affecting the work and activities of human rights defenders;

(c) Procedural safeguards, including in criminal cases against human rights defenders, are in place in accordance with international human rights law in order to avoid the use of unreliable evidence, unwarranted investigations and procedural delays, thereby effectively contributing to the expeditious closing of all unsubstantiated cases, with individuals being afforded the opportunity to lodge complaints directly with the appropriate authority;

(d) Any provision or decision that may interfere with the enjoyment of human rights must respect fundamental principles enshrined in international law so that they are lawful, proportionate, non-discriminatory and necessary in a democratic society;

(e) Information held by public authorities is proactively disclosed, including on grave violations of human rights, and that transparent and clear laws and policies provide for a general right to request and receive such information, for which public access should be granted, except for narrow and clearly defined limitations;

(f) That provisions do not prevent public officials from being held accountable, and that penalties for defamation are limited in order to ensure proportionality and reparation commensurate to the harm done;

(g) Legislation aimed at preserving public morals is compatible with international human rights law;

(h) Legislation does not target activities of individuals and associations defending the rights of persons belonging to minorities or espousing minority beliefs;

(i) Dissenting views may be expressed peacefully;

12.   Expresses particular concern about systemic and structural discrimination and violence faced by women human rights defenders, and calls upon States to integrate a gender perspective in their efforts to create a safe and enabling environment for the defence of human rights;

13.	Reaffirms the right of everyone, individually and in association with others, to unhindered access to and communication with international bodies, in particular the United Nations, its representatives and mechanisms in the field of human rights, including the Human Rights Council, its special procedures, the universal periodic review mechanism and the treaty bodies, as well as regional human rights mechanisms;
14.	Strongly calls upon all States:

(a) To refrain from, and ensure adequate protection from, any act of intimidation or reprisals against those who cooperate, have cooperated or seek to cooperate with international institutions, including their family members and associates;

(b) To fulfil the duty to end impunity for any such acts of intimidation or reprisals by bringing the perpetrators to justice and by providing an effective remedy for their victims;

(c) To avoid legislation that has the effect of undermining the right reaffirmed in paragraph 13 above;

15.	Reaffirms the necessity for inclusive and open dialogue between civil society actors, particularly human rights defenders, and the United Nations in the field of human rights and, in this context, underlines that participation by civil society should be facilitated in a transparent, impartial and non-discriminatory manner;
16.	Underlines the value of national human rights institutions, established and operating in accordance with the Paris Principles, in the continued monitoring of existing legislation and consistently informing the State about its impact on the activities of human rights defenders, including by making relevant and concrete recommendations;
17.	Stressing in particular the valuable contribution of national human rights institutions, civil society and other stakeholders in providing input to States on the potential implications of draft legislation when such legislation is being developed or reviewed to ensure that it is in compliance with international human rights law;

18.	Invites leaders in all sectors of society and respective communities, including political, social and religious leaders, and leaders in business and media, to express public support for the important role of human rights defenders and the legitimacy of their work;

HRC RESOLUTION 21/12 ON THE SAFETY OF JOURNALISTS

8.	Calls upon States to promote a safe and enabling environment for journalists to perform their work independently and without undue interference, including by means of (a) legislative measures; (b) awareness-raising in the judiciary, law enforcement officers and military personnel, as well as journalists and civil society, regarding international human rights and humanitarian law obligations and commitments relating to the safety of journalists; (c) the monitoring and reporting of attacks against journalists; (d) publicly condemning attacks; and (e) dedicating necessary resources to investigate and prosecute such attacks;...

Regional Instruments

AFRICAN (BANJUL) CHARTER ON HUMAN AND PEOPLES' RIGHTS (BANJUL CHARTER)

2.	Every individual shall be entitled to the enjoyment of the rights and freedoms recognized and guaranteed in the present Charter without distinction of any kind such as race, ethnic group, color, sex, language, religion, political or any other opinion, national and social origin, fortune, birth or other status.
4.	Human beings are inviolable. Every human being shall be entitled to respect for his life and the integrity of his person. No one may be arbitrarily deprived of this right.
6.	Every individual shall have the right to liberty and to the security of his person. No one may be deprived of his freedom except for reasons and conditions previously laid down by law. In particular, no one may be arbitrarily arrested or detained.
9.	1. Every individual shall have the right to receive information. 2. Every individual shall have the right to express and disseminate his opinions within the law.
10.	1. Every individual shall have the right to free association provided that he abides by the law. 2. Subject to the obligation of solidarity provided for in 29 no one may be compelled to join an association.
11.	Every individual shall have the right to assemble freely with others. The exercise of this right shall be subject only to necessary restrictions provided for by law in particular those enacted in the interest of national security, the safety, health, ethics and rights and freedoms of others.
13.	1. Every citizen shall have the right to participate freely in the government of his country, either directly or through freely chosen representatives in accordance with the provisions of the law.

AFRICAN CHARTER ON THE RIGHTS AND WELFARE OF THE CHILD	
3.	Every child shall be entitled to the enjoyment of the rights and freedoms recognized and guaranteed in this Charter irrespective of the child's or his/her parents' or legal guardians' race, ethnic group, colour, sex, language, religion, political or other opinion, national and social origin, fortune, birth or other status.
4.	1. In all actions concerning the child undertaken by any person or authority the best interests of the child shall be the primary consideration.
7.	Every child who is capable of communicating his or her own views shall be assured the rights to express his opinions freely in all matters and to disseminate his opinions subject to such restrictions as are prescribed by laws.
8.	Every child shall have the right to free association and freedom of peaceful assembly in conformity with the law.
10.	No child shall be subject to arbitrary or unlawful interference with his privacy, family home or correspondence, or to the attacks upon his honour or reputation, provided that parents or legal guardians shall have the right to exercise reasonable supervision over the conduct of their children. The child has the right to the protection of the law against such interference or attacks.
13.	1. Every child who is mentally or physically disabled shall have the right to special measures of protection in keeping with his physical and moral needs and under conditions which ensure his dignity, promote his self-reliance and active participation in the community.
PROTOCOL TO THE AFRICAN CHARTER ON HUMAN AND PEOPLES' RIGHTS ON THE RIGHTS OF WOMEN IN AFRICA (MAPUTO PROTOCOL)	
4.	1. Every woman shall be entitled to respect for her life and the integrity and security of her person.

9.	1. States Parties shall take specific positive action to promote participative governance and the equal participation of women in the political life of their countries through affirmative action, enabling national legislation and other measures to ensure that:...
	c) women are equal partners with men at all levels of development and implementation of State policies and development programmes .
	2. States Parties shall ensure increased and effective representation and participation of women at all levels of decision-making.
18.	2. States Parties shall take all appropriate measures to:
	a) ensure greater participation of women in the planning, management and preservation of the environment and the sustainable use of natural resources at all levels;
23.	The States Parties undertake to:...
	b) ensure the right of women with disabilities to freedom from violence, including sexual abuse, discrimination based on disability and the right to be treated with dignity.
25.	States Parties shall undertake to:
	a) provide for appropriate remedies to any woman whose rights or freedoms, as herein recognised, have been violated;
	b) ensure that such remedies are determined by competent judicial, administrative or legislative authorities, or by any other competent authority provided for by law.

AFRICAN CHARTER ON DEMOCRACY, ELECTIONS AND GOVERNANCE

12.	State Parties shall...
	3. Create conducive conditions for civil society organizations to exist and operate within the law.

27.	State Parties shall commit themselves to...
	2. Fostering popular participation and partnership with civil society organizations;
28.	State Parties shall ensure and promote strong partnerships and dialogue between government, civil society and private sector.

DECLARATION OF PRINCIPLES ON FREEDOM OF EXPRESSION IN AFRICA

I.	1. Freedom of expression and information, including the right to seek, receive and impart information and ideas, either orally, in writing or in print, in the form of art, or through any other form of communication, including across frontiers, is a fundamental and inalienable human right and an indispensable component of democracy. 2. Everyone shall have an equal opportunity to exercise the right to freedom of expression and to access information without discrimination.
II.	1. No one shall be subject to arbitrary interference with his or her freedom of expression. 2. Any restrictions on freedom of expression shall be provided by law, serve a legitimate interest and be necessary and in a democratic society.
IV.	1. Public bodies hold information not for themselves but as custodians of the public good and everyone has a right to access this information, subject only to clearly defined rules established by law.

AMERICAN DECLARATION ON THE RIGHTS AND DUTIES OF MAN

I.	Every human being has the right to life, liberty and the security of his person.
II.	All persons are equal before the law and have the rights and duties established in this Declaration, without distinction as to race, sex, language, creed or any other factor.
IV.	Every person has the right to freedom of investigation, of opinion, and of the expression and dissemination of ideas, by any medium whatsoever.

| XXI. | Every person has the right to assemble peaceably with others in a formal public meeting or an informal gathering, in connection with matters of common interest of any nature. |
| XXII. | Every person has the right to associate with others to promote, exercise and protect his legitimate interests of a political, economic, religious, social, cultural, professional, labor union or other nature. |

AMERICAN CONVENTION ON HUMAN RIGHTS (ACHR)

| 1. | (1) The States Parties to this Convention undertake to respect the rights and freedoms recognized herein and to ensure to all persons subject to their jurisdiction the free and full exercise of those rights and freedoms, without any discrimination for reasons of race, color, sex, language, religion, political or other opinion, national or social origin, economic status, birth, or any other social condition. |
| 13. | 1. Everyone has the right to freedom of thought and expression. This right includes freedom to seek, receive, and impart information and ideas of all kinds, regardless of frontiers, either orally, in writing, in print, in the form of art, or through any other medium of one's choice. |

2. The exercise of the right provided for in the foregoing paragraph shall not be subject to prior censorship but shall be subject to subsequent imposition of liability, which shall be expressly established by law to the extent necessary to ensure:

a. respect for the rights or reputations of others; or

b. the protection of national security, public order, or public health or morals.

3. The right of expression may not be restricted by indirect methods or means, such as the abuse of government or private controls over newsprint, radio broadcasting frequencies, or equipment used in the dissemination of information, or by any other means tending to impede the communication and circulation of ideas and opinions....

	5. Any propaganda for war and any advocacy of national, racial, or religious hatred that constitute incitements to lawless violence or to any other similar action against any person or group of persons on any grounds including those of race, color, religion, language, or national origin shall be considered as offenses punishable by law.
15.	The right of peaceful assembly, without arms, is recognized. No restrictions may be placed on the exercise of this right other than those imposed in conformity with the law and necessary in a democratic society in the interest of national security, public safety or public order, or to protect public health or morals or the rights or freedom of others.
16.	1. Everyone has the right to associate freely for ideological, religious, political, economic, labor, social, cultural, sports, or other purposes.
	2. The exercise of this right shall be subject only to such restrictions established by law as may be necessary in a democratic society, in the interest of national security, public safety or public order, or to protect public health or morals or the rights and freedoms of others.
	3. The provisions of this article do not bar the imposition of legal restrictions, including even deprivation of the exercise of the right of association, on members of the armed forces and the police.
23.	1. Every citizen shall enjoy the following rights and opportunities:
	a. to take part in the conduct of public affairs, directly or through freely chosen representatives;...
	2. The law may regulate the exercise of the rights and opportunities referred to in the preceding paragraph only on the basis of age, nationality, residence, language, education, civil and mental capacity, or sentencing by a competent court in criminal proceedings.

| 25. | 1. Everyone has the right to simple and prompt recourse, or any other effective recourse, to a competent court or tribunal for protection against acts that violate his fundamental rights recognized by the constitution or laws of the state concerned or by this Convention, even though such violation may have been committed by persons acting in the course of their official duties. |

2. The States Parties undertake:

a. to ensure that any person claiming such remedy shall have his rights determined by the competent authority provided for by the legal system of the state;

b. to develop the possibilities of judicial remedy; and

c. to ensure that the competent authorities shall enforce such remedies when granted.

INTER-AMERICAN CONVENTION ON THE PREVENTION, PUNISHMENT AND ERADICATION OF VIOLENCE AGAINST WOMEN (CONVENTION OF BELEM DO PARA)

| 4. | Every woman has the right to the recognition, enjoyment, exercise and protection of all human rights and freedoms embodied in regional and international human rights instruments. These rights include, among others:... |

c. The right to personal liberty and security;...

e. The rights to have the inherent dignity of her person respected and her family protected;

f. The right to equal protection before the law and of the law;

g. The right to simple and prompt recourse to a competent court for protection against acts that violate her rights;

h. The right to associate freely;

i. The right of freedom to profess her religion and beliefs within the law; and

j. The right to have equal access to the public service of her country and to take part in the conduct of public affairs, including decision-making.

5. Every woman is entitled to the free and full exercise of her civil, political, economic, social and cultural rights, and may rely on the full protection of those rights as embodied in regional and international instruments on human rights. The States Parties recognize that violence against women prevents and nullifies the exercise of these rights.

6. The right of every woman to be free from violence includes, among others:

a. The right of women to be free from all forms of discrimination; and

b. The right of women to be valued and educated free of stereotyped patterns of behavior and social and cultural practices based on concepts of inferiority or subordination.

INTER-AMERICAN CONVENTION ON THE ELIMINATION OF ALL FORMS OF DISCRIMINATION AGAINST PERSONS WITH DISABILITIES

III. To achieve the objectives of this Convention, the states parties undertake:

1. To adopt the legislative, social, educational, labor-related, or any other measures needed to eliminate discrimination against persons with disabilities and to promote their full integration into society, including, but not limited to:

a) Measures to eliminate discrimination gradually and to promote integration by government authorities and/or private entities in providing or making available goods, services, facilities, programs, and activities such as employment, transportation, communications, housing, recreation, education, sports, law enforcement and administration of justice, and political and administrative activities;

INTER-AMERICAN DEMOCRATIC CHARTER

4. Transparency in government activities, probity, responsible public administration on the part of governments, respect for social rights, and freedom of expression and of the press are essential components of the exercise of democracy.

   The constitutional subordination of all state institutions to the legally constituted civilian authority and respect for the rule of law on the part of all institutions and sectors of society are equally essential to democracy.

OAS DECLARATION OF PRINCIPLES ON FREEDOM OF EXPRESSION

1. Freedom of expression in all its forms and manifestations is a fundamental and inalienable right of all individuals. Additionally, it is an indispensable requirement for the very existence of a democratic society.

2. Every person has the right to seek, receive and impart information and opinions freely under terms set forth in Article 13 of the American Convention on Human Rights. All people should be afforded equal opportunities to receive, seek and impart information by any means of communication without any discrimination for reasons of race, color, sex, language, religion, political or other opinions, national or social origin, economic status, birth or any other social condition.

4. Access to information held by the state is a fundamental right of every individual. States have the obligation to guarantee the full exercise of this right. This principle allows only exceptional limitations that must be previously established by law in case of a real and imminent danger that threatens national security in democratic societies.

ARAB CHARTER ON HUMAN RIGHTS	
3.	1. Each State party to the present Charter undertakes to ensure to all individuals subject to its jurisdiction the right to enjoy the rights and freedoms set forth herein, without distinction on grounds of race, colour, sex, language, religious belief, opinion, thought, national or social origin, wealth, birth or physical or mental disability. 2. The States parties to the present Charter shall take the requisite measures to guarantee effective equality in the enjoyment of all the rights and freedoms enshrined in the present Charter in order to ensure protection against all forms of discrimination based on any of the grounds mentioned in the preceding paragraph. 3. Men and women are equal in respect of human dignity, rights and obligations within the framework of the positive discrimination established in favour of women by the Islamic Shariah, other divine laws and by applicable laws and legal instruments. Accordingly, each State party pledges to take all the requisite measures to guarantee equal opportunities and effective equality between men and women in the enjoyment of all the rights set out in this Charter.
14.	1. Everyone has the right to liberty and security of person. No one shall be subjected to arbitrary arrest, search or detention without a legal warrant.
21.	I. No one shall be subjected to arbitrary or unlawful interference with regard to his privacy, family, home or correspondence, nor to unlawful attacks on his honour or his reputation. 2. Everyone has the right to the protection of the law against such interference or attacks.
23.	Each State party to the present Charter undertakes to ensure that any person whose rights or freedoms as herein recognized are violated shall have an effective remedy, notwithstanding that the violation has been committed by persons acting in an official capacity.

24.	Every citizen has the right:
	1. To freely pursue a political activity.
	2. To take part in the conduct of public affairs, directly or through freely chosen representatives...
	5. To freely form and join associations with others.
	6. To freedom of association and peaceful assembly.
	7. No restrictions may be placed on the exercise of these rights other than those which are prescribed by law and which are necessary in a democratic society in the interests of national security or public safety, public health or morals or the protection of the rights and freedoms of others.
32.	1. The present Charter guarantees the right to information and to freedom of opinion and expression, as well as the right to seek, receive and impart information and ideas through any medium, regardless of geographical boundaries.
	2. Such rights and freedoms shall be exercised in conformity with the fundamental values of society and shall be subject only to such limitations as are required to ensure respect for the rights or reputation of others or the protection of national security, public order and public health or morals.
35.	1. Every individual has the right to freely form trade unions or to join trade unions and to freely pursue trade union activity for the protection of his interests.
	2. No restrictions shall be placed on the exercise of these rights and freedoms except such as are prescribed by the laws in force and that are necessary for the maintenance of national security, public safety or order or for the protection of public health or morals or the rights and freedoms of others.
40.	1. The States parties undertake to ensure to persons with mental or physical disabilities a decent life that guarantees their dignity, and to enhance their self-reliance and facilitate their active participation in society.

CHARTER OF FUNDAMENTAL RIGHTS OF THE EUROPEAN UNION	
1.	Human dignity is inviolable. It must be respected and protected.
3.	1. Everyone has the right to respect for his or her physical and mental integrity.
6.	Everyone has the right to liberty and security of person.
7.	Everyone has the right to respect for his or her private and family life, home and communications.
11.	1. Everyone has the right to freedom of expression. This right shall include freedom to hold opinions and to receive and impart information and ideas without interference by public authority and regardless of frontiers.
12.	1. Everyone has the right to freedom of peaceful assembly and to freedom of association at all levels, in particular in political, trade union and civic matters, which implies the right of everyone to form and to join trade unions for the protection of his or her interests.
21.	1. Any discrimination based on any ground such as sex, race, colour, ethnic or social origin, genetic features, language, religion or belief, political or any other opinion, membership of a national minority, property, birth, disability, age or sexual orientation shall be prohibited. 2. Within the scope of application of the Treaties and without prejudice to any of their specific provisions, any discrimination on grounds of nationality shall be prohibited.
23.	Equality between women and men must be ensured in all areas, including employment, work and pay. The principle of equality shall not prevent the maintenance or adoption of measures providing for specific advantages in favour of the under-represented sex.

24.	1. Children shall have the right to such protection and care as is necessary for their well-being. They may express their views freely. Such views shall be taken into consideration on matters which concern them in accordance with their age and maturity. 2. In all actions relating to children, whether taken by public authorities or private institutions, the child's best interests must be a primary consideration.
26.	The Union recognises and respects the right of persons with disabilities to benefit from measures designed to ensure their independence, social and occupational integration and participation in the life of the community.
47.	Everyone whose rights and freedoms guaranteed by the law of the Union are violated has the right to an effective remedy before a tribunal in compliance with the conditions laid down in this Article.

EUROPEAN CONVENTION ON HUMAN RIGHTS (*ECHR*)

1.	The High Contracting Parties shall secure to everyone within their jurisdiction the rights and freedoms defined in Section I of this Convention.
5.	1. Everyone has the right to liberty and security of person.
8.	1. Everyone has the right to respect for his private and family life, his home and his correspondence. 2. There shall be no interference by a public authority with the exercise of this right except such as is in accordance with the law and is necessary in a democratic society in the interests of national security, public safety or the economic wellbeing of the country, for the prevention of disorder or crime, for the protection of health or morals, or for the protection of the rights and freedoms of others.
10.	1. Everyone has the right to freedom of expression. This right shall include freedom to hold opinions and to receive and impart information and ideas without interference by public authority and regardless of frontiers. This Article shall not prevent States from requiring the licensing of broadcasting, television or cinema enterprises.

2. The exercise of these freedoms, since it carries with it duties and responsibilities, may be subject to such formalities, conditions, restrictions or penalties as are prescribed by law and are necessary in a democratic society, in the interests of national security, territorial integrity or public safety, for the prevention of disorder or crime, for the protection of health or morals, for the protection of the reputation or rights of others, for preventing the disclosure of information received in confidence, or for maintaining the authority and impartiality of the judiciary.

11.

1. Everyone has the right to freedom of peaceful assembly and to freedom of association with others, including the right to form and to join trade unions for the protection of his interests.

2. No restrictions shall be placed on the exercise of these rights other than such as are prescribed by law and are necessary in a democratic society in the interests of national security or public safety, for the prevention of disorder or crime, for the protection of health or morals or for the protection of the rights and freedoms of others. This Article shall not prevent the imposition of lawful restrictions on the exercise of these rights by members of the armed forces, of the police or of the administration of the State.

13.

Everyone whose rights and freedoms as set forth in this Convention are violated shall have an effective remedy before a national authority notwithstanding that the violation has been committed by persons acting in an official capacity.

14.

The enjoyment of the rights and freedoms set forth in this Convention shall be secured without discrimination on any ground such as sex, race, colour, language, religion, political or other opinion, national or social origin, association with a national minority, property, birth or other status.

16.

Nothing in Articles 10, 11 and 14 shall be regarded as preventing the High Contracting Parties from imposing restrictions on the political activity of aliens.

COE FRAMEWORK CONVENTION FOR THE PROTECTION OF NATIONAL MINORITIES	
3.	2. Persons belonging to national minorities may exercise the rights and enjoy the freedoms flowing from the principles enshrined in the present framework Convention individually as well as in community with others.
4.	1. The Parties undertake to guarantee to persons belonging to national minorities the right of equality before the law and of equal protection of the law. In this respect, any discrimination based on belonging to a national minority shall be prohibited.
7.	The Parties shall ensure respect for the right of every person belonging to a national minority to freedom of peaceful assembly, freedom of association, freedom of expression, and freedom of thought, conscience and religion.
9.	1. The Parties undertake to recognise that the right to freedom of expression of every person belonging to a national minority includes freedom to hold opinions and to receive and impart information and ideas in the minority language, without interference by public authorities and regardless of frontiers. The Parties shall ensure, within the framework of their legal systems, that persons belonging to a national minority are not discriminated against in their access to the media.
15.	1. The Parties shall create the conditions necessary for the effective participation of persons belonging to national minorities in cultural, social and economic life and in public affairs, in particular those affecting them.
OAS DECLARATION OF CHAPULTEPEC	
Principle 2	Every person has the right to seek and receive information, express opinions and disseminate them freely. No one may restrict or deny these rights.
OSCE BISHKEK DECLARATION (Freedom of the media)	
2.	Governments should ensure that citizens as members of the different linguistic and cultural groups represented in the society have the right and the opportunity to freely express their views and preserve their language and culture via media.

APPENDIX B: TREATIES, DECLARATIONS AND OTHER INSTRUMENTS

The international law and principles setting out the standards for the right to dissent are found in the following international instruments (numbers of States Parties indicated is current to June 2016).

United Nations (UN) Treaties, Declarations and Other Instruments

The UDHR

- *Universal Declaration of Human Rights ("UDHR")*, adopted 10 Dec. 1984, U.N. Doc. A/810, at 71 (1948), online <http://www.un.org/en/documents/udhr/>.

UN Treaties

- *Vienna Convention on the Law of Treaties* ("Vienna Convention"), adopted 23 May 1969, entered into force 27 Jan. 1980, U.N. Doc. A/CONF. 39/26, reprinted in 8 ILM 679 (1969), online <https://treaties.un.org/doc/Publication/UNTS/Volume%201155/volume-1155-I-18232-English.pdf>. 114 States Parties.

- *International Covenant on Civil and Political Rights ("ICCPR")*, adopted 16 Dec. 1966, entered into force 23 March 1976, U.N. Doc. A/6316, 999 U.N.T.S. 171, online <http://www.ohchr.org/EN/ProfessionalInterest/Pages/CCPR.aspx>. 168 States Parties.

- *Optional Protocol to the International Covenant on Civil and Political Rights*, adopted 16 Dec. 1966, entered into force 23 March 1976, U.N. Doc. A/6316, 999 U.N.T.S. 171, online <http://www1.umn.edu/humanrts/instree/b4ccprp1.htm>. 115 States Parties.

- *International Covenant on Economic, Social and Cultural Rights ("ICESCR")*, adopted 16 Dec. 1966, entered into force 3 Jan. 1976, U.N. Doc. A/6316, 999 U.N.T.S. 3, online <http://www.ohchr.org/EN/ProfessionalInterest/Pages/CESCR.aspx>. 162 States Parties.

- *Optional Protocol to the International Covenant on Economic, Social and Cultural Rights*: resolution/adopted by the General Assembly, adopted 10 December 2008, entered into force 5 May 2013, GA Res. 832, UN GAOR, 63rd Session, UN Doc A/RES/63/117 (2008), online <http://www.ohchr.org/EN/ProfessionalInterest/Pages/OPCESCR. aspx>. 14 States Parties.

- *Convention against Torture and Other Cruel, Inhuman or Degrading Treatment or Punishment ("CAT"),* adopted 10 Dec. 1984, entered into force 26 June 1987, U.N. Doc. A/39/51, at 197 (1984), online <http:// www.ohchr.org/EN/ProfessionalInterest/Pages/CAT.aspx>. 155 States Parties.

- *Optional Protocol to the Convention against Torture and other Cruel, Inhuman or Degrading Treatment or Punishment,* adopted 18 December 2002, entered into force on 22 June 2006, A/RES/57/199, online <http://www.ohchr.org/en/ProfessionalInterest/Pages/OPCAT. aspx>. 72 States Parties.

- *Convention on the Elimination of All Forms of Discrimination against Women ("CEDAW"),* adopted 18 December 1979, entered into force 3 September 1981, UN Doc. A/34/46, at 193 (1979), online <http:// www.ohchr.org/EN/ProfessionalInterest/Pages/CEDAW.aspx>. 188 States Parties.

- *Optional Protocol to the Convention on the Elimination of All Forms of Discrimination Against Women,* adopted 6 October 1999, entered into force on 22 Dec. 2000, United Nations, Treaty Series, vol. 2131, p. 83, online <http://www.un.org/womenwatch/daw/cedaw/protocol/text. htm>. 104 States Parties.

- *International Convention on the Elimination of All Forms of Racial Discrimination* ("CERD"), adopted 21 December 1965, entered into force 4 January 1969, U.N. Doc. A/6014 (1966), online <http://www. ohchr.org/EN/ProfessionalInterest/Pages/CERD.aspx>. 177 States Parties.

- *Convention on the Rights of the Child ("CRC"),* adopted 20 Nov. 1989, entered into force 2 Sept. 1990, U.N. Doc. A/44/49, at 166 (1989), online <http://www.ohchr.org/en/professionalinterest/pages/crc. aspx>. 194 States Parties.

- *Optional Protocol to the Convention on the Rights of the Child on a Communications Procedure*, adopted 19 December 2011, entered into force 14 April 2014, A/RES/66/138, online <https://treaties.un.org/doc/source/signature/2012/ctc_4-11d.pdf>. 11 States Parties.

- *Convention relating to the Status of Refugees*, adopted 28 July 1951, entered into force 22 April 1954, United Nations, Treaty Series, vol. 189, p. 137, online <http://www.ohchr.org/EN/ProfessionalInterest/Pages/StatusOfRefugees.aspx>. 145 States Parties.

- UN General Assembly, *Protocol Relating to the Status of Refugees*, adopted 31 January 1967, entered into force 4 October 1967, United Nations, Treaty Series, vol. 606, p. 267, online <http://www1.umn.edu/humanrts/instree/v2prsr.htm>. 146 States Parties.

- *International Convention on the Protection of the Rights of All Migrant Workers and Members of their Families ("ICRMW")*, adopted 18 December 1990, entered into force 1 July 2003, A/RES/45/158, online <http://www2.ohchr.org/english/bodies/cmw/cmw.htm>. 47 States Parties.

- *International Convention for the Protection of all Persons from Enforced Disappearance*, adopted 20 December 2006, entered into force 23 December 2010, United Nations, Treaty Series, vol. 2716, p. 3, online <http://www.ohchr.org/Documents/ProfessionalInterest/disappearance-convention.pdf>. 52 States Parties.

- *Convention on the Rights of Persons with Disabilities*, adopted 13 December 2006, entered into force 3 May 2008, United Nations, Treaty Series, vol. 2515, p. 3, online <http://www.un.org/disabilities/convention/conventionfull.shtml>. 167 States Parties.

- International Labour Organization (ILO), *Convention concerning Freedom of Association and Protection of the Right to Organise*, C87, adopted 09 July 1948, entered into force 04 July 1950, online <http://www.ilo.org/dyn/normlex/en/f?p=normlexpub:12100:0::no::p12100_instrument_id:312232>. 153 States Parties.

Other UN Instruments

- *United Nations Declaration on the Rights of Indigenous Peoples*, adopted 2 October 2007, by a majority of 143 states in favour, 4 votes against (Australia, Canada, New Zealand and the U.S.A.) and 11 abstentions (Azerbaijan, Bangladesh, Bhutan, Burundi, Colombia, Georgia, Kenya, Nigeria, Russian Federation, Samoa and Ukraine), A/RES/61/295, online <http://www.un.org/esa/socdev/unpfii/documents/DRIPS_en.pdf>. Canada and the other 3 States who voted against the Declaration have all since reversed their position.

- *Declaration on the Right and Responsibility of Individuals, Groups and Organs of Society to Promote and Protect Universally Recognized Human Rights and Fundamental Freedoms*, adopted 9 December 1998, A/RES/53/144, online <http://www.ohchr.org/EN/ProfessionalInterest/Pages/RightAndResponsibility.aspx>.

- *Declaration on the Elimination of All Forms of Intolerance and of Discrimination Based on Religion or Belief*, adopted 25 November 1981, A/RES/36/55, online <http://www.un.org/documents/ga/res/36/a36r055.htm>.

- *Declaration on the Rights of Persons Belonging to National or Ethnic, Religious and Linguistic Minorities*, adopted 18 December 1992, A/RES/47/135, online <http://www.un.org/documents/ga/res/47/a47r135.htm>.

- *Declaration on the Right to Development,* adopted 4 December 1986, A/RES/41/128, online <http://www.un.org/documents/ga/res/41/a41r128.htm>

- *U.N. Human Rights Council Resolution on the Independence and impartiality of the judiciary, jurors and assessors, and the independence of lawyers*, adopted without a vote on 7 June 2013, A/HRC/23/L.9, online <http://ap.ohchr.org/documents/dpage_e.aspx?si=A/HRC/23/L.9>.

- *Basic Principles on the Role of Lawyers,* unanimously adopted by the Eighth United Nations Congress on the Prevention of Crime and the Treatment of Offenders, Havana, 27 August to 7 September 1990, U.N. Doc. A/CONF.144/28/Rev.1 at 118 (1990), online <http://www1.umn.edu/humanrts/instree/i3bprl.htm>.

- *The Durban Declaration and Programme of Action,* adopted by consensus at the 2001 World Conference against Racism (WCAR) 31 August to 8 September 2001, online <http://www.un.org/en/durbanreview2009/ddpa.shtml>.

- *The Public's Right To Know: Principles On Freedom Of Information Legislation,* June 1999, E/CN.4/2000/63, Annex II, online <https://documents-dds-ny.un.org/doc/UNDOC/GEN/G00/102/59/PDF/G0010259.pdf?OpenElement>.

- *Basic Principles on the Use of Force and Firearms by Law Enforcement Officials,* adopted by the Eighth United Nations Congress on the Prevention of Crime and the Treatment of Offenders, Havana, Cuba, 27 August to 7 September 1990, online <http://www.ohchr.org/EN/ProfessionalInterest/Pages/UseOfForceAndFirearms.aspx>.

- *Code of Conduct for Law Enforcement Officials,* 5 February 1980, A/RES/34/169, online <http://www.ohchr.org/EN/ProfessionalInterest/Pages/LawEnforcementOfficials.aspx>.

- *Guidelines for the Effective Implementation of the Code of Conduct for Law Enforcement Officials,* 24 May 1989, Economic and Social Council resolution 1989/61, annex, online <http://www.coe.int/t/dg1/legalcooperation/economiccrime/cybercrime/cy%20activity%20Interface2006/un%20Guidelines%20CoC%20Law%20Enforcement%20Officers.pdf>.

- *Basic Principles and Guidelines on the Right to a Remedy and Reparation for Victims of Gross Violations of International Human Rights Law and Serious Violations of International Humanitarian Law,* adopted 16 December 2005, A/RES/60/147, online <http://www.ohchr.org/EN/ProfessionalInterest/Pages/RemedyAndReparation.aspx>.

- *Guidelines on the Role of Prosecutors,* adopted by the Eighth United Nations Congress on the Prevention of Crime and the Treatment of Offenders, Havana, Cuba, 27 August to 7 September 1990, online <http://www.ohchr.org/EN/ProfessionalInterest/Pages/RoleOfProsecutors.aspx>.

- *Basic Principles on the Independence of the Judiciary,* adopted by the Seventh United Nations Congress on the Prevention of Crime and the

Treatment of Offenders held at Milan from 26 August to 6 September 1985, and endorsed by General Assembly resolutions 40/32 of 29 November 1985 and 40/146 of 13 December 1985, online <http:// www.ohchr.org/EN/ProfessionalInterest/Pages/IndependenceJudiciary. aspx>.

- General Assembly resolution 68/181, *Promotion of the Declaration on the Right and Responsibility of Individuals, Groups and Organs of Society to Promote and Protect Universally Recognized Human Rights and Fundamental Freedoms: protecting women human rights defenders,* A/RES/68/181 (18 December 2013), online <http://www. un.org/en/ga/search/view_doc.asp?symbol=A/RES/68/181>.

- UN General Assembly, Human Rights Council resolution 30/9, *Equal participation in political and public affairs,* adopted without a vote, 1 October 2015, A/HRC/RES/30/9, online <https://documents-dds-ny.un.org/doc/UNDOC/GEN/G15/232/93/PDF/G1523293. pdf?OpenElement>.

- UN General Assembly, Human Rights Council resolution 25/38, *The promotion and protection of human rights in the context of peaceful protests,* adopted by a vote (31 in favour, 9 against, 7 abstentions), 28 March 2014, A/HRC/RES/25/38, online <http://www.ohchr.org/ Documents/Issues/Executions/A-HRC-RES-25-38.pdf>.

- UN General Assembly, Human Rights Council resolution 22/10, *Promotion and protection of human rights in the context of peaceful protests,* adopted without a vote, 21 March 2013, A/HRC/RES/22/10, online <https://documents-dds-ny.un.org/doc/UNDOC/GEN/ G13/128/40/PDF/G1312840.pdf?OpenElement>.

- UN General Assembly, Human Rights Council resolution 19/35, *Promotion and protection of human rights in the context of peaceful protests,* adopted without a vote, 23 March 2012, A/HRC/RES/19/35, online <https://documents-dds-ny.un.org/doc/RESOLUTION/GEN/ G12/131/38/PDF/G1213138.pdf?OpenElement>.

- UN General Assembly, Human Rights Council resolution 12/16, *Freedom of opinion and expression,* adopted without a vote, 2 October 2009, A/HRC/RES/12/16, online <https://documents-dds-

ny.un.org/doc/RESOLUTION/GEN/G09/166/89/PDF/G0916689.
pdf?OpenElement>.

- UN General Assembly, Human Rights Council resolution 24/5, *The rights to freedom of peaceful assembly and of association,* adopted without a vote, 26 September 2013, A/HRC/RES/24/5, online <https:// documents-dds-ny.un.org/doc/UNDOC/GEN/G13/178/33/PDF/ G1317833.pdf?OpenElement>.

- UN General Assembly, Human Rights Council resolution 21/16, *The rights to freedom of peaceful assembly and of association,* adopted without a vote, 27 September 2012, A/HRC/RES/21/16, online <https://documents-dds-ny.un.org/doc/RESOLUTION/GEN/ G12/174/63/PDF/G1217463.pdf?OpenElement>.

- UN General Assembly, Human Rights Council resolution 15/21, *The rights to freedom of peaceful assembly and of association,* adopted without a vote, 30 September 2010, A/HRC/RES/15/21, online <https://documents-dds-ny.un.org/doc/UNDOC/GEN/G10/166/98/ PDF/G1016698.pdf?OpenElement>.

- UN General Assembly, Human Rights Council resolution 24/24, *Cooperation with the United Nations, its representatives and mechanisms in the field of human rights,* adopted by vote, 27 September 2013 [31 in favour, 1 against, 15 abstentions], A/HRC/ RES/24/24, online <https://documents-dds-ny.un.org/doc/UNDOC/ GEN/G13/180/27/PDF/G1318027.pdf?OpenElement>.

- UN General Assembly, Human Rights Council resolution 24/21, *Civil society space: creating and maintaining, in law and in practice, a safe and enabling environment,* adopted without a vote, 27 September 2013, A/HRC/RES/24/21, online <https://documents-dds-ny.un.org/ doc/UNDOC/GEN/G13/179/57/PDF/G1317957.pdf?OpenElement>.

- UN General Assembly, Human Rights Council resolution 31/32, *Protecting human rights defenders, whether individuals, groups or organs of society, addressing economic, social and cultural rights,* Adopted as orally revised by a recorded vote (33 to 6, with 8 abstentions), 24 March 2016, A/HRC/RES/31/32, online <https:// documents-dds-ny.un.org/doc/UNDOC/GEN/G16/083/21/PDF/

G1608321.pdf?OpenElement>.

- UN General Assembly, Human Rights Council resolution 22/6, *Protecting human rights defenders,* adopted without a vote, 21 March 2013, A/HRC/RES/22/6, online <http://ap.ohchr.org/documents/ dpage_e.aspx?si=A/HRC/RES/22/6>.

- UN General Assembly, Human Rights Council resolution 21/12, *Safety of Journalists,* adopted without a vote, 27 September 2012, A/HRC/RES/21/12, online <https://documents-dds-ny.un.org/doc/ RESOLUTION/GEN/G12/174/10/PDF/G1217410.pdf?OpenElement>.

African Union (AU) Treaties and Other Instruments

AU Treaties

- *African (Banjul) Charter on Human and Peoples' Rights* (*"Banjul Charter"*), June 27, 1981, OAU Doc. CAB/LEG/67/3 rev. 5, 21 I.L.M. 58 (1982), entered into force 21 October 1986, online <http://www.achpr. org/instruments/achpr/>. 53 States Parties.

- *African Charter on the Rights and Welfare of the Child,* July 11, 1990, OAU Doc. CAB/LEG/24.9/49, entered into force Nov. 29, 1999, online <http://www.achpr.org/instruments/child/>. 41 States Parties.

- *Protocol to the African Charter on Human and Peoples' Rights on the Rights of Women in Africa,* 11 July 2003, entered into force 25 November 2005, online <http://www.achpr.org/instruments/women-protocol/>. 28 States Parties.

- *Protocol to the African Charter on Human and Peoples' Rights on the Establishment of an African Court on Human and Peoples' Rights,* adopted 10 June 1998, entered into force 25 January 2004, online <http://www.achpr.org/instruments/court-establishment/>. 24 States Parties.

- *African Charter on Democracy, Elections and Governance,* 30 January 2007, entered into force 15 February 2012, online <http://www.achpr. org/instruments/charter-democracy/>. 24 States Parties.

Other African Union Instruments

- *Guidelines and Measures for the Prohibition and Prevention of Torture, Cruel, Inhuman or Degrading Treatment or Punishment in Africa* ("The Robben Island Guidelines"), adopted by the African Court on Human and Peoples' Rights during its 32nd ordinary session, October 2002, online <http://www.achpr.org/sessions/32nd/resolutions/61>.

- *Declaration of Principles on Freedom of Expression in Africa*, adopted by the African Commission on Human and Peoples' Rights, 32nd Session, 17 - 23 October, 2002: Banjul, The Gambia, online <http://hrlibrary.umn.edu/achpr/expressionfreedomdec.html>.

Organization of American States (OAS) Treaties, Declarations and Other Instruments

OAS Treaties

- *American Convention on Human Rights* ("ACHR"), "Pact of San Jose", Costa Rica, 22 November 1969, entered into force 18 July 1978, O.A.S. Treaty Series No. 36, 1144 U.N.T.S. 123, online <http://www.oas.org/dil/treaties_B-32_American_Convention_on_Human_Rights.htm>. 25 States ratified/acceded, but 2 States later renounced their ratification (Trinidad and Tobago, Venezuela). (9 States, including Canada and the U.S.A., have not ratified the Convention).

- *American Declaration on the Rights and Duties of Man* ("American Declaration"), adopted by the Ninth International Conference of American States, Bogotá, Colombia, 2 May 1948, OEA/Ser.L./V/11.71, at 17 (1988), online <http://www.oas.org/dil/1948%20American%20Declaration%20of%20the%20Rights%20and%20Duties%20of%20Man.pdf>.

- *Charter of the Organization of American States*, 30 April 1948, O.A.S. Treaty Series No. 36, 1144 U.N.T.S. 123, entered into force 13 Dec. 1951, amended 1967, 1985, 14 Dec. 1992, 10 June 1993, online <http://www.oas.org/dil/treaties_A-41_Charter_of_the_Organization_of_American_States.pdf>. 35 States Parties.

- *Inter-American Convention On The Prevention, Punishment And*

Eradication Of Violence Against Women "Convention Of Belem Do Para", adopted 06 September 1994, entered into force 03 May 1995, online <http://www.oas.org/juridico/english/treaties/a-61.html>. 32 States Parties.

- *Inter-American Convention on the Elimination of all Forms of Discrimination against Persons with Disabilities*, adopted 8 June 1999, entered into force 14 September 2001, online <http://www.oas.org/juridico/english/treaties/a-61.html>. 32 Sates Parties.

Other OAS instruments

- *Inter-American Democratic Charter*, adopted 11 September 2001, <http://www.oas.org/en/democratic-charter/pdf/demcharter_en.pdf>.

- *Declaration of Principles on Freedom of Expression*, adopted by the Inter-American Commission on Human Rights at its 108th regular sessions in October 2000, online <http://www.oas.org/en/iachr/expression/showarticle.asp?artID=26>.

- *Chapultepec Declaration*, adopted by the Hemisphere Conference on Free Speech Mexico City March 11, 1994, online <http://www.oas.org/en/iachr/expression/showarticle.asp?artID=60>.

Council of Europe (COE): Treaties and Other Instruments

COE Treaties

- *European Convention on Human Rights ("ECHR")*, Nov. 4, 1950, 213 U.N.T.S. 222, entered into force 3 September 1953, online <http://conventions.coe.int/treaty/Commun/QueVoulezVous.asp?NT=005&CM=7&DF=24/07/2012&CL=ENG>. 47 States Parties. Ratification is required for entry into the European Union.

- *Charter of Fundamental Rights of the European Union*, proclaimed at the Nice European Council on 7 December 2000, entered into force 01 December 2009, online <*http://eur-lex.europa.eu/legal-content/EN/TXT/HTML/?uri=CELEX:12012P/TXT&from=EN*>.

- *Framework Convention for the Protection of National Minorities,* adopted 10 November 1994 by the Committee of Ministers of the Council of Europe, entered into force 1 February

- 1998, ETS No.157, online <http://www.coe.int/en/web/minorities/text-of-the-convention>. (The *Framework Convention* may be ratified by member States of the Council of Europe, and non-member States may join at the invitation of the Committee of Ministers. Accession to the Convention is obligatory, at least politically, for States that apply for membership in the Council of Europe.) 39 Member States.

Other European Instruments

- Organization for Security and Co-operation in Europe, Bishkek Declaration, (Fifth Central Asia Media Conference "Media in Multi-Cultural and Multi-Lingual Societies", Bishkek, Kyrgyzstan, 17-18 September 2003), online <http://www.osce.org/fom/42521?download=true>.

Other Instruments

- *Arab Charter on Human Rights,* adopted by the League of Arab States, 22 May 2004, entered into force 15 March 2008, online <http://hrlibrary.umn.edu/instree/loas2005.html>.

APPENDIX C: OTHER RESOURCES

- Office of the United Nations High Commissioner for Human Rights, *Human Rights Standards and Practice for the Police: Expanded Pocket Book on Human Rights for the Police*, Professional Training Series No. 5/Add.3. UN Doc HR/P/PT/5/Add.3 (2004), online <http://www.ohchr.org/Documents/Publications/training5Add3en.pdf>.

- OSCE Office for Democratic Institutions and Human Rights (ODIHR), *Handbook on Monitoring*

- *Freedom of Peaceful Assembly* (Warsaw: 2011), online <http://www.osce.org/odihr/82979>.

- Geneva Academy of International Humanitarian Law and Human Rights, *Academy Briefing No. 5: Facilitating Peaceful Protests* (January 2014), online <http://www.geneva-academy.ch/academy-publications/academy-briefings/1084-the-international-code-of-conduct-for-private-security-service-providers>.

Lawyers' Rights Watch Canada

Lawyers' Rights Watch Canada (LRWC) is a committee of Canadian lawyers who promote human rights and the rule of law by providing support internationally to human rights defenders in danger. LRWC promotes the implementation and enforcement of international standards designed to protect the independence and security of human rights defenders around the world. In its work, LRWC:

- Campaigns for lawyers whose rights, freedoms or independence are threatened as a result of their human rights advocacy;

- Produces legal analyses of national and international laws and standards relevant to human rights abuses against lawyers and other human rights defenders; and

- Works in cooperation with other human rights organizations.

Around the world, lawyers and others who defend human rights are often singled out as targets of repression, much of which is perpetrated by governments or government-controlled agencies. Criminal offences against human rights defenders occur with alarming frequency. In addition, authorities use existing laws and legal procedures to prosecute or otherwise intimidate advocates representing unpopular clients or causes, often in violation of international standards. Methods used to silence, intimidate or punish advocates are often illegal pursuant to the law of the state itself.

LRWC seeks to identify illegal actions against advocates, campaign for the cessation of such actions, and lobby for the implementation of effective immediate and long-term remedies.

LRWC was incorporated as a non-profit society on June 8, 2000 and Lawyers' Rights Watch (Legal Research) Canada – LRW(LR)C – was incorporated January 2, 2002, pursuant to the provisions of the Canada Corporations Act. LRWC is run by volunteers and funded solely by membership fees and donations from individuals. Donations are gratefully accepted.

www.lrwc.org

CPSIA information can be obtained
at www.ICGtesting.com
Printed in the USA
LVOW05s0828271217
559935LV00005B/2/P